The Revolutionary Rhetoric of *Hamilton*

The Revolutionary Rhetoric of *Hamilton*

Edited by Luke Winslow, Nancy J. Legge, and Jacob Justice

LEXINGTON BOOKS
Lanham • Boulder • New York • London

Published by Lexington Books
An imprint of The Rowman & Littlefield Publishing Group, Inc.
4501 Forbes Boulevard, Suite 200, Lanham, Maryland 20706
www.rowman.com

86-90 Paul Street, London EC2A 4NE

Copyright © 2022 by The Rowman & Littlefield Publishing Group, Inc.

All rights reserved. No part of this book may be reproduced in any form or by any electronic or mechanical means, including information storage and retrieval systems, without written permission from the publisher, except by a reviewer who may quote passages in a review.

British Library Cataloguing in Publication Information Available

Library of Congress Cataloging-in-Publication Data

Names: Winslow, Luke, 1980– editor. | Legge, Nancy J., editor. | Justice, Jacob, 1991– editor.
Title: The revolutionary rhetoric of Hamilton / edited by Luke Winslow, Nancy J. Legge and Jacob Justice.
Description: Lanham : Lexington Books, [2022] | Includes bibliographical references and index.
Identifiers: LCCN 2022026848 (print) | LCCN 2022026849 (ebook) |
  ISBN 9781666914443 (cloth) | ISBN 9781666914467 (paperback) | ISBN 9781666914450 (ebook)
Subjects: LCSH: Miranda, Lin-Manuel, 1980– Hamilton. | Hamilton, Alexander, 1757–1804. | Narration (Rhetoric) | Race in musical theater. | History in popular culture—United States—History—21st century. | Musicals—Political aspects—United States—History—21st century.
Classification: LCC ML410.M67976 R48 2022 (print) | LCC ML410.M67976 (ebook) | DDC 792.1/4—dc23/eng/20220708
LC record available at https://lccn.loc.gov/2022026848
LC ebook record available at https://lccn.loc.gov/2022026849

LW: Dedicated to the faculty, staff, and students at San Diego State University—a community of excellence.

NJL: Dedicated to Jim, Alexis, and Jake: my "seconds" who understand the moment and the movement.

JJ: Dedicated to Talya, Mom, and Dad for imparting a lifelong love of music and history.

Contents

Acknowledgments ix

Introduction: Turning the World Upside Down 1
    Nancy J. Legge, Jacob Justice, and Luke Winslow

SECTION I: REVELATIONS ABOUT HISTORY 13

Chapter 1: "If You Had to Choose": *Hamilton*, Public Memory, and
    the Hamilton-Jefferson Rivalry 15
    Talya Peri Slaw and Jacob Justice

Chapter 2: Washington Says Good-Bye: Examining "One Last
    Time" through Public Memory 31
    Jessica L. Gehrke

Chapter 3: The Rhetorical Significance of John Laurens in
    Hamilton: An American Musical 47
    Nancy J. Legge

Chapter 4: Da Da Da Dat Da: The Rhetorical Construction of
    Hamilton's Mad Monarch 67
    Sarah Mayberry Scott

SECTION II: REVELATIONS ABOUT RACE 85

Chapter 5: Casting as a Rhetorical Act: Color-Purposeful Casting
    and *Hamilton*'s Anti-White Casting Call 87
    Ailea G. Merriam-Pigg

Chapter 6: *Hamilton*'s Revolutionary Aesthetic: Race, Hip-Hop,
    and the American Style 101
    Luke Winslow and Jonathan Veal

Chapter 7: *Hamilton*, Social Revolution, and the Black Lives
    Matter Movement   117
Caleb George Hubbard

SECTION III: REVELATIONS ABOUT SOCIOPOLITICAL ISSUES   135

Chapter 8: Immigrants: Getting the Job Done, Then and Now   137
Judith P. Roberts

Chapter 9: The Sphere Where It Happens: Reading *Hamilton*'s
    Representations of the Public/Private Sphere as Gendered,
    Restraining, and Revolutionary   149
Erika M. Thomas

SECTION IV: REVELATIONS ABOUT BROADWAY   167

Chapter 10: Who Lives, Who Dies, He Tells the Story: Hip-Hop,
    Antagonist-Narrators, and the Impact of Musical Genre on
    Storytelling   169
Max Dosser and Kevin Pabst

Chapter 11: Aaron Burr vs. Mike Pence: Curtain Speeches and
    Controversy   185
Ryan Louis

Chapter 12: *Hamilton* and the Genre of the Politicized Broadway
    Musical: Following the Rhetorical Tradition, Twisting the
    Rhetorical Tradition   203
Theodore F. Sheckels

Index   217

About the Authors   223

Acknowledgments

Luke Winslow would like to thank Dr. Trischa Goodnow for providing the initial inspiration for the project. Thanks also to Jonathan Veal, and his brilliant cohort of San Diego State University graduate students, for their passion, curiosity, and community. And special thanks to my co-editors and fellow authors included here for displaying the tenacity, creativity, and patience needed to bring this project to completion.

Nancy J. Legge would like to thank Jim, Alexis, and Elisa, who read earlier drafts of my essay and provided invaluable feedback. Thanks to my students in Rhetorical Criticism and the Rhetoric of Popular Culture, who listened to different versions of my analysis and asked thoughtful questions. Finally, I would like to raise a glass to my co-editors, Luke and Jacob. We began the project as strangers who shared a passion for *Hamilton*. We completed the project as colleagues who learned that together we can overcome adversity and never lose that passion. I am forever grateful for their strong work ethic, excellent critical eyes, and camaraderie.

Jacob Justice would like to thank Dr. Trischa Goodnow for her leadership in initiating this project. I would also like to thank fellow editors Luke and Nancy for believing in the project and helping to move it forward despite numerous setbacks, as well as the contributing authors for standing by the project. I am also thankful for my colleagues at the Department of Writing and Rhetoric at the University of Mississippi. And special thanks to Talya Slaw for introducing me to *Hamilton* and for her constant support.

Introduction

Turning the World Upside Down

Nancy J. Legge, Jacob Justice, and Luke Winslow

In August 2015, *Hamilton: An American Musical* arrived on Broadway, chronicling the life of Alexander Hamilton, the first secretary of state, beginning with his childhood in the Caribbean and ending with his death in a duel with then vice president Aaron Burr. In between, the show explores Hamilton's arrival in New York City, his role in the Revolutionary War, his career in politics, his political scandals, and his family life. The show lays bare many of Hamilton's faults as much as it details his many accomplishments. *Hamilton* dramatizes the nation's founding and its key historical figures through songs, music, and choreography that has captivated audiences. The show has sustained an unprecedented amount of popularity, largely because of its unique approach to representing American history onstage, including the show's unconventional storytelling, unprecedented casting, and innovative integration of rap and hip-hop music (Rowe, 2018). Most of the central characters in the show are non-White. Lin-Manuel Miranda—who wrote the music, book, and lyrics while also playing the titular role of Hamilton during the musical's first year—explained his intentions:

> This is a story about America then, told by America now, and we want to eliminate any distance. Our story should look the way our country looks. Then we found the best people to embody these parts. I think it's a very powerful statement without having to be a statement. (Van Evra, 2019)

Hamilton has since become a generation-defining pop culture phenomenon, winning eleven Tony Awards, seven Olivier Awards (the UK equivalent of the Tony Awards), a Grammy, and a Pulitzer Prize for Drama. Miranda also won a MacArthur "genius grant." Adam Gopnik of the *New Yorker* described *Hamilton* as the defining "musical of the Obama era, as much as '*Camelot*' was of the Kennedy era" (Gopnik, 2016). But as Obama left office and Donald Trump assumed the presidency, *Hamilton* grew to become an even greater cultural and political force.

In July 2020, *Hamilton* premiered on the streaming service Disney+, making the show accessible for millions of viewers who would never see it on Broadway. The release, originally scheduled for October 2021, was moved up as the coronavirus pandemic lockdowns forced the world into social isolation and shuttered theaters, cinemas, and travel. *Hamilton* also premiered on Disney+ soon after the murder of George Floyd by a Minneapolis police officer and political protests against racial injustice and police violence raged across the country. Further, the contentious presidential election between Donald Trump and Joe Biden was raising new questions about the future of American democracy (Chang, 2020; Paulson, 2020). Sensing an opportunity, Disney decided to release *Hamilton* into this climate. It paid off. In the first ten days on Disney+, "2.7 million households streamed *Hamilton*, exceeding the number who saw the show on Broadway or on any stage" (Frankel, 2020).

On Disney+, *Hamilton*'s cultural force expanded far beyond the elite circles of Broadway. New public conversations emerged about *Hamilton* whitewashing American history, including heated debates about Miranda's portrayal of the Founding Fathers and the show's representations of slavery (Dunn, 2020). Critic Wesley Morris wrote, "The show advanced a conversation that we're now having more vociferously than even four or five years ago, when we didn't have a president who openly mourned the removal of Confederate iconography" (Goodman, 2020). Along with journalists and art critics, *Hamilton*'s impact has also been explored by scholars of philosophy, history, and rhetoric. *Hamilton and Philosophy: Revolutionary Thinking* (2017) considered the show's philosophical questions, including the morality of honor, the implications of heroes who own slaves, and the historical accuracy of the show. *Historians on Hamilton: How a Blockbuster Musical Is Restaging America's Past* (2018) focused a historical lens on "what the musical got right and wrong" about Hamilton and other characters and whether the musical was as "revolutionary" as it claimed to be. *Rhetoric, Politics, and Hamilton: An American Musical* (2021), edited by Drury and Drury, included essays exploring the link between *Hamilton*, public memory, social identity, and democracy.

Our book offers a unique extension to the public conversations and scholarly research on *Hamilton*. The extant scholarly literature was written before the summer of 2020, when George Floyd's killing sparked the most significant protests against racial injustice in American history and changed the American public's reception of *Hamilton* (Srikanth, 2020). Lin-Manuel Miranda encouraged the new public conversation, tweeting that critiques of his show were "all fair game" in this new historical moment (2020). The extant *Hamilton* research does not consider the show's wider audience and the reemergence of racial unrest after George Floyd. Several of the chapters in this book directly address popular culture and racial turmoil, offering a fresh intervention into an unprecedented historical moment.

Near the end of the first act, *Hamilton* features a song called "Yorktown (The World Turned Upside Down)," based on legend about the British troops singing the song after their defeat at the Battle of Yorktown (Provan, 2018). The American Revolution challenged the world order. In like manner, *Hamilton* reflected and shaped a changing world order in the twenty-first century. In this book, the authors explore how *Hamilton* turned ideas upside down by encouraging audiences to see and interpret the world in new ways. Specifically, the book examines how *Hamilton* challenged conventional conceptions of theater, race, politics, and American history, especially the show's revolutionary capacity to promote social criticism, influence public memory, and shape community-building. *Hamilton* is an exemplar of popular culture's potential and, more specifically, musical theater's capacity to spark difficult and profound conversations about political controversies and ongoing injustices. As such, *Hamilton* is ripe for rhetorical analysis.

THE RHETORIC OF POPULAR CULTURE

Some may dismiss *Hamilton* as trivial entertainment—nothing more and nothing less. They may assume that popular culture is an empty distraction and certainly not worthy of scholarly attention and analysis. The reality, however, is that popular culture texts communicate messages about what is "normal" or "abnormal," "acceptable" or "unacceptable," "valuable" or "not valuable." Popular culture is pervasive. We all participate in popular culture every day: we listen to podcasts, read the news, watch films, stream music, and have conversations with our friends about the latest memes or TikTok videos. As we participate, we come to understand what is valued, accepted, and normal. We also learn what is problematic, laughable, or otherwise unacceptable. Popular culture is so pervasive that we often engage with it and are influenced by it, without thinking. This is precisely why it should not be dismissed as trivial or unimportant. Popular culture "has the persuasive power to shape beliefs and behaviors" (Sellnow, 2018, p. 7). To dismiss it as "a distraction" or "empty" or "not worthy" of inquiry dismisses essential ways that we communicate, create meaning, and understand cultural values.

Historically, many scholars did not consider popular culture worthy of inquiry. The ancient Greeks and Romans, medieval courtiers, Renaissance theologians, political thinkers in the emerging democracies of the eighteenth century, and critical scholars of the 1800s and 1900s placed a premium on the culture of the ruling class. As recently as the 1970s, there was no place for the study of popular culture in the conventional university curriculums because popular culture was still considered to be a vulgar and essentially commercial medium, appealing to the lowest common denominator (Mukerji and Schudson, 1991). Instead, scholars focused their analyses on legal rulings, political speeches, and public policy decisions.

Early perceptions of popular culture as debased and insignificant were influenced by Edward Burnett Tylor's and Matthew Arnold's definitions of culture in the late nineteenth century. Tylor took an anthropological attitude toward cultural studies, defining all the customs and mores of a group as "culture." However, he argued it was only at the highest stage of an explicitly formulated sequence of progressive human development that "culture" could flower (Stocking, 1982). Tylor placed savagery and barbarism as the lowest grades on his scale and European culture (of which he was a part) at the top, as the end product of all cultural development and the most perfect form of human achievement. Matthew Arnold continued to use Tylor's preference for high culture. But for Arnold, there was no "popular culture." The savagery and barbarism of the common people was not culture at all, but an activity fit for anarchy. Arnold instead preferred and studied the "sweetness and light" produced by the ruling elite (Cruz, 1999). The responsibility of guiding the masses away from their vulgar day-to-day influences fell on the ruling elite, who were to educate the masses out of their cultural ignorance.

Yet high culture was not accessible to the masses. Elites had self-interest in keeping the masses in the dark. According to sociologist Herbert J. Gans (1999), the elite who supported high culture "rejected popular participation in elite activities" and had little interest in providing access to high culture to non-elites (p. 73). Gans explains that until the twentieth century, "upper income groups were frequently opposed to educating lower ones, for they were fearful that literacy would only lead to revolution and the loss of their privileges" (p. 73).

This preservation of high culture by the elite while simultaneously blocking access to it reflects a political agenda. Popular culture is in continuous tension with high culture (Mukerji and Schudson, 1991). Author John Seabrook (2000) argued that separating culture into highbrow and lowbrow is itself a political act meant to render culture into class. For this reason, guardians of the elite saw popular culture as a threat. They saw threats from novels in the eighteenth century which attracted women readers in droves; from mass circulation of newspapers in the late nineteenth century which attracted the working class; from nickelodeons in the early twentieth century which attracted new immigrants to the United States; from comic books in the 1940s and 1950s which attracted the young; and of course, in the twenty-first century, from an iconoclastic hip-hop musical attracting new audiences to the theater for the first time. Popular culture texts were recognized as potential vehicles for those without power to communicate ideas and challenge ways of thinking. That these popular texts threatened the political power of the elite illustrates how politics transcends the courtroom and the Senate floor.

Indictments of popular culture took a different form in the twentieth century. Influential Marxist thinkers, members of the Frankfurt School including Max Horkheimer, Theodor Adorno, Herbert Marcuse, Leo Lowenthal, and Erick Fromm argued that hegemony from above, and not contestation from below, defined most popular culture. Although these thinkers held divergent ideas, most characterized popular culture as a distortion of reality camouflaging unequal power relations and producing passive and politically debilitated audiences. Despite their admiration of high art, Horkheimer and Adorno in particular argued that most popular culture artifacts eventually became commodities and that culture itself had been transformed into an industry—an industry that did not guide us toward a blissful life or moral responsibility but exhorted its audience to "toe the line" (Adorno, 2005, p. 107). Mass commodification meant that there was no struggle, only top-down influence, leaving audiences with only two options: buying or not buying (Macdonald, 2005). These scholars in the Frankfurt School argued that the masses were dupes, brainwashed into conformity by the culture industry: a conformity that replaced consciousness and hindered the ability of the masses to engage in political struggle (Debord, 2005).

The Frankfurt School was wise to expose how the ruling elite might use popular culture to monopolize culture into an industry of consumption, turning art into commodities and producing passive consumers. Popular culture often does provide consumers a fake way to overcome injustice and oppression by obscuring race, class, and gender and turning politics into entertainment (Lipsitz, 1990). Many have argued that popular culture constructs hierarchies of power through subtle mechanisms of control that promote a way of life in which elite interests are assumed to be "natural" and "commonsense." Rather than using police dogs and fire hoses to make sure everyone knows who is in charge, hegemonic forms of influence come through in everyday media consumption. It is in popular culture that hegemony arises and where hegemony is secured (Hall, 1981).

And yet, many popular culture texts, including the debates about the messages in and influences of *Hamilton*, point to a more complicated relationship between hegemony and popular culture. What the Frankfurt School missed in overestimating the power of the elite in popular culture was the *process* by which relations of dominance and subordination are articulated. Hegemony is never a fixed, once-and-for-all achievement. It is an innately unstable process that must be continually renewed, re-created, defended, and modified (Eagleton, 1991). No sooner are power relations established than they start to come apart, as excluded individuals and groups struggle to create new alliances capable of transforming inequitable power relations. Hegemony is a temporary solution that must be remade each day. This often takes place in popular culture, where people are not passive consumers but active participants. The current debates about the positive and negative influences of *Hamilton* (many of which are detailed in the chapters in this book) reflect this tension and ongoing struggle. In this way, popular culture can also be the site of struggle from below, offering moments of contestation and resistance. Stuart Hall put it well:

> I think there is a continuous and necessarily uneven and unequal struggle, by the dominate culture, constantly to disorganize and reorganize popular culture; to enclose and confine its definitions and forms within a more inclusive range of dominant forms. There are points of resistance; there are also moments of supersession; this is the dialectical cultural struggle. In our times it goes on continuously, in the complex line of resistance and acceptance, refusal and capitulation, which make the field of culture a sort of constant battlefield. A battlefield where no-once-for-all victories are obtained, but where there are always strategic positions to be won and lost. (1981, p. 233)

Hamilton's cultural impact reveals how the Frankfurt School might have been blinded to the *struggle* of popular culture. Like an athletic contest that is deemed "not a game" because one side is so dominant, those in power controlled the struggle over the marginalized and nonaligned so much that many missed the struggle in the first place. The upper class defined culture in advantageous terms, valorizing their cultural activities as the locus of a genuine, "autonomous" aesthetic production, while labeling what the masses did as vulgar and debased (Jameson, 1979, p. 133). Just as Broadway theater was once thought to be "better" art than rap music, the "seal of approval" was given to the activities that met the standards established by those in power. But the rules and standards evolve. Today, many problems of racism may be managed in Ava DuVernay's films. Sexism may be managed in romance novels where some women use the act of reading to carve out for themselves private time in the face of domestic demands (Brummett, 2006; Radway, 1984). The ways that *Hamilton* was first received are different than the ways that it is currently discussed. All of these changes reveal an ongoing conversation about the influential messages in popular culture. Popular culture, and

Hamilton in particular, functions as a site of struggle, where conversations about culture values are located.

Popular culture often operates between hierarchies of power imposed from above and the resistance and contestation from below. It can be emancipatory or dominating—a site of transformational work on social and political anxieties or a tool of oppression. Many look to popular culture with the assumption that conventional institutions like politics, religion, and the law cannot offer effective means of resistance because they are controlled by the ruling elite. The master's tools cannot dismantle the master's house, and so the groups not allowed on the Senate floor, who are marginalized, can look to popular culture for resistance. The potential for the marginalized and voiceless to use *Hamilton* to struggle against the powerful is a wonderful example of bottom-up political work that can be done in popular culture. There, in the everyday texts of popular culture, is where empowerment and disempowerment can be managed. It is clear the marginalized and nonaligned can use popular culture as a form of resistance and contestation by carving out for themselves places of comfort and by finding sites of struggle in one of the only places where their voices are not muted.

But a skeptic may yet wonder if popular culture distracts people from the "real" political organization and issues of political economy. Some may suggest that popular culture may work as a *substitute* for politics—a way of posing imaginary solutions to real-life problems (see Lipsitz, 1990). Instead of marching in a BLM rally or writing a letter to the editor, one can turn on Disney+. Terry Eagleton articulated this skeptical stance when he wrote, "Watching television for long stretches confirms individuals in passive, isolated, privatized roles and consumes a good deal of time that could be put to productive political uses" (1991, p. 35).

Others may wonder how culture can be a political practice in a society where world-spanning corporations like Apple, Meta, and News Corp dominate the global cultural market, where resistance seems to be appropriated and marketed, and even the most radical politics can take the form of celebrity endorsement (Denning, 2004). If watching Disney+ is understood as a form of cultural resistance, haven't we lost any sense of effective politics? But the messages communicated in popular culture texts can and have provided transformational ideas and actions on social and political anxieties (Jameson, 1979).

Popular culture texts including *Hamilton* address some of these qualms by highlighting how modernization has expanded the location of "real" political work from the Senate floor and courtrooms to television screens and smartphones. The declining social influence of the political parties, social organizations, and religious institutions points to a cultural transition disrupting our sense of place. If we want to understand how people are influenced and how public affairs are nudged in one direction or another, we need to look more at what is happening beyond traditional levers of power. The decline in traditional political, social, and religious engagement has created a void that popular culture has filled. This means that the texts which were once considered insignificant have replaced the ones thought to be the sole influence on moral, aesthetic, and political value.

Leo Tolstoy argued the public decisions shaping history are not made by ruling elites alone but by the everyday experiences of millions of people who organically and chaotically shape destiny from the bottom up. Understanding *Hamilton*'s rhetorical impact begins with recognizing that ruling elites exert only partial influence over political progress. It is not the politicians in the White House alone who influence us. It is also the rhetoric of our everyday experiences that influences us (Brummett, 2006). For this reason, when a cultural artifact seems to be screaming, "There is no need to look over here; there is no rhetoric going on over here," we ought to take a closer look. Hegemonies are hidden. That is what makes them hegemonic. And when they are well-disguised, it takes a deft critic to root them out: a critic willing to dig into *The Bachelor* and *Succession* to think about the way those programs not only entertain but influence; a critic working like an anthropologist when watching a *Star Wars* reboot because beneath the surface, the films provide audiences with the possibility of additional meanings telling a larger story than itself; a critic willing to shine a light on the texts of everyday living that go beyond culture to the politics of culture.

The forthcoming chapters challenge the notion that the State of the Union address and the *New York Times* op-ed are the only places where public conversations are shaped. Understanding popular culture in this way can be a useful tool for seeing the rhetorical dimensions of our world more richly and clearly. From this scholarly foundation, the forthcoming chapters deploy a range of theoretical perspectives, lenses, and methodological tools to illuminate *Hamilton*'s political and cultural significance. Showing the flexibility of rhetorical studies and adjacent disciplines, the chapters in this book treat *Hamilton* as a public memory artifact shaping social understandings of American history, an intervention into debates about racial inequality provoked by the Black Lives Matter movement, a window into societal attitudes toward immigrants and gender relations, and an instigator of evolution within the musical theater genre.

Introduction

CHAPTER OVERVIEW

Section I explores how *Hamilton* challenges our traditional thinking about history. In chapter 1, Talya Peri Slaw and Jacob Justice explore the ways that *Hamilton* urges viewers to reconsider the roles of Alexander Hamilton and Thomas Jefferson in our history and collective public memory. In chapter 2, Jessica L. Gehrke considers how *Hamilton* helps us reinterpret the significance of Washington's Farewell Address. In chapter 3, Nancy J. Legge examines the significance of the Laurens Interlude in the show. She argues that the show does not ignore slavery but presents the issue as an uncomfortable reality. The scene is a metaphor for the ways that Hamilton and the Founding Fathers consciously ignored slavery while building the country. In chapter 4, Sarah Mayberry Scott examines how *Hamilton* influences how King George III is remembered and discussed, arguing that the king's portrayal reinforces stereotypes about mental illness.

In Section II of the book, the authors explore ways that *Hamilton* challenges traditional thinking about race. In chapter 5, Ailea Merriam-Pigg explores the deliberate choices made in original and subsequent casting for the show and the backlash that followed, which accused the *Hamilton* casting call of being "anti-White." Merriam-Pigg suggests that the call was a deliberate attempt to decenter Whiteness in theater, with implications for performers and future casting calls. Chapter 6 examines the aesthetic of *Hamilton*. Luke Winslow and Jonathan Veal argue that some aspects of Black style were reinvented in *Hamilton* to appeal to and resonate with White audiences who might attend the show. In chapter 7, Caleb George Hubbard contends that two social revolutions, the American Revolution in *Hamilton* and the Black Lives Matter movement, are interrelated. He suggests that *Hamilton* provides a platform for Black Lives Matter as well as instructions for making long-term social changes. Black Lives Matter, in turn, demands accountability from the nation for unfulfilled promises of freedom and justice.

Section III of the book considers some ways that *Hamilton* challenges traditional ways of thinking about some social and political issues, especially immigration and gender. In chapter 8, Judith P. Roberts argues that the show's elevation of immigrants in public rhetoric spilled over to current public discourse, urging audiences to fight for pro-immigrant policies and for immigrants. In chapter 9, Erika M. Thomas looks at some gender dynamics in the show and argues that they illustrate ongoing tensions of power and politics in relationships.

Section IV of the book examines how *Hamilton* challenges basic assumptions about musical theater. In chapter 10, Max Dosser and Kevin Pabst examine how the role of the narrator is challenged and transformed in

Hamilton. Chapter 11 involves the function of "curtain speeches." Ryan Louis focuses on the November 2016 performance of *Hamilton* that Vice President–elect Mike Pence attended and the curtain call delivered to him by the cast. He examines the subsequent controversy that ensued about the proper role of performers, theater, and the interaction between entertainment and politics. In chapter 12, Theodore F. Sheckels considers how *Hamilton* altered our conceptualizations of musical theater. He suggests that *Hamilton* is both traditional and revolutionary, deviating from tradition so that an aesthetic or political point can be made.

Ultimately, *Hamilton* has encouraged each of us to think more critically about our most complicated social challenges. *Hamilton* is a rich artifact that has inspired us to turn traditional ways of thinking upside down and consider varied, and sometimes controversial, interpretations of history, politics, social issues, and theater. It is our hope that these chapters do likewise for the reader, challenging assumptions and sparking new conversations while also appreciating the artistic excellence of this generational cultural force.

REFERENCES

Adorno, T. W. (2005). "Culture Industry Reconsidered." In *Popular Culture: A Reader*, edited by R. Guins and O. Z. Cruz. Thousand Oaks, CA: Sage Publications.

Brummett, B. (2006). *Rhetoric in Popular Culture*. Thousand Oaks, CA: Sage Publications.

Chang, J. (2020). "Review: From Broadway to Disney+, 'Hamilton' Speaks Brilliantly to a Time of Fear and Protest." *Los Angeles Times*, June 30, 2020. https://www.latimes.com/entertainment-arts/movies/story/2020-06-30/hamilton-review-lin-manuel-miranda-disney.

Cruz, J. (1999). *Culture on the Margins: The Black Spiritual and the Rise of American Cultural Interpretation*. Princeton, NJ: Princeton University Press.

Debord, G. (2005). "The Commodity as Spectacle." In *Popular Culture: A Reader*, edited by R. Guins and O. Z. Cruz. Thousand Oaks, CA: Sage Publications.

Denning, M. (2004). *Culture in the Age of Three Worlds*. London and New York: Verso.

Dunn, M. (2020). "How *Hamilton* Became the First Musical of the Trump Era." Writing Stage, November 17, 2020. https://thewritingstage.com/2020/11/16/how-hamilton-became-the-first-musical-of-the-trump-era/.

Eagleton, T. (1991). *Ideology: An Introduction*. London and New York: Verso.

Frankel, D. (2020). "Disney Plus 'Hamilton' Viewership Exceeds Those Who've Seen It Live, Research Company Says." Next TV, July 20, 2020. https://www.nexttv.com/news/disney-plus-hamilton-viewership-exceeds-those-whove-seen-it-live-research-company-says.

Gans, H. J. (1999). *Popular Culture and High Culture: An Analysis and Evaluation of Taste*. New York: Basic Books.

Goodman, S. (2020). "Debating 'Hamilton' as It Shifts from Stage to Screen." *New York Times*, July 10, 2020. https://www.nytimes.com/2020/07/10/movies/hamilton-critics-lin-manuel-miranda.html.

Gopnik, A. (2016). "'Hamilton' and the Hip-Hop Case for Progressive Heroism." *The New Yorker*, February 5, 2016. https://www.newyorker.com/news/daily-comment/hamilton-and-the-hip-hop-case-for-progressive-heroism.

Hall, S. (1981). "Notes on Deconstructing 'the Popular.'" In *People's History and Socialist Theory*, edited by Samuel Raphael. London: Routledge.

Jameson, F. (1979). "Reification and Utopia in Mass Culture." *Social Text* 1, 130–48.

Lipsitz, G. (1990). *Time Passages: Collective Memory in American Popular Culture*. Minneapolis: University of Minnesota Press.

Macdonald, D. (2005). "A Theory of Mass Culture." In *Popular Culture: A Reader*, edited by R. Guins and O. Z. Cruz. Thousand Oaks, CA: Sage Publications.

Miranda, L. [@Lin_Manuel]. (2020). "Appreciate you so much, @brokeymcpoverty. All criticisms are valid. The sheer tonnage of complexities and failings of these people I couldn't get. Or wrestled with but cut. I took 6 years and fit as much as I could in a 2.5 hour musical. Did my best. It's all fair game." [Tweet]. Twitter. July 6, 2020. https://twitter.com/Lin_Manuel/status/1280120414279290881.

Mukerji, C. and M. Schudson (1991). *Rethinking Popular Culture: Contemporary Perspectives in Cultural Studies*. Berkeley: University of California Press.

Paulson, M. (2020). "'Hamilton' Is Coming to the Small Screen. This Is How It Got There." *New York Times*, June 25, 2020. https://www.nytimes.com/2020/06/25/movies/hamilton-movie-disney-streaming.html.

Provan, J. (2018). "Legend Holds That the British Fifes and Drums Played 'The World Turned Upside Down' as the Redcoats Marched Out from Behind Their Ramparts to Stack Their Arms at Washington's Feet. But Did It Actually Happen?" MilitaryHistoryNow.com, May 29, 2018. https://militaryhistorynow.com/2018/05/29/the-world-turned-upside-down-did-the-british-really-play-the-sardonic-melody-during-the-yorktown-surrender/.

Radway, J. A. (1984). *Reading the Romance: Women, Patriarchy, and Popular Literature*. Chapel Hill: University of North Carolina Press.

Rowe, B. (2018). "Why Is *Hamilton* So Successful?" Medium, November 22, 2018. https://medium.com/@brianrowe_70270/why-is-hamilton-so-successful-71e1752257f6.

Seabrook, J. (2000). *Nobrow: The Culture of Marketing; the Marketing of Culture*. New York: Vintage.

Sellnow, D. D. (2018). *The Rhetorical Power of Popular Culture*, 3rd ed. Los Angeles, CA: Sage Publications.

Srikanth, A. (2020). "No, Twitter Hasn't Canceled *Hamilton*—Although Some Are Calling for It." *The Hill*, July 6, 2020. https://thehill.com/changing-america/enrichment/arts-culture/506012-no-twitter-hasn't-exactly-cancelled-hamilton-although.

Stocking, G. W. (1982). *Race, Culture, and Evolution: Essays in the History of Anthropology*. Chicago: University of Chicago Press.

Van Evra, J. (2019). "*Hamilton*: 15 Fascinating Facts about the Biggest Musical of All." *CBCnews*. CBC/Radio Canada, October 30, 2019. https://www.cbc.ca/radio/q/blog/hamilton-15-fascinating-facts-about-the-biggest-musical-of-all-time-1.5341556.

SECTION I

Revelations about History

Chapter 1

"If You Had to Choose"

Hamilton, *Public Memory*, and the Hamilton-Jefferson Rivalry

Talya Peri Slaw and Jacob Justice

On May 12, 2009, Lin-Manuel Miranda performed at the White House Evening of Poetry, Music, and the Spoken Word. As the recently inaugurated Barack Obama looked on from the audience, Miranda introduced a selection about a historical figure that, according to Miranda, "embodies hip-hop: treasury secretary Alexander Hamilton." For many reasons, Hamilton is not a person whose life and ideology are an obvious match with hip-hop music. Nonetheless, Miranda's 2009 preview of what would become *Hamilton: An American Musical* foreshadowed one of the musical's key accomplishments: the rehabilitation and revitalization of an often overlooked and complex historical figure, Hamilton.

Hamilton's counterintuitive yet innovative choice to retell America's origin myth using hip-hop music and a multicultural cast made the show a cultural phenomenon. As a result, the musical's "remarkable success" has "restored Hamilton's reputation in the American mind to a status not seen since Reconstruction" (Knott, 2018, p. 552). *Hamilton* has proven such a potent cultural force that the musical is credited with spurring efforts to preserve Hamilton's portrait on the $10 bill (Phillips, 2016).

Although the musical is beloved by people of all political persuasions, *Hamilton* has special significance for progressive liberals, as the show is widely interpreted as a metaphor for Obama's America that celebrates "previously marginalized people" shouldering "the responsibility and burden of American history" (Gopnik, 2016, para. 4). Lin-Manuel Miranda's novel reinterpretation has transformed Hamilton into a "hero of the progressive left" (Isenberg, 2016, para. 1) and an "unlikely icon of democratic inclusiveness" (Stoller, 2017, para. 3). Further cementing popular associations between Hamilton and liberalism, the musical's lyrics were paraphrased by Hillary Clinton in her presidential nomination acceptance speech at the 2016 Democratic National Convention (Poniewozik, 2016), and a remix of the song "My Shot" from the *Hamilton* soundtrack served as the exit music for then senator Kamala Harris's presidential campaign launch rally in January 2019 (Scott, 2019).

Hamilton's newfound status as a liberal hero is puzzling. For much of the nation's history, Alexander Hamilton was reviled "as the founding's villain—the man who sought to foist a crown upon the nation and to subvert Jeffersonian democracy" (Knott, 2004, para. 2). Moreover, Democrats traditionally identified Hamilton's archnemesis Thomas Jefferson as the father of the Democratic Party. For decades, Democrats and historians drew a direct "line from Jefferson to Roosevelt to Kennedy" (Burstein, 2015, p. 37). According to this narrative, the Democratic Party is defined by its centuries-long commitment to championing the rights of common folk against the predatory forces of big business and corruption (Schlesinger, 1953).

Hamilton's cultural impact can be elucidated by examining how the musical revises public memories of Alexander Hamilton and Thomas Jefferson. *Hamilton* deconstructs mythologization of Jefferson while inventing a new mythology that centers the contribution of immigrants and minorities to the nation's greatness. We argue that *Hamilton* revolutionizes the story of America's founding to account for the contemporary nation's growing diversity and to render this origin story compatible with an inclusive, community-oriented interpretation of the American Dream myth. In this chapter, we demonstrate that a key means through which *Hamilton* reframes the American Dream mythology is its portrayal of the rivalry between Hamilton and Jefferson, who serve as symbolic proxies for contemporary liberals and conservatives in the ongoing debate over the proper role and size of government. We explain the qualities of *Hamilton*—in terms of music, lyrics, choreography, staging, and costuming—that enable the show to reimagine Founding Era public memories.

In advancing this argument, we treat *Hamilton* as a public memory text that revises historical understandings of Hamilton, Jefferson, and the American Revolution. By public memory, we refer to collective understandings of the past that publics develop to comprehend a society's past, present, and future as manifested in popular culture, art, memory sites, and memorials (Bodnar, 1992). We argue that *Hamilton* reshapes public memory by serving as a memorial to Hamilton, an influential but often overlooked figure, and by challenging the tendency of much American public memory to venerate Jefferson. Rather than analyze solely the musical's historical accuracy, we investigate how *Hamilton* encourages a specific set of remembrances of these pivotal historical figures.

That *Hamilton* is an intervention into public memory is beyond dispute. The show's staging features cast members observing the show's proceedings from U-shaped, two-story balconies, acting as stand-ins for contemporary students of history. Often, ensemble members or even lead actors and actresses stand on these balconies, watching as pivotal scenes unfold from above, serving as agents of memory to emphasize scenes as significant. Moreover, the show's lyrics "consciously refer to the shaping of historical memory" (Monteiro, 2018, pp. 59–60). Early in the show, a young Hamilton dreams about a coming day "when our children tell our story" (Miranda and McCarter, 2016, p. 35). Later in *Hamilton*, Hamilton's heartbroken wife Eliza sings, "I'm erasing myself from the narrative" while burning letters (p. 238). Elsewhere in the show, George Washington reminds Hamilton that "history has its eyes on you" and kicks off the final musical number by stating "you have no control" over "who tells your story" (pp. 120, 280). Through thoughtful staging and lyrical choices, *Hamilton* argues that "history" is not an objective record of past events but is instead subject to ongoing negotiation, interpretation, and argument. The musical is keenly self-aware that it advances a partial understanding of history while occluding others.

An important contribution of *Hamilton* to public memory is to present Hamilton as a more appropriate source of inspiration for contemporary progressives than Jefferson. The musical attempts to salvage American history by providing a hero worthy of a rapidly diversifying nation where many denizens are increasingly skeptical of the founding generation for its complicity in slavery and other injustices. We develop this argument in four parts. First, we explain how public memory of Jefferson has evolved across history. Second, we outline the tenets of the American Dream myth and debates over how to interpret this myth. Third, we argue that *Hamilton* juxtaposes qualities of Hamilton and Jefferson to present Hamilton as a founder of American progressivism and an exemplar of the American Dream. Fourth, we conclude by reflecting on the significance of *Hamilton* as a public memory text.

PUBLIC MEMORIES OF THE FOUNDING ERA

Public memory can be defined as how "a public or society understand[s] both its past, present, and, by implication, its future" (Bodnar, 1992, p. 15). Through public memory, societies create a "sense of collectivity" and shared history to cement group identities and foster community (Phillips, 2007, p. 3; Gillis, 1996). Public memory is flexible: societies may craft collective memories and shared historical narratives to confront contemporary problems and respond to societal needs (Halbwachs, 1992). Finally, public memory is also a struggle over power that can serve political ends, as memory texts "instruct" audiences "about what is to be valued in the future as well as in the past" (Blair, Jeppeson, and Pucci, 1991, p. 263).

A particularly important area of public memory research is charting how historical remembrances of certain individuals can evolve over time. Attention to shifts in public memories of historical figures can elucidate how these individuals are taken up as either heroes or villains to function as a narrative resource for contemporary rhetors to advance their goals (Browne, 1999). Perhaps no figure in American history better illustrates the fluid nature of public memory than Thomas Jefferson, whose memory "has been recast and reconstituted" for ideological purposes countless times (Burstein, 2015, p. 24; Cogliano, 2006). For over a century, Jefferson served for "Democrats as Lincoln has for decades served the Republicans: the formal symbol of the party's legendary beginnings" (Peterson, 1962, p. 448). The Democratic Party's celebration of Jefferson persisted throughout the twentieth century and into the new millennium. As recently as 2007, Barack Obama spoke at a Jefferson-Jackson dinner held in Iowa and lionized the Democratic Party as "the party of Jefferson and Jackson, of Roosevelt and Kennedy" and promised that corporations "will not drown out the voices of the American people when I am President" (Obama, 2007, paras. 8–13).

Yet by President Obama's second term, the Democratic Party's tradition of celebrating Jefferson was waning. The conservative movement increasingly asserted itself as the rightful heirs of the Jeffersonian tradition (Burstein, 2015). Moreover, with public memory of Jefferson increasingly defined by the contradiction between his status as "the foremost expositor of human freedom and equality in eighteenth-century America" and his ownership "of approximately six hundred African slaves" (Cogliano, 2006, p. 12), American liberals were searching for a new hero that could redeem the nation's violent past while charting a path to a more progressive future.

COMPETING AMERICAN DREAM INTERPRETATIONS

Hamilton posits the first treasury secretary as a crucial source of inspiration for modern progressives by presenting Hamilton as the embodiment of the American Dream. In this section, we outline key tenets of the American Dream myth and ongoing debates over how to interpret this narrative. *Hamilton* unabashedly declares that realizing the American Dream requires energetic government and a commitment to inclusivity, weighing in on contemporary political disputes.

The Individualistic and Community-Oriented American Dream Myths

Merrill Peterson, prolific Jefferson historian, once declared that "the classic dialogue of American politics" is "the dialogue of Jefferson and Hamilton" (1962, p. 210). For decades, the canonical origin story of the Democratic Party positioned Jefferson as the party's heroic father figure. Within such narratives, Hamilton and Jefferson were "archetypal antagonists, whose opposite principles were Monarchical and Democratical" (p. 21). Jefferson was remembered as a champion of individual liberty, with Hamilton reduced to a negative symbol of big government run amok.

Just as political movements have fought over ownership of Jefferson, there is a long-standing debate about whether individualistic or community-oriented values are the key to unlocking the American Dream. The American Dream is a sacred-secular myth that can be defined as "the promise that all Americans have a reasonable chance to achieve success as they define it—material or otherwise—through their own efforts, and to attain virtue and fulfillment through success" (Hochschild, 1995, p. xi). Although the nation has struggled to make the dream available to all, this myth serves as the nation's "guiding mythology" (Samuel, 2012, p. 1).

Conservatives have historically advanced an individualistic interpretation where "enactment of personal values ensures fulfillment of the American Dream," while liberals advanced a community-oriented interpretation presenting "societal values (and policies flowing from them) as the key to achievement of the American Dream" (Rowland and Jones, 2007, p. 432). The former interpretation presents government as an obstacle to individual flourishing; the latter views government action as necessary to achieve the American Dream where markets fail to create equitable prosperity. This debate mirrors the "Jefferson-Hamilton dichotomy," which symbolizes "essential differences in domestic policy prescriptions" (Burstein, 2015, p. 59).

The Inclusive and Exclusive American Dream Myths

Nativism has become a dominant force in American politics, a trend encapsulated by the election of President Donald Trump in 2016. Although conservatives and liberals have long disagreed about whether individual or community values best secured the American Dream, both interpretations of the American Dream myth were rooted in a fundamentally inclusive worldview, maintaining faith that the American Dream can be made available to all (Chait, 2018). Departing from this consensus, a debate is underway about how inclusive or exclusive the American Dream should be. The *inclusive* American Dream myth is defined by optimism and openness toward immigrants, while the *exclusive* or *nationalist* variant espouses a dystopian outlook and hostility toward noncitizens. Trump's "hoard-the-pie, pull-up-the-drawbridge" nationalism reduces politics to a zero-sum game where frightening Others threaten to steal the American Dream from "real" Americans (Friedman, 2019, para. 14). Trump's rhetoric stokes anxieties about the crumbling of this dream and tells Americans that the dream needs to be protected from unworthy and dangerous outsiders. In the next section, we explain how *Hamilton* the musical revises public memories of the Hamilton-Jefferson rivalry to advocate for an optimistic, inclusive, community-oriented interpretation of the American Dream.

HAMILTON, JEFFERSON, AND THE AMERICAN DREAM

Hamilton intervenes into these arguments over how to properly realize the American Dream and thus reframes public memory of the American Revolution, by elevating Hamilton as the original American progressive and recasting Jefferson as a kindred spirit to small government conservatives. This reframing is accomplished through a series of juxtapositions. First, *Hamilton* contrasts the distinct governing philosophies of Hamilton and Jefferson. Second, *Hamilton* creates an analogy between Hamilton's compromising political style and that of President Obama, in turn presenting Jefferson as an obstructionist in the vein of contemporary Republicans. Third, *Hamilton* contrasts Hamilton and Jefferson's character and background by arguing that Hamilton's immigrant upbringing is the embodiment of the American Dream while dismissing Jefferson as a privileged slaveholder. Fourth, *Hamilton* lionizes its titular character as a hero that contemporary liberals can identify with by symbolically linking him to America's boisterous cities, while presenting Jefferson as a provincial defender of the rural South.

Governing Philosophies

Hamilton, at its core, is an affirmation of the community-oriented American Dream myth, arguing that government intervention is crucial to securing the American Dream. In the musical, Hamilton vocally advocates energetic government to bring states together and uplift all Americans. Jefferson, in contrast, argues for passive government that affords greater independence to states.

As the first act of *Hamilton* draws to a close in "Non-Stop," audiences watch Hamilton transition from soldier to public servant. Hamilton implies that his motivation for entering politics results from concern about the new nation's struggling economy ("This colony's economy's increasingly stalling"; Miranda and McCarter, 2016, p. 137). Hamilton's solution, even prior to becoming treasury secretary and battling with Thomas Jefferson, is "strong central democracy" (Miranda and McCarter, 2016, p. 138).

This argument is expanded in the Cabinet Battles, as Hamilton defends his views against Jefferson's opposition. In "Cabinet Battle #1," Jefferson begins by referencing his own words in the Declaration of Independence, stating "life, liberty, and the pursuit of happiness / we fought for these ideals, we shouldn't settle for less" (Miranda and McCarter, 2016, p. 161). Jefferson then lays out his argument against establishing a national bank, asserting that such a plan would foster corruption by benefiting "the very seat of government where Hamilton sits" (Miranda and McCarter, 2016, p. 161). Here, Jefferson offers his skepticism about big government, noting that a national bank would expand the power of the central government. Jefferson is primarily concerned about the individual states maintaining their independence from the national government. This "every state for itself" mentality instructs audiences that Jefferson subscribes to a more individualistic interpretation of the American Dream.

Hamilton's verse in "Cabinet Battle #1" is a line-by-line response to Jefferson, beginning with "Thomas, that was a real nice declaration / Welcome to the present, we're running a real nation" (Miranda and McCarter, 2016, p. 161). According to Hamilton, it is not enough to aspire to worthy ideals such as life, liberty, and happiness. Instead, Hamilton argues, it takes government action to help ensure those ideals become reality. Hamilton, ignoring Jefferson's contention about states' rights, argues that the young nation needs "aggressive and competitive" economic policy rather than "a sedative" (Miranda and McCarter, 2016, p. 161). The implication of Hamilton's argument is that only through a strong union of states can the United States of America succeed.

In "Hurricane," Hamilton personalizes this vision of the American Dream. As his life crumbles in the aftermath of the devastating Reynolds Pamphlet, Hamilton recounts his origin story as a source of strength. When his hometown was destroyed by a hurricane when Hamilton was a teenager, he worked hard to recover from the destruction, writing "his way out" (Miranda and McCarter, 2016, p. 232). However, Hamilton credits his success to the community that raised him, recounting how his hometown "passed a plate around" and "raised enough" money for Hamilton to pay for passage to New York (Miranda and McCarter, 2016, p. 232). *Hamilton* emphasizes Hamilton's prolific work ethic, but his grittiness alone is not enough to guarantee success. Instead, Hamilton's individual successes are owed to community sacrifices. Hamilton's gracious reflection on the collective roots of his individual accomplishments is a powerful illustration of President Obama's community-oriented interpretation of the American Dream myth. Speaking in Osawatomie, Kansas, Obama articulated this theme by declaring that "we're the greatest nation on Earth" because "our success has never just been about survival of the fittest. It's about building a nation where we're all better off. We pull together. We pitch in. We do our part" (Obama, 2011).

Political Style

Hamilton further argues that Hamilton is the proper inspiration for modern progressives by creating a direct analogy between the Hamilton-Jefferson rivalry and President Obama's contentious relationship with congressional Republicans. Specifically, *Hamilton* portrays Hamilton and Jefferson as representing two competing political styles: Hamilton represents pragmatic liberalism, whereas Jefferson represents hyper-partisan obstructionism. Invoking a popular understanding of the Obama administration among liberals, Hamilton gradually learns the value of compromise despite confronting resistance from obstinate political rivals. By contrast, Jefferson, in his fierce opposition to Hamilton's agenda, serves as a stand-in for the conservative backlash against the Obama administration.

The policy debates throughout *Hamilton*'s second act operate as a clever restaging of Obama-era disputes and a showcase for the competing political styles of Hamilton and Jefferson. Hamilton begins the second act with grand ambitions of establishing a strong central government and a national bank. In "Cabinet Battle #1," Jefferson derides Hamilton's plan as "an outrageous demand" that is "too many damn pages for any man to understand" (Miranda and McCarter, 2016, p. 161). By complaining about the page length of Hamilton's proposals, Miranda's Jefferson bears more in common with modern congressional Republicans than the historical Jefferson, who was a voracious reader. A common Republican complaint against President Obama's signature Affordable Care Act (ACA), made memorably by Senator Mitch McConnell (R-Kentucky), was that the bill was too long and therefore impossible to implement (Kessler, 2013). In *Hamilton*, Jefferson is ventriloquized by Miranda to parrot anti-Obama talking points, portraying Jefferson's disagreements with Hamilton as motivated by petty grievances and cynical partisanship. Echoing long-standing Democratic criticisms of Republican efforts to oppose the ACA, Hamilton complains that Jefferson and James Madison "don't have a plan, they just hate mine" (Miranda and McCarter, 2016, p. 163). Whereas Hamilton's arguments for expanded government appear to be rooted in sincere conviction, Jefferson's counterarguments are presented as rooted in ignorance and his personal antipathy to Hamilton, invoking the Republican Party's relentless obstruction of the first Black president.

Hamilton's response to Jefferson's obstruction is revealing. Although Hamilton initially asserts that "we need bold strokes," he ultimately accedes to Washington's command to "convince more folks" (Miranda and McCarter, 2016, p. 163). In "The Room Where It Happens," Hamilton strikes a compromise for the betterment of the nation. In a backroom deal, Hamilton, Jefferson, and Madison negotiate the creation of a national bank in exchange for the nation's capital being located near Virginia. By swallowing his pride, or rather holding his nose and closing his eyes, and negotiating with his rivals, Hamilton rises above partisanship to achieve concrete results. Hamilton emerges from this crucible of partisanship as a progressive hero who embodies Obama's maxim that "democracy requires compromise" (Obama, 2016).

Like Obama, Hamilton is also subjected to vicious personal attacks about his background. For example, in "Washington On Your Side," Jefferson, Madison, and Aaron Burr sing, "This immigrant isn't somebody we chose," using Hamilton's immigrant status to delegitimize him (Miranda and McCarter, 2016, p. 200). Lin-Manuel Miranda argued that Jefferson's xenophobic attacks are meant to parallel the racist backlash against Obama:

> The direct line I can pull on the most is between Hamilton's life story and the immigrant narrative in our country. The fact that immigrants have to work twice as hard just to get here, but that also, at some point, it's going to be thrown in your face as a negative. In Hamilton's case, it was Jefferson and Madison writing basically the same things you would hear about Obama during election cycles: "How do we really know where he's from?" (qtd. in Binelli, 2016)

In *Hamilton*, Miranda reads contemporary partisan dynamics onto the past, portraying Jefferson as a proto–Tea Party conservative who obstructs and delegitimizes Hamilton using the same tactics employed by Republicans against Obama.

Hamilton's and Jefferson's competing political styles are also reflected in the musical's choreography (created by Andy Blankenbuehler). Hamilton, the proponent of compromise, rarely, if ever, dances alone. Instead, he either sings solos while stationary or dances with the ensemble, as if he, too, is part of the ensemble. In contrast, Jefferson, portrayed as an aloof obstructionist, is much flashier and often performs his own dance moves in front of the ensemble. When the audience first meets Jefferson during "What'd I Miss," he makes a show of triumphantly striding down the staircase. At the bottom of the stairs, Jefferson waits for the ensemble to be assembled in a straight line before he begins strutting in front of them, as though to distinguish himself. Though Jefferson doesn't often have solo choreography in the show, he does have a signature move: his high-stepping strut that he uses to move across the stage in front of the ensemble. In *Hamilton*, the choreography reinforces the differences in political style between Hamilton and Jefferson, showing Hamilton as willing to work together with the ensemble, a part of a larger whole, while Jefferson performs choreography in front of and apart from the ensemble, representing his showmanship and unwillingness to work together. For politically astute audiences, the implications are clear: progressives who value teamwork and achieving concrete results should look to Hamilton, rather than Jefferson, as their inspiration.

Character and Upbringing

A third way that *Hamilton* contrasts Hamilton and Jefferson is in their character development. *Hamilton* presents Hamilton's journey from squalor to treasury secretary as the enactment of the community-oriented American Dream myth. The musical juxtaposes this backstory against Jefferson's, who is portrayed as an ivory tower intellectual. In addition, the show also portrays Jefferson as a hypocrite slaveholder, while Hamilton the fierce abolitionist works hard to create a better nation for all people.

The show opens by highlighting Hamilton's American Dream success story: a child born into poverty, without parents or prospects, who nonetheless becomes an essential figure in the founding of the United States. According to Miranda, "The ten-dollar founding father without a father / Got a lot farther by working a lot harder" (Miranda and McCarter, 2016, p. 16). Hamilton's unrelenting work ethic is a recurring point of emphasis. In fact, Hamilton is so ceaseless in his work that he "writes like he's running out of time" (Miranda and McCarter, 2016, p. 137).

In contrast, Jefferson is presented as an ivory tower intellectual, interested in abstract ideals but unwilling to work toward them. In "Cabinet Battle #1," Hamilton criticizes Jefferson's elitism and absence from the Revolutionary War, telling his rival, "Don't lecture me about the war, you didn't fight in it" (Miranda and McCarter, 2016, p. 161). The fictional Hamilton's criticism of Jefferson as overly idealistic and detached is consonant with pragmatic themes running throughout Obama's rhetoric. In *The Audacity of Hope*, for example, Obama wrote that "the pursuit of ideological purity . . . keeps us from finding new ways to meet the challenges we face as a country" (Obama, 2006, p. 40).

This difference in character is accentuated in costuming. During the first act, Hamilton is dressed similarly to the ensemble. He starts in the same neutral-toned base and then is handed a brown coat to put on. This distinguishes Hamilton from the ensemble but is similar to what the other named American characters are wearing. Once the war commences, he wears a military uniform that matches the other characters' costumes. Finally, only after the war, and in a position of greater power, does he wear his signature dark green outfit. The green costume is striking but a far cry from the flashiness of Jefferson's costume. When the audience first encounters Jefferson, by contrast, he is in a bright purple velvet costume. Not only does Jefferson stand out, but he also looks "out of touch . . . with the new country and what's happening on the ground" (Semuels, 2015).

A second way that Hamilton's and Jefferson's characters are contrasted is by highlighting Hamilton's status as an immigrant. Hamilton repeatedly emphasizes his pride in this immigrant background. The most famous instance of this in *Hamilton*, of course, is in "Yorktown" when Hamilton and Lafayette share a high five after saying, "Immigrants: we get the job done" (Miranda and McCarter, 2016, p. 121). By many accounts, this is the show's most famous line, regularly getting a standing ovation and enormous applause from live audiences (Frank and Kramnick, 2016). Later, as Hamilton is dying from gunshot wounds, he explicitly links his immigrant status to the American Dream myth, calling America "a place where even orphan immigrants can leave their fingerprints and rise up" (Miranda and McCarter, 2016, p. 273).

An additional way that Jefferson and Hamilton are differentiated is by their views on slavery. In Miranda's telling, Hamilton is a staunch abolitionist who believes, "We'll never be free until we end slavery" (Miranda and McCarter, 2016, p. 122). Jefferson, however, is criticized for being a slave owner. In the audience's first introduction to Jefferson, they see the ensemble hurriedly cleaning, assuming the role of Monticello's enslaved population. As they line up to greet Jefferson, Jefferson says, "Sally be a lamb, darlin', won't cha open it?" in regard to a letter from Washington, a direct reference to Jefferson's relationship with Sally Hemings (Miranda and McCarter, 2016, p. 152). In "Cabinet Battle #1," Hamilton attacks Jefferson's character by calling attention to his ownership of enslaved people. Although Jefferson boasts about the agricultural productivity of the South, Hamilton remarks: "We know who's really doing the planting" (Miranda and McCarter, 2016, p. 161). Though *Hamilton*'s criticism of slavery leaves much to be desired, Jefferson's status as a slave owner is used to vilify him, positioning Hamilton, in contrast, as committed to equality in the new nation.

Regional Loyalties

Hamilton further positions Hamilton as a progressive hero by framing him as the embodiment of the promise represented by America's diverse and vibrant urban communities. *Hamilton* casts Hamilton and Jefferson as exemplars of their respective geographical regions. Hamilton is lionized as a true urbanite who embodies the grit and tenacity of New York City and, therefore, America. By contrast, Jefferson is synonymized with the rural South and is portrayed as a parochial sectionalist whose true loyalties are with his region, not the nation as a whole.

Hamilton has been recognized as a love letter to Miranda's hometown, and "a celebration of New York's immigrant history and its centrality to the nation's history" (Harris, 2018, p. 71). The "greatest city in the world" looms large over many scenes throughout the musical (Miranda and McCarter, 2016, p. 45). In the musical's opening moments, New York is framed as a symbol of hope and opportunity, as Burr, acting as narrator, sings, "In New York, you can be a new man" (Miranda and McCarter, 2016, p. 17). Later in the musical, New York is where Hamilton performs valorous deeds in the Revolutionary War, falls in love, receives his education, practices law, and distinguishes himself as a thinker and politician. Throughout the musical, Hamilton emerges as a true New York success story and a product of the can-do spirit that the city embodies.

By contrast, Jefferson is linked to the agrarian South. The conflict between Hamilton, Jefferson, and Madison is framed as partly a regional rivalry. When Jefferson returns stateside in "What'd I Miss," Madison laments, "I've been fighting for the South alone / Where have you been?" (Miranda and McCarter, 2016, p. 153). Jefferson is portrayed as so provincial that he questions why southern states should feel any sense of responsibility to their neighbors, asking, "If New York's in debt, why should Virginia bear it?" (Miranda and McCarter, 2016, p. 161). Later in the musical, Jefferson and Madison declare themselves "Southern motherfuckin' Democratic Republicans," emphasizing their regional loyalties (Miranda and McCarter, 2016, p. 200). Like the historical Jefferson, Miranda's Jefferson waxes poetic about the virtues of the self-sufficient yeoman farmer. Jefferson unfavorably compares Hamilton, who "primps and preens and dresses like the pits of fashion," to "our poorest citizens, our farmers," who "live ration to ration / As Wall Street robs 'em blind in search of chips to cash in" (Miranda and McCarter, 2016, p. 199). According to Jefferson, modest farmers, who through their hard labor produce material goods, are the true embodiment of the American Dream, in contrast to idle speculators in northern cities.

The urban/rural divide invoked by *Hamilton* has contemporary salience, as a major fault line of current American politics is the polarization of urban and rural voters (McKee, 2008). Although historically the Democratic Party echoed Jefferson's romanticization of hardworking farmers, the modern Democratic Party is powered by diverse voters in cities (Thompson, 2019). The 2020 presidential election, for example, "further cemented America's urban-rural political divide," as urban and suburban areas trended toward Joe Biden while Donald Trump dominated in rural areas (Skelley and Wiederkehr, 2021). The stark geographical and cultural divides between Democrats and

Republicans sparked a testy debate over whether small-town Americans or city dwellers best embody the "real America" (Grier, 2018).

Hamilton argues that immigrants and urbanites are quintessential American heroes, despite the storied American political tradition of pastoral nostalgia made famous by Jefferson. In doing so, the musical reframes the American Dream myth and offers counsel to contemporary progressives. Although Jefferson was once considered the father of the Democratic Party, *Hamilton* suggests that Hamilton better embodies the progressive worldview and presents him as a kindred spirit to the contemporary urbanites that fuel Democratic turnout. *Hamilton* places immigrants and cities at the center of the American story, creating a usable history for modern urban liberals.

CONCLUSION

Hamilton is part of an ongoing reevaluation of American history and a search for heroes untainted by involvement with slavery, in the hopes of recovering "a *relatable* founding, full of behavior and ideas and values modern [audiences] can embrace as their own" (Waldstreicher and Pasley, 2018, p. 143). Moreover, *Hamilton* has "changed the modern American political landscape" and public memory of the American Revolution (Lauer, 2020, para. 5). Lyra D. Monteiro, an assistant professor of history at Rutgers University, Newark, told the *New York Times* that *Hamilton* is not only "an amazing piece of theater" but something that audiences (mis)interpret "as a piece of history" (qtd. in Schuessler, 2016, para. 10).

In this essay, we outlined how *Hamilton* has reshaped public memory and explained how Alexander Hamilton was transformed from "the founding's villain" into an icon of multicultural liberalism (Knott, 2004, para. 2). *Hamilton* has all but finalized a move away from the previous iteration of liberal mythology that positioned Thomas Jefferson as the father of the Democratic Party and the "the Father of Democracy" itself (Peterson, 1962, p. 68). Thanks to *Hamilton*, this privileged position in the imagination of American liberals is now occupied by Alexander Hamilton, who in Lin-Manuel Miranda's interpretation was an eighteenth-century forebearer of contemporary liberalism: an immigrant who opposed slavery, advocated energetic government to empower communities, supported political compromise, and was deeply rooted in the urban environment that he arose from. *Hamilton* offers modern liberals a founding hero they can take pride in, whose values align with an interpretation of the American Dream myth that beseeches Americans to take responsibility for the well-being of their communities and to espouse openness and hospitality to others.

REFERENCES

Binelli, M. (2016). "'Hamilton' creator Lin-Manuel Miranda: The Rolling Stone interview." *Rolling Stone*, June 1, 2016. https://www.rollingstone.com/culture/culture-news/hamilton-creator-lin-manuel-miranda-the-rolling-stone-interview-42607/.

Blair, C., M. S. Jeppeson, and E. Pucci Jr. (1991). "Public Memorializing in Postmodernity: The Vietnam Veterans Memorial as Prototype." *Quarterly Journal of Speech* 77, no. 3, 263–88.

Bodnar, J. (1992). *Remaking America: Public Memory, Commemoration, and Patriotism in the 20th Century*. Princeton, NJ: Princeton University Press.

Browne, S. H. (1999). "Remembering Crispus Attucks: Race, Rhetoric, and the Politics of Commemoration." *Quarterly Journal of Speech* 85, no. 2, 169–87.

Burstein, A. (2015). *Democracy's Muse: How Thomas Jefferson Became an FDR Liberal, a Reagan Republican, and a Tea Party Fanatic, All the While Being Dead*. Charlottesville: University of Virginia Press.

Chait, J. (2018). "The GOP Is Trump's Personality Cult. Could Democrats Do the Same?" *New York Magazine*, June 27, 2018. http://nymag.com/intelligencer/2018/06/trump-made-the-gop-a-personal-cult-could-democrats-do-that.html.

Cogliano, F. D. (2006). *Thomas Jefferson: Reputation and Legacy*. Edinburgh, UK: Edinburgh University Press.

Frank, J., and I. Kramnick. (2016). "What 'Hamilton' Forgets about Hamilton." *New York Times*, June 10, 2016. https://www.nytimes.com/2016/06/11/opinion/what-hamilton-forgets-about-alexander-hamilton.html.

Friedman, T. L. (2019). "Is America Becoming a Four-Party State?" *New York Times*, February 19, 2019. https://www.nytimes.com/2019/02/19/opinion/four-party-america-politics.html.

Gillis, J. R., ed. (1996). *Commemorations: The Politics of National Identity*. Princeton, NJ: Princeton University Press.

Gopnik, A. (2016). "'Hamilton' and the Hip-Hop Case for Progressive Heroism." *The New Yorker*, February 5, 2016. https://www.newyorker.com/news/daily-comment/hamilton-and-the-hip-hop-case-for-progressive-heroism.

Grier, P. (2018). The Deep Roots of America's Rural-Urban Political Divide. *Christian Science Monitor*, December 26, 2018. https://www.csmonitor.com/USA/Politics/2018/1226/The-deep-roots-of-America-s-rural-urban-political-divide.

Halbwachs, M. (1992). *On Collective Memory*. Chicago: University of Chicago Press.

Harris, L. M. (2018). "The Greatest City in the World? Slavery in New York in the Age of Hamilton." In *Historians on Hamilton: How a Blockbuster Musical Is Restaging America's Past*, edited by Renee C. Romano and Claire Bond Potter, 71–93. Newark, NJ: Rutgers University Press.

Hochschild, J. L. (1995). *Facing Up to the American Dream: Race, Class, and the Soul of the Nation*. Princeton, NJ: Princeton University Press.

Isenberg, N. (2016). "Liberals Love Alexander Hamilton. But Aaron Burr Was a Real Progressive Hero." *Washington Post*, March 30, 2016. https://www.washingtonpost

.com/posteverything/wp/2016/03/30/liberals-love-alexander-hamilton-but-aaron-burr-was-a-real-progressive-hero/.

Kessler, G. (2013). "How Many Pages of Regulations for 'Obamacare'?" *Washington Post*, May 15, 2013. http://wapo.st/10xvxpM?tid=ss_tw.

Knott, S. F. (2004). "The Man Who Made Modern America." *Claremont Review of Books* IV, no. 4. https://claremontreviewofbooks.com/the-man-who-made-modern-america/.

Knott, S. F. (2018). "The Four Faces of Alexander Hamilton: Jefferson's Hamilton, Hollywood's Hamilton, Miranda's Hamilton, and the Real Hamilton." *American Political Thought* 7, 543–64.

Lauer, A. (2020). "Six Ways 'Hamilton' Directly Impacted American Politics." InsideHook. July 2, 2020. https://www.insidehook.com/article/arts-entertainment/how-hamilton-musical-changed-american-politics.

McKee, S. C. (2008). Rural Voters and the Polarization of American Presidential Elections. *PS: Political Science and Politics* 41, no. 1, 101–8.

Miranda, L. M., and J. McCarter (2016). *Hamilton: The Revolution*. New York: Grand Central Publishing.

Monteiro, L. D. (2018). "Race-Conscious Casting and the Erasure of the Black Past in *Hamilton*." In *Historians on Hamilton: How a Blockbuster Musical Is Restaging America's Past*, edited by Renee C. Romano and Claire Bond Potter, 58–70. Newark, NJ: Rutgers University Press.

Obama, B. (2006). *The Audacity of Hope*. New York: Crown Publishers.

Obama, B. (2007). Speech at the Jefferson-Jackson dinner. American Rhetoric, November 7, 2007. https://www.americanrhetoric.com/speeches/barackobama/barackobamajeffersonjacksondinner.htm.

Obama, B. (2011). Remarks by the President on the economy in Osawatomie, Kansas. White House Office of Press Secretary, December 6, 2011. https://obamawhitehouse.archives.gov/the-press-office/2011/12/06/remarks-president-economy-osawatomie-kansas.

Obama, B. (2016). Remarks by the President at Howard University commencement ceremony. White House Office of Press Secretary, May 7, 2016. https://obamawhitehouse.archives.gov/the-press-office/2016/05/07/remarks-president-howard-university-commencement-ceremony.

Peterson, M. D. (1962). *The Jefferson Image in the American Mind*. New York: Oxford University Press.

Phillips, A. (2016). "How Politics and Hip-Hop Saved the Hamilton $10 Bill—and Put Harriet Tubman on the $20." *Washington Post*, April 20, 2016. https://www.washingtonpost.com/news/the-fix/wp/2016/04/20/how-politics-and-hip-hop-saved-the-hamilton-10-bill-and-put-harriet-tubman-on-the-20/.

Phillips, K. R., ed. (2007). *Framing Public Memory*. Tuscaloosa: University of Alabama Press.

Poniewozik, J. (2016). "Her Shot: Hillary Clinton Shares a Vision of America Out of 'Hamilton.'" *New York Times*, July 30, 2016. https://www.nytimes.com/2016/07/30/arts/television/hillary-clinton-speech-democratic-national-convention-hamilton.html

Rowland, R. C., and J. M. Jones. (2007). "Recasting the American Dream and American Politics: Barack Obama's Keynote Address to the 2004 Democratic National Convention." *Quarterly Journal of Speech* 93, no. 4, 425–48.

Samuel, L. R. (2012). *The American Dream: A Cultural History*. Syracuse, NY: Syracuse University Press.

Schlesinger, A. M. (1953). *The Age of Jackson*. Boston, MA: Little and Brown Company.

Schuessler, J. (2016). "'Hamilton' and History: Are They in Sync?" *New York Times*, April 11, 2016. https://www.nytimes.com/2016/04/11/theater/hamilton-and-history-are-they-in-sync.html.

Scott, R. (2019). "Sen. Kamala Harris Kicks Off 2020 Campaign Criticizing Trump and Calling for Unity." ABC News, January 27, 2019. https://abcnews.go.com/Politics/sen-kamala-harris-kicks-off-2020-campaign-criticizing/story?id=60668277

Semuels, A. (2015). "How *Hamilton* Recasts Thomas Jefferson as a Villain." *The Atlantic*, August 19, 2015. https://www.theatlantic.com/entertainment/archive/2015/08/how-hamilton-recasts-thomas-jefferson-as-a-villain/401669/.

Skelley, G., and A. Wiederkehr. (2021). "How the Frost Belt and Sun Belt Illustrate the Complexity of America's Urban-Rural Divide." FiveThirtyEight, January 27, 2021. https://fivethirtyeight.com/features/how-the-frost-belt-and-sun-belt-illustrate-the-complexity-of-americas-urban-rural-divide/.

Stoller, M. (2017). "The Hamilton Hustle." *The Baffler*. https://thebaffler.com/salvos/hamilton-hustle-stoller.

Thompson, D. (2019). "How Democrats Conquered the City." *The Atlantic*, September 13, 2019. https://www.theatlantic.com/ideas/archive/2019/09/brief-history-how-democrats-conquered-city/597955/.

Waldstreicher, D., and J. L. Pasley. (2018). "*Hamilton* as Founders Chic: A Neo-Federalist, Antislavery Usable Past?" In *Historians on Hamilton: How a Blockbuster Musical Is Restaging America's Past*, edited by Renee C. Romano and Claire Bond Potter, 137–66. Newark, NJ: Rutgers University Press.

Chapter 2

Washington Says Good-Bye

Examining "One Last Time" through Public Memory

Jessica L. Gehrke

The musical *Hamilton* is a cultural phenomenon that "has taken Broadway and the world by storm" (Vine, 2018, para. 1) since its premiere on August 6, 2015. It received a record sixteen Tony nominations and won eleven Tony Awards and a Pulitzer Prize (Vankin, 2017). Lin-Manuel Miranda also expanded the musical's reach by developing a Hamildrop series that provided new musical content related to *Hamilton* that was released throughout 2018 (Kaufman, 2017). In both the musical and the Hamildrop series, Miranda constructs historical interpretations of America's early history with the goal of creating a relevant historical tale, saying, "This is a story about America then, told by America now" (Delman, 2015, para. 2). This goal also suggests that the musical and the works associated with it, such as the Hamildrop series, can also be viewed as political commentary. The use of Washington's Farewell Address in *Hamilton* demonstrates how public memory is malleable and activated by present concerns (Blair, Dickinson, and Ott, 2010).

I focus on two songs related to each other and Washington's Farewell Address within the *Hamilton* sphere that demonstrate how context can influence our understanding of the past to make sense of the present: "One Last Time" and "One Last Time (44 Remix)." "One Last Time" is part of the score of the musical *Hamilton*, and Miranda frames the writing of the Farewell Address through the theme of "teach them how to say good-bye" as Washington and Hamilton are singing the song together (Miranda and Jackson, 2015). "One Last Time (44 Remix)" was released in December 2018 as part of the Hamildrop series. Christopher Jackson (the original performer of Washington in the musical), former president Barack Obama, and BeBe Winans perform the song (*Hamilton*, 2018). I argue that through these two songs, Miranda used the aspects of the historical Farewell Address to frame what American leadership should look like today. Specifically, he utilized historical context and the musical's story to promote a particular vision of leadership for today's audience in "One Last Time" but leaves "One Last Time (44 Remix)" open to interpretation by the audience even as it shares some common themes with the musical's version. As a stand-alone song, however, the remix's interpretation can be shaped by present politics and individual perceptions. To understand how the use of history shapes our present interpretations of the Farewell Address, I will first provide background for the Farewell Address. Then I will explore how public memory provides a useful lens to explore Miranda's presentation of the past because of *Hamilton*'s popularity, historical basis, and interest in telling a story relevant to today.

BACKGROUND OF THE FAREWELL ADDRESS

As an example of public address, Washington's Farewell Address is noteworthy in its own right. The speech is recognized as part of the American rhetorical canon, as suggested by its inclusion in different speech anthologies (e.g., Reid, 1988; Reid and Klumpp, 2015; Suriano, 1993). Scholars are interested in the Farewell Address as well; interest ranges from whole books about its development (Malanson, 2015) to discussions of why Hamilton was not credited as an author (Chernow, 2004; Malanson, 2014). But most pertinent to this analysis is the context surrounding the Farewell Address, which influences how the text is used in *Hamilton* to demonstrate the transition of power.

The Farewell Address was written because George Washington wanted to step down from office, but he also needed to balance his desire to leave office with the needs of the country. Many people assumed he would serve as president longer; in fact, many assumed Washington would remain president for as long as he lived (Chernow, 2004). At this point in history, a democratic society with a peaceful turnover of power was not the norm. Washington's choice to leave office was unheard of as "he surrendered power in a world where leaders had always grabbed for more" (Chernow, 2004, p. 505). In addition, because he was still popular among the people and there was no precedent to only serve two terms, Washington also "knew he had to announce publicly his desire to not be re-elected" (Reid and Klumpp, 2015, p. 188). As Washington was the first leader for the new United States, his leaving office was more than deciding to not run for president. He was the first president and, therefore, had to consider how to tell citizens he was not going to remain president while assuring them that the country could continue under new leadership.

Washington had served as president because he was willing to help develop the newly formed country, but he also had a goal of leaving office. In fact, "his closest friends and advisors knew that Washington had longed for retirement almost since the day he took office in 1789 and that he had attempted to step down at the end of his first term before reluctantly agreeing to stand for reelection" (Malanson, 2015, p. 2). He even asked James Madison to draft a farewell address toward the end of his first term. At the end of his second term, Washington still wanted to leave office, and this time, he would not be persuaded to stay. However, he did want to provide his guidance to help the country continue as it dealt with political issues.

Historical records demonstrate that Washington and his contemporaries faced significant challenges as they developed a new government. His second term was more challenging than the first four years. During his second term, there was fierce partisan battle over how the United States should approach international affairs. For instance, "his opposition to aid for the French Revolution, his suppression of the Whiskey Revolution, and his perceived pro-British leanings in the settlement of differences with England through the 1794 Jay Treaty" had many upset with his leadership choices (Suriano, 1993, p. 16). In fact, Ron Chernow (2004) argued that "beneath its impartial air, the farewell address took dead aim at the Jeffersonian romance with France" (p. 506). Because "Washington's second term was marked by more disputes, an increasingly bitter partisan rhetoric and a solidifying of political parties" (Reid, 1988, p. 187), Washington wanted to provide his final thoughts to help direct the country's future, drawing on his experience and concerns from his time in office. This context informed the key themes within the Farewell Address. Washington focused on the issues affecting the United States within his address: partisanship that could irrevocably tear the country apart, concern over the rise of political parties, and becoming too involved with international affairs.

To provide this direction about the issues facing the country and to persuade the country to accept his resignation, Washington turned to Hamilton to help write the Farewell Address. Although Hamilton was no longer serving in the cabinet, Hamilton had become one of Washington's "most trusted and likeminded advisor[s]" (Malanson, 2015, p. 27), and the two men had developed a strong friendship (Chernow, 2004, p. 505). Therefore, Hamilton was a natural choice for Washington to send James Madison's original version of the Farewell Address, from Washington's first term, to make revisions. Because of the issues plaguing the second term, the two men moved on from the version written by Madison to write a new version that would better reflect their current political situation and Washington's goals.

In addition to its historical background, the Farewell Address has rhetorical significance. Michael J. Hostetler (2002) argued that the complex text is a cultural symbol that "still calls Americans to the unfinished process of national character building" (p. 404). In addition, the Farewell Address set the stage for how Americans would view interactions with each other and with foreign nations. As a cultural symbol, therefore, the Farewell Address provides an opportunity for the presenter(s) to use the text to "recollect [its] meaning for a new moment" (Gaffey, 2015, p. 342). Because of its place within the rhetorical canon and the opportunities for the text to be repurposed, understanding how the Farewell Address was developed and its purpose helps us better understand how its meaning was adapted within *Hamilton* and the Hamildrop series. Miranda made choices about how to present the Farewell Address, which, through careful study, can provide insights about how current issues affect how the songs frame the Farewell Address's meaning for us today. To understand this framing, I turn to how public memory can help us understand how the songs advance particular viewpoints about the past to influence the future.

PUBLIC MEMORY

Public memory can serve as a useful lens to understand how context affects each presentation of these three artifacts, conceptualizing a specific meaning for the Farewell Address within its own historical situation. Although the two fields are related, the study of public memory differs from the study of history. Kendall R. Phillips (2004) explained:

> History, with its apparent claims to accuracy and objectivity, is—or at least had been—viewed as implying a singular and authentic account of the past. Memory, on the other hand, is conceived in terms of multiple, diverse, mutable, and competing accounts of past events. (p. 2)

Historians do recognize the role of public memory, including its usefulness in studying artifacts like *Hamilton*, as Renee C. Romano and Claire Bond Potter (2018) argued:

> We believe historians need to take *Hamilton* seriously because it has already demonstrated its enormous potential to shape what Americans know and understand about both the man and this era. Although professional historians are sometimes reluctant to admit it, television, movies, fictional works, museums, and family lore often shape people's perceptions of the past more than scholarship does. (p. 8)

Understanding the roles of history and cultural influences together provide opportunities to examine how we construct and challenge the past to achieve specific goals, or in other words, how we use public memory to advance specific agendas.

Because we construct public memory, it is rhetorical; Phillips (2004) argued that "to speak of memory . . . is to speak of a highly rhetorical process" (p. 2). In this rhetorical process, context plays an important role in how we shape history as "rhetorical legibility is predicated in publicly recognizable symbolic activity *in context*. That is, rhetoric typically understands discourses, events, objects, and practices as timely, of the moment, specific, and addressed to—or constitutive of—particular audiences in particular circumstances" (Blair, Dickinson, and Ott, 2010, p. 4, emphasis in original). Valerie Lynn Schrader's (2017; 2019) work also demonstrates how public memory can be applied to musical theater. She also has studied *Hamilton* to explain how the musical suggests Hamilton should be remembered and that it offers life lessons for the audience, depending on which character(s) the audience member identifies with (Schrader, 2019). Her work illustrates that as musicals present history, they also provide opportunities to consider how theatrical productions create public memory, working with the audience to develop meaning. These meanings, however, are informed and limited by what individuals understand about what they have experienced.

Miranda's choices about how to present the Farewell Address highlight how context affects the rhetorical construction of history to meet the needs of the present. As an academic field, history has traditionally focused on objectivity and accuracy (Thelen, 1989). Yet Miranda sacrificed or adjusted historical facts to advance a compelling story (Miranda and McCarter, 2016). An issue of the *Journal of the Early Republic* examines these choices, from its historical representation of Hamilton to the musical's position within musical theater (Kelly, 2017). Joanne B. Freeman (2017) argued that the musical is problematic because it provides inaccurate history to viewers. Some choices may be understandable to better tell a story within time constraints, such as the inaccurate presentation of Burr and Hamilton's interactions. However, she argued other choices are more damaging for the audience's accurate understanding of Hamilton as a historical figure, such as the musical's depiction of Hamilton as an abolitionist when in reality, his wife's family (and by extension, Hamilton) owned slaves (Freeman, 2017, pp. 253–56). Moreover, Freeman (2017) posits that this musical is the first time Hamilton is a "folk hero," because in reality, he was not liked by his contemporaries (p. 260). The presentation of Hamilton in the musical, therefore, creates questions about the accuracy of the show's history even with the understanding that Miranda was creating a story for Broadway.

Historians' discussions of the musical also recognize that Miranda, as the author, is constructing a specific view of history for the time he lives in. Nancy Isenberg (2017) stated that "Miranda's goal was not to rewrite history. Indeed, his play has more to do with contemporary politics" (p. 298). Isenberg (2017) recognized that the context of current political issues, such as Miranda's view of immigration, could affect how Miranda shaped his depiction of Hamilton (Hogeland, 2018; Monteiro, 2018). However, researchers have also recognized that "*Hamilton* needs to be explored as a historical phenomenon in its own right" (Romano and Potter, 2018, p. 6). The musical and its related products offer rich opportunities to take up this charge. For this analysis, I focus on the songs "One Last Time" and "One Last Time (44 Remix)," which provide an opportunity to consider not only how the musical presents history but also how a specific text is understood and reconceptualized in different contexts to address current issues. I turn next to how these two songs reflect or ignore historical context to provide commentary on current events.

TWO SONGS, DIFFERENT CONTEXTS

"One Last Time" in *Hamilton* and "One Last Time (44 Remix)" are markedly different from the original Farewell Address as well as different from each other. The original Farewell Address is addressing the current political situation and helping the American people accept Washington's resignation. The song "One Last Time" is part of how *Hamilton* demonstrates Hamilton and Washington's relationship and reflects the importance of Washington voluntarily leaving a powerful position. The remix, however, is part of a 12-month series called "Hamildrops." The content was described as "new Hamilton content, dropping every month in 2018" (Hamildrops). At least one purpose of the series is to "to provide Hamil-heads with tons of new material over the next year" (Kaufman, 2017, para. 1). The songs vary from the Decemberists singing "Ben Franklin's Song" to Miranda and Ben Platt singing a mash-up of songs from *Hamilton* and *Dear Evan Hansen* to "Weird Al" Yankovic singing "The Hamilton Polka" (Hamildrops). Here, "One Last Time (44 Remix)" is part of an eclectic mix designed specifically for *Hamilton* fans to offer new ways to consume content related to the show.

Out of the all the *Hamilton* material, this is one of the few songs Miranda chose to focus on twice. This repeated use of the Farewell Address is notable as "groups tell their past to themselves as others as ways of understanding, valorizing, justifying, excusing, or subverting conditions or beliefs of their current moment" (Blair, Dickinson, and Ott, 2010, p. 6). I argue Miranda appears to use his interpretation of "One Last Time" within the musical to address how he views both Washington's presidency and Hamilton's role within it as important facets of American history. The remix highlights Miranda's respect for former president Obama and possibly hints at his concerns with former president Trump. With each conceptualization, new layers of meaning are added to the song and the Farewell Address. Because of both presentations' popularity, audiences may be using the songs to decide how to interpret both American history as well as current and past presidents.

To study these songs, I engaged with the original address and the song lyrics. I studied the Farewell Address, listened to the soundtrack of *Hamilton* and the song "One Last Time" multiple times, reviewed the CD liner notes and noted differences between the songs' lyrics using the liner notes, attended a live performance of *Hamilton*, and listened to "One Last Time (44 Remix)" multiple times to understand key themes and note repeated phrases. In addition, by researching the Farewell Address, the musical's development, and contexts surrounding these songs, I found that the transfer of power and societal issues are reflected in the songs' message.

THEMES WITHIN THE SONGS

Both songs are affected by their contexts, with "One Last Time" being one part of the story of Hamilton and Washington within the musical while "One Last Time (44 Remix)" is a stand-alone song designed to help promote *Hamilton*. In both cases, they develop similar themes reflecting on how leaders should leave office and building on the show's arguments about immigration to frame interpretations of the past based on the current political climate.

"Teach Them to Say Good-Bye": How Leaders Leave Office

Both "One Last Time" and "One Last Time (44 Remix)" reflect Washington's desire to leave office while providing guidance for the country, and the songs incorporate the Farewell Address's goal of helping the country adjust to the idea that Washington would step down from office. Each song emphasizes the idea of "teach them how to say good-bye" as Washington directs the country "one last time." However, in the musical, the Farewell Address is not just a chance for Washington to share his thoughts or provide guidance about governing. Rather, "One Last Time" is about framing Washington's legacy to influence how he will be remembered by Hamilton and the country's citizens. For Washington, the Farewell Address is his final opportunity to serve his country as the American people learn how to let a president retire after his faithful service. This goal is realized as Washington and Hamilton use the Farewell Address to connect the ideas of "teaching them how to say good-bye" and "one last time" to the concept of Washington "going home."

Both versions of "One Last Time" frame Washington as a man who knows when to lead and when to leave office. For instance, Washington shares he will use his position "to move them along" so the nation "will outlive me when I'm gone" (Miranda and Jackson, 2015). Additionally, in the musical, when Washington announces he is not going to run for a third time, Hamilton responds in disbelief, asking "if this is the best time," and claims "as far as the people are concerned / you have to serve, you could continue to serve" (Miranda and Jackson, 2015). Washington, however, is adamant that it is his time to leave office. By outlining these concerns and highlighting Washington's response of "teach them how to say good-bye," the musical recognizes that the Farewell Address needs to help citizens accept Washington's resignation. The concerns raised by Hamilton are also reflected in the Farewell Address, such as when Washington requested people "not disapprove my determination to retire" (Reid and Klumpp, 2015, p. 189). Throughout the musical version of "One Last Time," Washington is portrayed as a leader who understands part of his legacy is knowing when to step down, and it frames his legacy for the audience attending *Hamilton*.

The remix also highlights how the choice to leave office is decided with the nation in mind. Both songs frame Washington's legacy as someone who was willing to do what was right for his country. Both the musical's version and the remix use the closing paragraphs to highlight Washington's humanity as he chose to leave office and asked the American people to accept his resignation. This text includes Washington acknowledging he is "too sensible of my defects not to think it probable that I may have committed many errors" but asking his audience to remember that he "spent forty-five years of my life dedicated to its service with an upright zeal" (Reid and Klumpp, 2015, p. 202). The songs then conclude with the reminder that Washington is teaching Americans how to say good-bye as he goes home to Mount Vernon. Washington, therefore, was a servant of his country who even used leaving office to serve democracy by setting the precedent for future leaders.

In "One Last Time," teaching the American public how to "say good-bye" reflects how, at the time, it was unheard of for a leader to willingly cede power. Miranda highlights the importance of Washington's decision, stating:

> Washington had an extraordinary American life. I think the most extraordinary thing he did was step down from the presidency, ensuring that this American experiment would continue without him. By modeling a peaceful transition from president to president, he puts us eons ahead of every other fledgling democracy on earth. (The Bush Center, 2017)

Because Miranda admires Washington's choice to resign, he emphasizes the idea of "teach them how to say good-bye" in both the musical and remix. The songs focus on the uniqueness of Washington's choice to leave office rather on than political situations, even as the musical's version acknowledges the concerns over partisanship and foreign relations that Washington discussed in detail within the original text. The focus, however, is clearly on what it means for a president to step down from office. By highlighting the unconventional choice of Washington, Miranda also sets up a reminder of what the peaceful transition of power means today, through the remix.

Based on the performers, notably former president Obama, "One Last Time (44 Remix)" can be used as a reminder for Americans to honor the peaceful transfer of power between presidents. President Obama's contribution is significant because of his ongoing connection to the musical. The first release of anything related to *Hamilton* was when Miranda presented a draft of "Alexander Hamilton" at the White House in May 2009. He had been invited to participate in a spoken word event, and he used the opportunity to share an early draft of what would become the introductory song of the musical (Estevez, 2018). Later, the cast of Hamilton provided a performance of select songs to then president Obama, then vice president Biden, and others in the White House on March 4, 2016. Obama's visual reaction to the performance was noted, especially as his term of service was ending, with one reporter noting, "Throughout the performance [of 'One Last Time'], the camera frequently cuts to the president, vice president, and first lady in the audience, and as Jackson holds the final note, Obama can be seen mouthing 'whoa' and leading the audience in a standing ovation" (Coggan, 2017, para. 2). At the end of the performance, Miranda and Obama embrace, and Obama concludes the performance by referencing knowing how to say good-bye (Hamilton, 2017).

In addition, the Hamilton YouTube channel video description for the performance of the song mentions that as they are "prepar[ing] for President Barack Obama's final days in office, we celebrate the profound legacy he leaves behind. . . . Teach 'em how to say good-bye" (Hamilton, 2017). The specific song, therefore, is linked to Obama as his presidency was ending. Obama's reading of the original Farewell Address in the Hamildrop version, along with the reference to his presidency with the number 44 in the title, provides a final connection between his presidency and how to interpret the Farewell Address.

These connections between former president Obama and the theme of "teaching them how to say good-bye" suggest that the remix could also be a way to help audiences process and accept the transfer of power between Obama and former president Trump. Although Americans knew Obama was going to leave office after serving two terms, it was generally assumed Hillary Clinton would win the 2016 election. After a contentious and bitterly divided election, Trump won the Electoral College. Although Trump's supporters rejoiced, many others struggled with what it meant that Trump won. With the deep political divisions within the country and Miranda's sensitivity to how the musical relates to current events, the song could serve as a transition for unhappy citizens. The remix provides a way for listeners to hear the message that the American way is for the former president to step aside after serving two terms.

The remix also helps frame Obama's legacy. The remix cuts the dialogue between the characters of Washington and Hamilton to introduce the theme of "teach them to say good-bye." By divorcing the song from the musical and having Obama read the Farewell Address, the song moves Washington and Hamilton out of the picture. By reading Washington's final comments about leaving office soon after he left office, Obama has the opportunity to connect Washington's sentiments to his legacy and help unhappy citizens use "One Last Time" as a way to accept Trump's presidency.

Because Washington's rationale for the address is presented within the musical and the remix, the different items show how memory is recontextualized to address current issues. Within the musical, Miranda is not only telling Hamilton and Washington's story but is also framing how we should understand Washington's decision to leave office. Through the remix, Washington's Farewell Address can reflect not only how to view the transition of power but how to accept a new, polarizing president. However, as I studied the context of "One Last Time," I determined it is also possible that the song could be used as commentary on immigration policy.

"The Vine and Fig Tree": A Place to Rest for Citizens and Immigrants

Studying the context of the development of "One Last Time," Miranda's views on immigration—as illustrated through other *Hamilton*-related material—and the political situation when the remix was released suggests that societal concerns like immigration also affect the song's message. To understand this possible connection, I examine how the phrase "the vine and the fig tree" is connected Washington's retirement and "One Last Time," Washington and immigration, and the remix.

Both songs use the phrase "the vine and the fig tree" to reflect that it is time for the president to leave office, using a favorite phrase of Washington. Washington often used the biblical image of the "vine and fig tree" to refer to "his fondness for Mount Vernon, his own, personal vine and fig tree" (Tsakiridis, 2021, para. 3). In the musical, the phrase transitions from Hamilton and Washington's debate over his retirement to quoting the Farewell Address. In the remix, this phrasing opens the song. The phrase's prominence connects the writing of the Farewell Address to the writing of lyrics and music. In fact, this reference was key to development of the song: "When he [Miranda] turned the Bible passage into a lyric, he built the phrase 'their own vine and fig tree' on the intervals that Chris sings best" (Miranda and McCarter, 2016, p. 207). Miranda emphasized the importance of Washington choosing to retire by developing the best musical portrayal of the phrase for Christopher Jackson, the original actor for George Washington. This phrase, both in its wording and musical arrangement, highlights the importance of having a place to work and then rest.

Miranda did not only connect the reference to a vine and fig tree to Washington's desire to retire in the musical; he also commented on the phrase's connection to immigration. To understand this connection, it is helpful to understand how the musical itself is connected to immigration. Immigration is an important theme within the musical, as Miranda chose to tell an overall positive story of the role of immigrants in founding America. Not only is Hamilton portrayed as an immigrant (Odom, Miranda, and Ensemble, 2015), but other characters also acknowledge how they serve America as immigrants. For instance, in the song "Yorktown (The World Turned Upside Down)," the characters state, "Immigrants: we get the job done" (Cast of *Hamilton*, 2015). In an interview, Miranda acknowledges the role immigration plays in the musical:

> It's a nice reminder that our best military commander was a French immigrant who came here to fight. The guy who organized us into regiments and literally wrote the Army handbook was [Friedrich Wilhelm] Von Steuben, a German guy who came here to help. Immigrants helped us win this war and have helped us every step since. (Hayes, 2015, para. 36)

Miranda also created a musical video in 2017 based on the song "Immigrants (We Get the Job Done)," originally from *The Hamilton Mixtape*, commenting on the problems of refusing to allow immigrants entrance to America (Kreps, 2017). Throughout his work on the musical and its related products, Miranda deliberately connected *Hamilton* to immigration. To understand how "One Last Time" may connect to immigration, however, we need to understand more about the context of the phrase "the vine and fig tree."

In addition to being a phrase Washington used to envision his own retirement, Washington used "the vine and fig tree" to refer to America as a land of refuge, which is highlighted in *Hamilton: The Revolution*, a book which provides insights into the musical's development. In this book, Miranda and McCarter (2016) noted that in 1790, when Washington "cited the verse in a letter to a Jewish community that had immigrated to Rhode Island to seek relief from prosecution, he was stating the principle that all men and women should find a safe haven in America, no matter who they are or where they came from" (p. 208). Although this letter is not part of the musical or the Farewell Address, Miranda and McCarter connected the image of a vine and fig tree, which illustrates Washington's desire to retire in peace in "One Last Time," to immigration in their discussion of the song "One Last Time." Moreover, Miranda and McCarter tied the development of the song to broader societal concerns, finding the song's meaning "took on additional weight" because of the 2015 shooting at the Emanuel AME Church in Charleston, South Carolina (2016, p. 208). Based on the musical's connection to immigration, Washington's historical use of the phrase, and what was taking place when the song was written, the context also informs how we can view the phrase "the vine and fig tree." Activated by past and current concerns, the songs also can be used to comment on who should have the right to reside in America—to have their own "vine and fig tree," just as Washington desired.

Public memory provides a useful lens to examine how the songs "One Last Time" and "One Last Time (44 Remix)" connect their themes to their contexts. Since *Hamilton* is positioned as a musical about America today, we should ask how the musical frames the past to help us understand the world today. Even as the songs reflect the historical construction of the Farewell Address and even quote its closing, as I examined the songs' backgrounds, development, and contexts, I noted that the songs are influenced by our interpretations of the present, and those interpretations will continue to change in the future.

PUBLIC MEMORY AND "ONE LAST TIME"

Blair, Dickinson, and Ott (2010) argued that "memory is historically and culturally specific; it has meant different things to people and cultures at different times and has been instrumentalized in the service of diverse cultural practices" (p.11). Even as "One Last Time" is part of the musical's presentation of history and "One Last Time (44 Remix)" is part of a promotional series separating songs from the musical's context, both songs provide opportunities to reflect on how Miranda frames the Farewell Address for today. In each situation, the address has been adapted to fit the needs of the show and its writers to make their own commentary about American leadership and their beliefs about societal concerns. As the Farewell Address's presentation shifts from a printed address in 1796 to part of a popular musical's score to a performance available on streaming platforms, the door opens for new interpretations, even as the theme of how to say good-bye is rooted in historical context.

Because public memory shifts based on present circumstances, there can be a longevity or parts that "stick," even if the reason why changes. For instance, as the Farewell Address was adapted for the musical and then the remix, an emphasis remained on how American presidents should step aside—a theme influenced by the novelty of Washington's choice to step down from office. However, in the musical, it becomes about teaching people to say good-bye, obscuring other important issues Washington addressed within his Farewell Address. In the remix, it became a way to frame one president's legacy and to accept a controversial new president taking over. Even as I was working on revising this chapter, after former president Trump's refusal to concede the 2020 election, false claims of widespread election fraud, and the invasion of the Capitol on January 6 (Helderman, Hsu, and Weiner, 2021; Zadrozny, 2020), the theme of "teach them how to say good-bye" was taking on a new meaning as we watched how the peaceful transfer of power was disrupted. Because public memory is activated by present concerns (Blair, Dickinson, and Ott, 2010, p. 6), context gives new meaning and possibilities to how "One Last Time" and "One Last Time (44 Remix)" can be used to reflect upon our current political situation and what we expect from our presidents.

The songs' subtle message about immigration, though activated by current concerns, is not as likely to have staying power. To understand the song's connection to immigration, one needs to understand specific and less familiar historical references and current societal influences on the song's development, in addition to the general *Hamilton* connections to immigration. The more obvious theme of how presidents should leave office can be more easily adapted by the present moment. In each case, however, public memory has been activated by current concerns even as the songs adapt to different moments in time, illustrating both its longevity and fleeting nature. Our current context ultimately will affect how we view "One Last Time" and the remix's presentation of Washington's Farewell Address, revealing how our current circumstances affect how we frame and use the past.

REFERENCES

Blair, C., G. Dickinson, and B. L. Ott. (2010). "Introduction: Rhetoric/Memory/Place." In *Places of Public Memory: The Rhetoric of Museums and Memorials*, edited by G. Dickinson, C. Blair, and B. L. Ott, 1–54. Tuscaloosa: University of Alabama Press.

The Bush Center. (2017). "Hamilton's America" [Video]. YouTube, March 18, 2017. https://www.youtube.com/watch?v=50vDxtBUDaQ.

Cast of Hamilton. (2015). "Yorktown (The World Turned Upside Down)" [Song]. On *Hamilton: An American Musical* [Album]. Atlantic Recording Corporation.

Chernow, R. (2004). *Alexander Hamilton*. New York: Penguin Books.

Coggan, D. (2017). "Watch *Hamilton* Cast Perform 'One Last Time' for President Obama at the White House." *Entertainment Weekly*, January 11, 2017. https://ew.com/theater/2017/01/11/hamilton-one-last-time-white-house-performance-barack-obama/.

Delman, E. (2015). "How Lin-Manuel Miranda Shapes History." *The Atlantic*, September 29, 2015. https://www.theatlantic.com/entertainment/archive/2015/09/lin-manuel-miranda-hamilton/408019/.

Estevez, M. (2018). "Happy Birthday, Lin-Manuel Miranda! A Look at the Original Rap Song That Gave Birth to 'Hamilton.'" *Billboard*, January 1, 2018. https://www.billboard.com/articles/columns/latin/8094406/happy-birthday-lin-manuel-miranda-original-hamilton-performance.

Freeman, J. B. (2017). "Will the Real Alexander Hamilton Please Stand Up?" *Journal of the Early Republic* 37, no. 2, 255–62.

Gaffey, A. J. (2015). "Recollecting Union: 'Rebel Flags' and the Epideictic Vision of Washington's Farewell Address." *Western Journal of Communication* 79, no. 3, 327–47. https://doi.org/10.1080/10570314.2015.1035399.

Hamilton. (2017). "'One Last Time'—*Hamilton* at the White House #ObamaLegacy" [Video], YouTube, January 10, 2017. https://www.youtube.com/watch?v=uV4UpCq2azs.

Hamilton. (2018). "Christopher Jackson, Barack Obama, Bebe Winans—One Last Time (44 Remix) [Official Audio]" [Video]. YouTube, December 20, 2018. https://www.youtube.com/watch?v=wFEL_0UFgIs.

Hamilton Hamildrops. (n.d.). "New *Hamilton* Content, Dropping Every Month in 2018." https://www.hamildrops.com/.

Hayes, C. (2015). "Billboard Cover: 'Hamilton' Creator Lin-Manuel Miranda, Questlove and Black Thought on the Runway Broadway Hit, Its Political Relevance, and Super-Fan Barack Obama." *Billboard*, July 30, 2015. https://www.billboard.com/articles/news/magazine-feature/6648455/hamilton-lin-manuel-miranda-questlove-black-thought-the-roots-chris-hayes-interview.

Helderman, R. S., S. S. Hsu, and R. Weiner. (2021). "'Trump Said to Do So' Accounts of Rioters Who Say the President Spurred Them to Rush the Capitol Could be Pivotal to Testimony." *Washington Post*, January 16, 2021. https://www.washingtonpost.com/politics/trump-rioters-testimony/2021/01/16/01b3d5c6-575b-11eb-a931-5b162d0d033d_story.html.

Hogeland, W. (2018). "From Ron Chernow's *Alexander Hamilton* to *Hamilton: An American Musical*." In *Historians on Hamilton: How a Blockbuster Musical Is Restaging America's Past*, edited by R. C. Romano and C. B. Potter, 17–41. Newark, NJ: Rutgers University Press.

Hostetler, M. J. (2002). "Washington's Farewell Address: Distance as Bane and Blessing." *Rhetoric and Public Affairs* 5, no. 3, 393–407.

Isenberg, N. (2017). "'Make 'Em Laugh': Why History Cannot Be Reduced to Song and Dance." *Journal of the Early Republic* 37, no. 2, 295–303.

Kaufman, G. (2017). "Lin-Manuel Miranda Announces 'Hamildrops' Series, Promising New Monthly 'Hamilton' Content for the Next Year." *Billboard*, December 14, 2017. https://www.billboard.com/articles/columns/pop/8070565/lin-manuel-miranda-hamildrops-monthly-series-decemberists-ben-franklin-song.

Kelly, C. E. (2017). "Introduction: Lin-Manuel Miranda's *Hamilton: An American Musical* and the Early American Republic." *Journal of the Early Republic* 37, no. 2, 251–53.

Kreps, D. (2017). "Lin-Manuel Miranda Releases 'Immigrants' Video from 'Hamilton Mixtape.'" *Rolling Stone*, June 28, 2017. https://www.rollingstone.com/music/music-news/lin-manuel-miranda-releases-immigrants-video-from-hamilton-mixtape-199515/.

Malanson, J. J. (2014). "'If I Had It in His Hand-Writing I Would Burn It': Federalists and the Authorship Controversy over George Washington's Farewell Address, 1808–1859." *Journal of the Early Republic* 34, no. 2, 219–42.

Malanson, J. J. (2015). *Addressing America: George Washington's Farewell and the Making of National Culture, Politics, And Diplomacy, 1796–1852* [eBook edition]. Kent, OH: Kent State University Press.

Miranda, L., and C. Jackson. (2015). "One Last Time" [Song]. On *Hamilton: An American Musical* [Album]. Atlantic Recording Corporation.

Miranda, L., and J. McCarter. (2016). *Hamilton: The Revolution (Being the Complete Libretto of the Broadway Musical, with a True Account of Its Creation, and Concise Remarks on Hip-Hop, the Power of Stories, and the New America.* New York: Grand Central Publishing.

Monteiro, L. D. (2018). "Race-Conscious Casting and the Erasure of the Black Past in *Hamilton*." In *Historians on Hamilton: How a Blockbuster Musical Is Restaging America's Past*, edited by R. C. Romano and C. B. Potter, 58–70. Newark, NJ: Rutgers University Press.

Odom, L., Jr., L. Miranda, and Ensemble. (2015). "Alexander Hamilton" [Song]. On *Hamilton: An American Musical* [Album]. Atlantic Recording Corporation.

Phillips, K. R. (2004). "Introduction." In *Framing Public Memory*, edited by K. R. Phillips, 1–14. Tuscaloosa: University of Alabama Press.

Reid, R. F. (1988). "Commentary and Washington's Farewell Address." In *Three Centuries of American Rhetorical Discourse: An Anthology and a Review*, edited by R. F. Reid, 186–201. Prospect Heights, IL: Waveland Press.

Reid, R., and J. F. Klumpp. (2015). "Commentary and Washington's Farewell Address." In *American Rhetorical Discourse*, 3rd ed., edited by R. Reid and J. F. Klumpp, 186–202. Prospect Heights, IL: Waveland Press.

Romano, R. C., and C. B. Potter (2018). "Introduction: History is Happening in Manhattan." In *Historians on Hamilton: How a Blockbuster Musical Is Restaging America's Past*, edited by R. C. Romano and C. B. Potter, 1–14. Newark, NJ: Rutgers University Press.

Schrader, V. L. (2017). "'Another National Anthem': Public Memory, Burkean Identification, and the Musical *Assassins*." *New Theatre Quarterly* 33, no. 4, 320–32. https://doi.org/10.1017/S0266464X1700046X.

Schrader, V. L. (2019). "'Who Tells Your Story?': Narrative Theory, Public Memory, and the *Hamilton* Phenomenon." *New Theater Quarterly* 35, no. 3, 261–74. https://doi.org/10.1017/S0266464X19000265.

Suriano, G. R. (1993). "Introduction to Farewell Address and Washington's Farewell Address." In *Great American Speeches*, edited by G. R. Suriano, 16–21. New York: Gramercy Book.

Thelen, D. (1989). "Memory and American History." *Journal of American History* 75, no. 4, 1117–29. https://doi.org/10.2307/1908632.

Tsakiridis, G. (2021). "Vine and Fig Tree." George Washington's Mount Vernon. https://www.mountvernon.org/library/digitalhistory/digital-encyclopedia/article/vine-and-fig-tree/.

Vankin, D. (2017). "A 'Hamilton' Timeline: How a Single Song Grew into a Global Musical Juggernaut." *LA Times*, August 10, 2017. https://www.latimes.com/entertainment/arts/theater/la-ca-cm-hamilton-history-timeline-20170813-htmlstory.html.

Vine, H. (2018). "Take a Look Back at *Hamilton*'s Opening Night on Broadway." *Playbill*, August 6, 2018. http://www.playbill.com/article/take-a-look-back-at-hamiltons-history-making-opening-night-on-broadway.

Zadrozny, B. (2020). "For Trump's 'Rigged' Election Claims, an Online Megaphone Awaits." NBC News, October 15, 2020. https://www.nbcnews.com/tech/tech-news/trump-s-rigged-election-claims-online-megaphone-awaits-n1243309.

Chapter 3

The Rhetorical Significance of John Laurens in *Hamilton: An American Musical*

Nancy J. Legge

When *Hamilton: An American Musical* premiered on Disney+ in July 2020, it became accessible to a significantly larger audience who, up until then, had only experienced the musical through hearing the original Broadway cast recording soundtrack or viewing publicly aired song performances. The increased access of Disney+ came with new debates about the show itself: within two days #CancelHamilton was trending on Twitter (Zonosa, 2020). Some issues that had been discussed since *Hamilton* premiered at The Public in January 2015 received a new airing with an increased audience (Peterson, 2020). These issues involved "a whole host of perceived problems," including its historical accuracy, the ways the play dealt with slavery, "the erasure of Black and Indigenous people," and "claims of revisionist history" (Zonasa, 2020, para. 3). This chapter considers an aspect of the #CancelHamilton discussion—how the show addresses slavery—by examining a unique and significant scene in the musical.

While seeing the show adds depth and dimension to the songs on the soundtrack, the album and the show are fundamentally the same. There are two major differences between the story told on the album and the story told in the live performance (Hein, 2020). One difference is in Act II, when Philip Hamilton dies and his mother, Eliza, screams after he takes his last breath (Mello, 2020). That scream is not on the soundtrack, as Lin-Manuel Miranda, the playwright, explained that he "needed" the audience to "see" that moment before they heard it (Miranda, July 4, 2020). The second and more significant difference is near the end of Act I. A song, "Tomorrow There'll Be More of

Us," is inserted between the songs "Dear Theodosia" and "Non-Stop" (Mello, 2020). Additionally, the song appears in a scene that is not on the recording. The scene contains a conversation, the *only* non-singing dialogue in the show, in which Eliza and Alexander Hamilton have a conversation about the death of his best friend, John Laurens.

These facts highlight this scene as both unique and important. And yet this scene has not been investigated nor significantly discussed in reviews of the show or in analyses about the show. The scene has been posted on YouTube, recorded from the Disney+ broadcast, where it is called "The Laurens Interlude" (cassiopeia, 2020). There is some discussion of the scene on YouTube, where posters emphasize their reactions to the scene. But there are no larger conversations about why the scene is added or its significance. As rhetorical critics, it is important to identify elements that are different or that "stand out" and to consider the rhetorical implications of those differences. Rhetoricians Hart, Daughton, and LaVally (2018) urge critics to examine patterns of what is said and to also consider "exceptions to patterns" (p. 68). This scene requires rhetorical investigation because it exhibits three exceptions: the scene is the only one not on the album, the scene contains a song not on the album, and the scene contains the *only* non-singing dialogue in the show.

This chapter investigates the rhetorical significance of the Laurens Interlude. Specifically, it argues that the scene functions as an indictment of how Hamilton (and the country's founders) ignored slavery to further their own interests. First, the chapter explores the ways that John Laurens is characterized by examining the lyrics Laurens sings. Next, the chapter details the Laurens Interlude. Third, the chapter conducts a rhetorical analysis using a narrative lens to examine the dialogue between the Hamiltons, the lines sung by the ghost of Laurens, the letter that Eliza reads, and the interaction between Alexander and Laurens. Finally, the chapter considers the rhetorical implications of this scene, especially as it relates to issues involving slavery. The chapter concludes by considering the social statements communicated in this scene, how they may add to the conversation about how *Hamilton: An American Musical* addresses slavery, and the impact that may have on some calls to #CancelHamilton (Romano, 2020).

THE CHARACTER OF JOHN LAURENS

John Laurens is introduced in the second song of the show, "Aaron Burr, Sir," when Burr and Hamilton enter a tavern and see three young revolutionaries (Lafayette, Mulligan, and Laurens). The three revolutionaries and Hamilton develop close ties, becoming a "band of brothers" brought together by their desire to fight for independence from England. One way to understand how we are invited to see John Laurens is to analyze the lyrics he sings, depicting things he cares about and how he sees the world. Laurens sings about seventy solo lines in the show. Those lines reflect four central themes: (1) friendship (especially with Hamilton); (2) willingness to fight for what is "right"; (3) concern for the future; and (4) playfulness. These themes, taken together, communicate how audiences understand "who" John Laurens is. Each trait will be explained and illustrated.

Friendship

A number of Laurens's lines express his fondness for Hamilton. Early in the show, as he observes Hamilton's quick wit and fluidity during "My Shot," Laurens suggests, "Let's get this guy in front of a crowd!" (Miranda and McCarter, 2016, p. 27). During much of the war, as illustrated in the song "Stay Alive," Laurens and Hamilton stay together in Washington's camp. Laurens explains how he viewed that time: "I stay at work with Hamilton. We write essays against slavery. And every day's a test of our camaraderie and bravery" (p. 97). Further, when Laurens is outraged about General Lee's disrespect of Washington, he and Hamilton lament that Lee should be held accountable. Hamilton explains that he has explicit orders to stand down, so Laurens steps up and challenges the general to a duel. As he prepares for the duel, Laurens confides his motivation: "Alexander, you're the closest friend I've got" (p. 98). He is willing to duel and put his life on the line for Hamilton!

Fighting for What Is "Right"

A second trait of Laurens is that he consistently fights for what he thinks is right. Laurens stands up for what he thinks is fair and fights for causes that he thinks are just. Laurens's friendship with Hamilton and Lee's disrespectful behavior lead Laurens to engage in a duel, illustrating that he literally fights for what he thinks is fair. He follows the rules for the fight, articulating proper etiquette for dueling, acknowledging that fairness is important. His willingness to fight extends beyond friendship to include fighting for justice, especially regarding sociopolitical causes: the war and slavery. He sings about the war: "I will gladly join the fight" (Miranda and McCarter, 2016, p. 35). He also encourages others to fight. In "My Shot," Laurens leads a chorus urging everyone to "Rise up!" and he wonders, "When are these colonies gonna rise up?" (p. 28). He urges others to fight for the cause of the war and to seek independence from England. Laurens also calls out Burr for not standing up for the cause and instead opting to lay low without speaking out. He challenges Burr to show courage and speak out in support of the war. Laurens suggests, "The revolution's imminent. What do you stall for?" (p. 23).

The most consistent cause that Laurens identifies with and fights for is emancipation. Hamilton identifies the band of brothers as "manumission abolitionists" (Miranda and McCarter, 2016, p. 27), and in "My Shot," Laurens has a solo that expresses his aspirations when he envisions coming to battle "on a stallion with the first black battalion" (p. 27). In almost every song that Laurens sings, he articulates his desire to end slavery. He articulates his plan to free slaves and fight along with black soldiers in the war. In "Yorktown," Hamilton and Laurens sing in unison, "We'll never be free until we end slavery" (p. 122). Laurens fights for causes important to him—fairness, the revolution, and centrally, the abolition of slavery and equal rights.

Concern for the Future

Hamilton, Laurens, Lafayette, and Mulligan are comrades, joined by the common cause of fighting for freedom from England and King George III. In "The Story of Tonight," they sing about their willingness to "gladly join the fight" (Miranda and McCarter, 2016, p. 35). Laurens's repetition of that line several times throughout Act I helps audiences understand that he knows what he is getting into. In the same song, he acknowledges his mortality, "I may not live to see our glory!" (p. 35). This line, sung several times in the first act, foreshadows his early and untimely death. Laurens also dreams of a time when his belief in the cause will be shared by many others and the revolution will grow. Laurens envisions a future when "there'll be more of us" willing to fight (p. 35). Finally, Laurens is clear about the rightness of the fight, believing that because the cause is an honorable one, those fighting today for independence would be evoked as heroes in the country's future. He promises that "[o]ur children will tell our story" (p. 35). Hamilton joins Laurens in his fight when they both sing during "Yorktown" that they must end slavery. Laurens anticipates when he'll "sally in" with the "first black battalion" (p. 27). Laurens envisions a future that is different, one that is hopeful and better for others, including slaves, but which may not include him. In this way, he is a visionary. He is willing to fight for that future, even recognizing that he may not see it.

Playfulness

In all of this, Laurens is a fun-loving tease. He is relentless with Burr. He taunts, "Well if it ain't the prodigy of Princeton College. Give us a verse, drop some knowledge" (Miranda and McCarter, 2016, p. 25). Laurens also shows his fun-loving nature when he jokes about Hamilton's reputation as a womanizer. He jokes that "if the tomcat can get married, there's hope for our ass after all" (p. 86). Burr is often the target of Laurens's needling. Even at the wedding reception for Alexander and Eliza, Laurens finds a way to pester Burr. When Burr comes to congratulate Hamilton, Laurens interrupts and asks, "What are you tryin' to hide, Burr? Well I heard you've got a special someone on the side, Burr" (p. 87). Laurens teases Burr when he talks about the rumors surrounding Burr's love life. Burr, clearly annoyed by Lauren's antics, tries to ignore the teasing. Laurens's fun-loving nature is not limited to poking fun of or teasing others. He highlights that part of the reason he is so much fun is that he loves to drink and party. In fact, drinking is a central way that he displays his character. He sings, "[N]o more sex for me, pour me another brew son!" (p. 25). Laurens sings several lines throughout Act I where he equates celebration and fun with drinking. When he wants to celebrate the band of brothers, he sings one recurring line: "[R]aise a glass to the four of us." Laurens has fun when he drinks with his friends and when he jokes with and about them. He recognizes the celebratory nature of these times by ordering more drinks. His partying nature is evoked when he exclaims, "Let's have another round" (p. 35).

John Laurens loved to drink, to tease, and to have fun. And yet he took friendship, the war, and slavery seriously. He was willing to put his life on the line for these issues; he recognized that his willingness to stand up for these causes might cost him his life. Audiences who are in tune with John Laurens are not surprised, then, to learn that he met an early death. But many audiences are likely surprised by the scene describing Laurens's death because, while the scene was foreshadowed in the lyrics, it was not part of the original Broadway cast recording. The next sections will describe the omitted scene and analyze it to consider the rhetorical significance of its inclusion in the live performances of the show.

DESCRIPTION OF THE OMITTED SCENE

The omitted scene is often referred to as the "Laurens Interlude" by dedicated fans of the show. It is one minute and seven seconds long. The scene begins as Alexander Hamilton finishes singing "Dear Theodosia," a duet with Aaron Burr. As that song comes to an end, the light goes off of Burr, and then Hamilton is shown sitting in his chair, smiling about the pride in his new country and his new son. Eliza Hamilton enters and tells Alexander that he's received a letter. He responds that he knows—"it's from John Laurens"—and says he will read it later (Miranda and McCarter, 2016, p. 131). She corrects him, holding the letter, explaining that it is from Henry Laurens, John's father. Hamilton, surprised and shaken, stands up and requests that she read the letter to him. The letter contains the news that John Laurens was killed in a skirmish with British troops in South Carolina, "one of the last casualties of the war." Henry Laurens laments, "As you know, John dreamed of emancipating and recruiting three thousand men for the first all-black military regiment. His dream of freedom for these men dies with him" (p. 131). At the same time that Eliza reads the letter, Lafayette and Mulligan are in the balcony of the scene, reading their own letters of the news and reacting. They both react to show sadness and distress, but their reactions are not spotlighted, as the lights are not on them. Additionally, John Laurens is on the right side of the stage and sings some lines, woven in between Eliza's and Alexander's dialogue. He is not part of the dialogue. Laurens's lines are from "The Story of Tonight," but in this scene the song is called "Tomorrow There'll Be More of Us" (p. 131). The scene is detailed below. Laurens's lines are in italics because they are sung, not spoken.

JL: *I may not live to see our glory*

EH: Alexander, there's a letter for you

AH: It's from John Laurens, I'll read it later

JL: *But I will gladly join the fight*

EH: No, it's from his father

AH: His father?

JL: *And when our children tell our story*

AH: Will you read it to me?

JL: *They'll tell the story of tonight*

EH: (reading) "On Tuesday the 27th my son was killed in a gunfight against British troops retreating from South Carolina. [AH hangs his head, shoulders moving] The war was already over. As you know, John dreamed of emancipating and recruiting three thousand men for the first all-black military regiment. His dream of freedom for these men dies with him."

JL: *Tomorrow there'll be MORE of US*

AH looks at John Laurens.

EH: Alexander?

JL turns to look at AH.

JL and AH lock eyes for 3 seconds

EH: Are you alright?

AH: I have so much work to do.

(Miranda and McCarter, p. 131)

The scene, omitted from the soundtrack but included in the live performance, contains a new song and spoken dialogue. The addition of this scene adds layers to the characters in the story and complexities to the overall arc of the storyline. But its inclusion "here" and "not there" should lead a critic to ask, "*Why* is this scene here?" That is, what does this scene uniquely communicate which therefore justifies its inclusion in the live performance of the show—what is its rhetorical function? It is the critic's job to unpack those layers and complexities to help get at the logic of this additional scene and work to uncover what is going on here (Hart, Daughton, and LaVally, 2018). The most appropriate way to analyze this scene is the narrative method. The Laurens Interlude tells the story of John Laurens's death and how the Hamiltons, Mulligan, and Lafayette learned of his death. The lens of narrative can provide the tools for unpacking some of the layers in this story. Before proceeding with the analysis, it is important to outline the central components of the narrative method.

Narrative Method

The systematic study of rhetoric began in ancient Greece and included the study of narrative. Since 467 BCE, when Sicilians overthrew King Hieron and established democratic rule, the study of rhetoric has included the study of narrative. Corax wrote in *Techne* that arguers should construct narratives which outlined their claims as more probable than the narratives of others (Gribas et al., 2017). Aristotle's *Poetics* (1984) included a discussion of narrative, highlighting that narratives should have clear beginnings, middles, and ends. In the twentieth century, rhetorical scholars including Kenneth Burke and Walter Fisher identified narrative as a central way ideas are communicated. Fisher (1987) contended that narrative is fundamental to how we understand the human experience. He suggested the narrative paradigm as an alternative to analyzing discourse from more traditional, rationalistic methods. To demonstrate the power of narrative analysis, Fisher analyzed the discourse of President Ronald Reagan. In contrast to the traditional reason-giving discourse of his predecessor, President Jimmy Carter, Reagan's rhetoric reflected a narrative that harkened back to the mythic hero of the American west and the "glory" of America's past. His story invited audiences to embrace his solution (and his candidacy). Reagan's stories consistently used terms such as "restore," "recapture," and "redeem" to create a vision of how we should view ourselves and our country (p. 151). Reagan's stories helped audiences accept his narrative, and his vision, of how things ought to be.

Foss (2017) suggests that narratives help us organize and understand experiences "so that we can make sense of the people, places, events, and actions we encounter in our lives" (p. 319). Many rhetorical scholars have used a narrative lens to help us understand how stories shape perspectives and influence audiences (Darsey, 2009; Dickinson, Ott, and Aoki, 2005; Lewis, 1987; Warnick, 1987; Farrell, 1985). By providing a series of events in a cohesive framework, narratives help us "sort through acts, characters, and situations so that a dominant central action or point emerges" (Foss, 1989, p. 229).

Narrative is different from other types of rhetorical events such as explicit arguments or other persuasive discourse. Further, because narratives "tell a story," audiences are often swayed to listen to a narrative without the same predisposition as those who are making overt persuasive appeals (Hart, Daughton, and LaVally, 2018). Nevertheless, because narratives tell a story from a particular perspective, through a specific lens, and by emphasizing particular ideas and not mentioning others, narratives are inherently persuasive. Narrative "involves strategic decisions," according to Hart, Daughton, and LaVally (2018), including which facts to stress, which characters to highlight, and when to punctuate the story. These choices are rhetorical elements that a critic should investigate. The Laurens Interlude is a story in and of itself, within the larger narrative of *Hamilton: An American Musical*, warranting an investigation of some of the strategic decisions made in telling this story about John Laurens.

Narrative Analysis

Foss (2017) suggests that critics should undertake a narrative analysis in three general steps. First, the critic should "identify the objective of the narrative" (p. 325). Second, the critic should consider the features of the narrative and how they help "accomplish the objective" (p. 325). Third, the critic should evaluate the narrative, using the concepts of narrative coherence and narrative fidelity. Once these steps have been completed, the critic can identify the theme of the narrative. This narrative analysis will use these steps to analyze the Laurens Interlude.

The Objective of the Narrative

The critic should begin by considering the "situation or condition" the story is addressing (Foss, 2017, p. 326). The focus in this step is to address the point of the story "from the perspective of the storyteller" (p. 326). This analysis begins with a question: "What is the point of the inserted scene, the Laurens Interlude?"

The most obvious objective of the Laurens Interlude is to tell the audience that Alexander Hamilton's best friend, John Laurens, died in one of the final battles of the Revolutionary War. But with a closer look, it becomes clear that the obvious answer is not the full objective of the scene. When other characters in the show die, if noted at all, it is revealed through a brief reference in a song. In the first song of the show, "Alexander Hamilton," audiences learn that Hamilton's mother died and his cousin committed suicide through lines in the song. There are not entire scenes dedicated to these events, despite their significant impacts on Hamilton's life. Additionally, in one of the last songs of the show, "The World Was Wide Enough," during the duel with Burr, Hamilton contemplates his own death and remembers people in his life who have died. He sings about seeing his mother and Washington in heaven, along with John Laurens (Miranda and McCarter, 2016). Critically, it is at this point in the play—near the end—that audiences learn of Washington's death; we could have learned of Laurens's death at the same time, in the same way. This point underscores the idea that there is more to the scene than merely presenting the information about Laurens's death to audiences.

A second objective for this scene may be to communicate how Hamilton avoided dealing with the news of his best friend's death. At the end of the scene, Hamilton says, "I have so much work to do." He exits quickly and Laurens's death is never discussed again. A common pattern in Hamilton's life is to work—to "write his way out" of difficult situations (Miranda and McCarter, 2016, p. 233). Hamilton's gift for writing, even as a young man, is what ultimately ensured his immigration to New York City from the Caribbean island of his birth. Later in his life (and in the show), he writes the Reynolds Pamphlet as a way to manage the difficult political situation of being accused of corruption. After Laurens died, the show moves to the song "Non-Stop," highlighting Hamilton's almost obsessive compulsion to work and write.

But, if the purpose of the Laurens Interlude is to show that Hamilton again managed his grief by writing, then the audience would only need the *news* of Laurens's death, which we get early in the scene, when Eliza reads the letter from Henry Laurens. Yet the scene continues well beyond the letter. What objective does Laurens's presence fulfill? Clearly, there is additional significance in the scene that has not been addressed with the two identified objectives. To expand the analysis, Foss (2017) urges the critic to examine some essential features of the narrative such as the setting, the characters, relationships, and the placement of the scene. Exploring these features can help further explain this unique scene.

The Features of the Narrative

What is the function of Laurens's appearance in the scene, singing those lines, and how do they help communicate the objective of the story? The first feature to examine is the setting (Foss, 2017). Laurens appears on the side of the stage—out of the main scene in Hamilton's house and the conversation between Eliza and Alexander. Laurens is in a white, ethereal light. Eliza does not see Laurens. Alexander acknowledges Laurens visually; he does not speak to him. One may interpret Laurens's presence as his ghost and/or Hamilton's incarnation of Laurens. This aspect of the setting highlights that Laurens's presence is important, even if (because?) he is only seen by Hamilton.

The next narrative feature involves examining the characters and relationships in the scene: John Laurens, Eliza, Alexander, and the letter written by Henry Laurens. John Laurens reiterates lines he has sung two previous times in the show and which capture the essence of who he is. He sings, "I may not live to see our glory," because he knows he could die young, as those who fight in wars are often aware of their potential mortality. He then sings, "But I will gladly join the fight," which reminds Hamilton and audiences that he fought "gladly." He believed in the war, and he should be viewed as a true patriot because he willingly gave his life for the cause. Laurens continues, "But when our children tell our story, they'll tell the story of tonight" (Miranda and McCarter, 2016, p. 131). He recognizes that the cause they are fighting is historic, that it will be discussed and remembered. He also highlights the importance of this moment and the decisions made "tonight." This scene is sequenced right after "Dear Theodosia," in which Burr and Hamilton consider the implications for their children of their victory over the British. Laurens, too, recognizes future generations will remember their struggles and bravery.

After those lines sung by Laurens, Eliza reads the letter written by Henry Laurens out loud to Alexander. In the letter, Henry asserts that abolition, the cause to which John dedicated his life, would die with John Laurens. Immediately after that claim (and the end of the letter), John Laurens sings, "Tomorrow there'll be more of us." The words stand as a refutation to his father's claim. The emphasis in Laurens's delivery is on the defiant phrase "more of us." His volume increases, he takes a step forward, and he clenches his fist to demonstrate emphasis. This emphasis is reinforced with the title of the song, "Tomorrow There'll Be More of Us." Those are the last words of John Laurens—a promise (or hope?) that the fight will continue because others will join the fight for abolition. John objects to his father's assertion that the cause of abolition will die with him. After Laurens's final words, he looks at Hamilton as if to say, "Right? There *will* be a continued fight!?" Hamilton stares back at Laurens in silence, as if he is considering his options. Oblivious to this interaction, Eliza asks, "Alexander, are you alright?"

The nonverbal interaction between Laurens and Hamilton at this point is significant. Laurens and Hamilton lock eyes for three long seconds. Hamilton has just heard that Henry Laurens, a prominent leader in the Revolution, has declared that emancipation will not be a cause for which the new country will fight. Hamilton hears the proclamation from his friend, John, who promises a growing fight for and commitment to abolition. The eye contact between Hamilton and Laurens highlights this juncture: Will he (and the country) agree with Henry Laurens and stop pursuing abolition, or will he (and the country) work to enact the vision of John Laurens? When Hamilton locks eyes with Laurens, he recognizes that his best friend would want him to fight for abolition. Wouldn't a true friend take up the mission that his best friend was willing to give his life for? Wouldn't a true patriot, committed to building a strong foundation for the new country, want to make sure that the problem of slavery was addressed?

After three seconds, Hamilton breaks eye contact with Laurens and provides his answer. He makes his choice and says to Eliza, "I have so much work to do" (Miranda and McCarter, 2016, p. 131). He turns and walks offstage. Hamilton literally and figuratively walks away from his friend's death and from the cause of abolition. Hamilton proclaims he has to get to work. And while Hamilton does do a lot of work in his remaining years, none of that work involves the cause that was closest to his best friend: abolition.

The abrupt ending of the scene is uncomfortable. Hamilton is grief-stricken, and that grief is palpable. Additionally, though, a significant flaw is revealed in the character of Alexander Hamilton: he will not address abolition. Instead, he turns to things that matter more to him. This is a clear signal to audiences that Hamilton is flawed. This is not how a best friend—or a patriot—should act.

The final feature to examine is the placement of the scene (Foss, 2017). The scene takes place immediately after the song "Dear Theodosia," featuring Hamilton and Burr sitting in their respective living spaces singing about the love they have for their children and the hopes they have about the future of those children in their new country. Audiences are asked to view Burr and Hamilton as multidimensional characters—fathers and patriots—who care deeply for their children and the country. These are men who promise to "build a strong foundation" for their children on which to build their futures (Miranda and McCarter, 2016, p. 128). The placement of the Laurens Interlude functions to remind audiences that these children would grow up in a world where slavery was a norm. The two fathers promise to build a "strong foundation" for the country; but that foundation included slavery. When the Founding Fathers, and these fathers in particular, built a country with slavery as a foundation, they assured that it was not a strong foundation at all, that it was a foundation that was destined to crumble. Slavery was, in fact, the very thing that would tear the country apart in a Civil War a few decades in the future (Badger, 2018; Loewen, 2011).

The Laurens Interlude ends and the next song, "Non-Stop," begins. In this song, Hamilton's obsessive work ethic is discussed and celebrated. Hamilton writes as if he's "running out of time," as he writes nearly every waking minute (Miranda and McCarter, 2016, p. 137). Hamilton has significant time and energy to dedicate to issues that matter to him. But he does not have the time to fight slavery. "Non-Stop" helps refocus Hamilton (and audiences) away from Laurens's death and abolition toward work that matters to him.

These features of the scene, including setting, characters, relationships (especially the nonverbal interaction between Hamilton and Laurens), and placement help to clarify the objective of this scene. This scene informs audiences about Laurens's death, and it also helps audiences understand that the problem of slavery was neglected in the nation's foundation. Audiences see that although Hamilton could have opted to take up the cause of abolition on behalf of his friend—and that his friend would have wanted him to—instead he literally turns his back on abolition and takes no action at all. Slavery persists for more than eighty years. The Laurens Interlude functions to highlight the choices that the nation's founders made about slavery: to consciously ignore it.

Evaluation of the Narrative

The next step in narrative analysis is to evaluate the story, assessing narrative coherence and narrative fidelity. Narrative coherence encourages the critic to examine whether the narrative is "internally consistent" (Foss, 2017, p. 337). Coherence is sometimes called "probability" and involves examining issues of "clarity, completeness, believability" (Hart, Daughton, and LaVally, 2018, p. 99). The concept of narrative fidelity, on the other hand, instructs the critic to evaluate the narrative's values, considering whether they are consistent with the audience and if the values in the narrative "ring true" (Foss, 2017, p. 337).

The Laurens Interlude reflects narrative coherence. All of the characters in the narrative are consistent with who they have been throughout the show. Hamilton is visibly shaken as Eliza reads the letter. Mulligan and Lafayette, in the balcony, are clearly bereaved with the news. The band of brothers fought together and had similar visions. The loss of Laurens was devastating. But that coherence is disrupted when Hamilton looks at Laurens and turns his back on him. The fact that Hamilton does not discuss Laurens's death or provide some tribute to him is unsettling. Instead, Hamilton opts to focus on his own work, which is a trait that he exhibits for the rest of the show (and throughout his life). Hamilton's character is driven to work "Non-Stop" while audiences are left to wonder about this choice to suppress his grief for losing Laurens. As Fisher (1987) posits, if a character's "actional tendencies contradict each other, change significantly, or alter in strange ways, the result is a questioning of character and a loss of characterological coherence" (p. 47).

This scene functions to reveal inconsistency in Hamilton's character: friend and not friend; grieving and ignoring that grief; working nonstop while not working on emancipation. The inconsistencies leave audiences uneasy about Hamilton's character.

The issue of narrative fidelity reinforces this unsettling feature of the scene. Fidelity concerns "the degree to which the values offered in the story ring true" with audiences (Sellnow, 2018, p. 56). Audiences judge a story as "ringing true" when good reasons are provided to embrace the values in the message and support "the consequences that result from adhering to or defying those values" (p. 56). While the narrative fidelity of what we know about Hamilton does hold—he wrote nonstop for the rest of his life and accomplished a great deal—the scene does not ring true for the value of friendship or the value of building a strong foundation for the country. This scene communicates that Hamilton turned his back on his friendship with Laurens and the cause to which Laurens was dedicated. The scene urges audiences to see Hamilton as flawed in his notions of friendship and in his willingness to ignore a central issue in founding the country: the role of slavery. Audiences may experience some dissonance; they may break with Hamilton's choices, finding it difficult to see Hamilton's reaction as acceptable. Seeger and Sellnow (2016) explain that "if the narrative derives conclusions that violate these [audience] expectations, it is less likely to be accepted" (p. 30). When Hamilton turns his back on Laurens, it reflects a significant violation of our understanding of friendship and loyalty. Laurens's character consistently demonstrated his dedication to Hamilton. As the Laurens Interlude exposes, Hamilton did not demonstrate a reciprocal loyalty to his friend. Additionally, Hamilton's silence on abolition violates audience expectations about what is just and right: slavery needed to be addressed when this country was founded. Hamilton exhibited no interest in ensuring that it was. Hamilton had a powerful hand in shaping the country, and he could have made slavery a sticking point had he opted to take up the cause (Kettler, 2020; Kelly, 2019). The Laurens Interlude violates narrative fidelity; many audience members may be uneasy with or reject Hamilton's actions in this scene because of the consequences of Hamilton's choice to reject both friendship and the importance of emancipation.

These breaks in both narrative coherence and narrative fidelity function to create a wedge between audiences and Alexander Hamilton. Some may realize that he is flawed because of the choices he made and the consequences of those choices. We see Laurens's death as tragic because he died young, needlessly (in a last skirmish), and it meant "an end" to the fight for abolition. This scene is an important one in breaking the mythology of Hamilton and the Founding Fathers, especially as it relates to slavery. This scene provides a fork in the road—Hamilton could help propel Laurens's dream of emancipation to reality or bury himself in his work. He opted for the latter, pursuing things that mattered to him, not to his best friend or to the long-term interests of his country. Audiences who view this scene may recognize the opportunity that Hamilton had to dedicate himself to the cause of fighting for emancipation. They may confront the reality of Hamilton's choice of self-interest over the interest of others. While he may have opposed slavery on principle, he did not advocate for its abolition, he did not rise up, and he focused on other priorities. The consequences of Hamilton's decision cannot be overstated. The Laurens Interlude communicates the turning point for that decision.

Narrative Theme

Analysis of the scene, its features, narrative coherence, and narrative fidelity help a critic determine a theme of the narrative. Foss (2017) explains that the critic's narrative analysis should help reveal the theme, or "the general idea illustrated by the narrative . . . what a narrative is about, and it points to the significance of the action" (p. 335). The dissonance that the Laurens Interlude communicates with audiences exposes a fundamental trait of Hamilton: he opts for selfishness instead of selflessness. This theme in evident in the scene; it is also a theme throughout the show. Hamilton consistently chooses his own desires rather than the desires of others. The Laurens Interlude helps audiences understand that Hamilton is not selfless; he may accomplish great things, but he consciously turned his back on his friend and on abolition. Many come to understand that Hamilton was too driven by self-interests to take on a cause as complicated and controversial as slavery. As Lin-Manuel Miranda acknowledges, Laurens's death "is the greatest What-If? in American history. A voice for emancipation from a surviving Revolutionary War veteran and a favorite of Washington: We'll never know what could have been" (Miranda and McCarter, 2016, p. 131). The Laurens Interlude encourages audiences to ponder "what if" and to experience frustration and anger with Hamilton for his inability and unwillingness to commit to the cause of abolition.

This narrative analysis of the Laurens Interlude helps to expose an additional tragedy of a story told in *Hamilton: An American Musical*. Foss (2017) suggests that the critic's investigation can help identify the *narrative type* of the story. This examination reinforces that the Laurens Interlude is a tragedy, a story "marked by unrealized expectations and the failure of the protagonist's dreams" (p. 335). This determination is not a surprise—almost everyone would understand that *Hamilton: An American Musical* is a tragedy. But this investigation reveals that the show is more than a tragedy because Hamilton's life is cut short in a duel with Vice President Aaron Burr. Studying the Laurens Interlude highlights that Laurens's death is also tragic, because aside from his death at an early age, as his father succinctly said, Laurens's dream of emancipation died with him. None of leaders in the Revolution would take up the cause of abolition. Additionally, this examination reveals that Hamilton could have been a voice for emancipation if he had looked the ghost of John Laurens in the eye and agreed to take up his cause. But Hamilton, along with all of the Founding Fathers, opted to stay silent on the issue of slavery. The tragedy of the Laurens Interlude emphasizes the culpability of this country's founders' willingness to turn their backs on the issue and forge ahead in building a nation despite, or perhaps because of, slavery. The country's foundation was far from "solid"; it was inherently flawed because it embraced and benefited from slavery.

CONCLUSION

This chapter began with a question about the rhetorical significance of including a scene in live productions that is omitted from the original Broadway cast recording. The scene includes the only spoken conversation in the show, a previously unheard song, and a significant nonverbal interaction between Hamilton and Laurens. These factors urge the critic to look at the scene to understand the significance of including it in the performances. While the song, and perhaps even the dialogue, could have been included on the album, the exchange between Hamilton and Laurens cannot be communicated without the visual and nonverbal elements of their interaction. Had the song "Tomorrow There'll Be More of Us" been included on the album, it may inappropriately focus our attention on the fact of Laurens's death rather than the tragedy of Hamilton turning his back on his friend and emancipation. Laurens's character emphasizes the desire for more people to join the cause of abolition. Hamilton looks Laurens in the eye and clearly rejects him by walking away and remaining silent. Saving this scene for those who are watching the show helps highlight the significance of this rejection; it helps viewers acknowledge and wrestle with the reality of our country's founders embracing slavery. First-time audiences are likely taken aback by this additional scene. The nonverbal elements are powerful, and the tension is palpable. Audiences may react with sadness, frustration, and dismay. Those who are uncomfortable with the scene may ponder, "What if things were different?" or "What if Hamilton had taken up Laurens's cause?" Others may understand that this flaw in Hamilton's choices should not be swept away or reasoned with.

Ultimately, a central function of the Laurens Interlude is to emphasize how Hamilton let Laurens's legacy and his dream for emancipation die. The scene helps create a wedge between Hamilton and audiences. Evaluating the story using the concepts of narrative coherence and narrative fidelity help expose Hamilton's reaction to Laurens's death as both consistent and inconsistent with his character. It is consistent for Hamilton to bury himself in his work. However, Hamilton's reaction is inconsistent with his friendship with Laurens and with his own desire to build a country with a strong foundation. Hamilton's choice for self-interest violates the values of friendship and emancipation that Laurens had persistently expressed and demonstrated. This scene helps to create a disruption in the identification with Hamilton and provides audiences with a window into a central flaw in the founding of the country.

When Disney+ premiered *Hamilton: An American Musical* in July 2020, conversations about *Hamilton* reemerged in the media and on social media platforms. Some of the conversations included criticisms about the musical. New audiences encountered and considered some ways that Hamilton and other Founding Fathers were portrayed. Some contended that *Hamilton: An American Musical* maintains and preserves a mythology about the infallibility of the Founding Fathers. Katherine J. Igoe (2020) argues that the issue of slavery is a central point of controversy about *Hamilton: An American Musical* because it does not explicitly deal with the fact that "a number of white historical figures in the musical, including perhaps Hamilton himself, owned slaves" (para. 2). Because the show does not openly critique slavery or the historical figures, it enables the Founders to emerge unscathed. In effect, these critiques hold, *Hamilton* condones the historical practices of slavery (Zonosa, 2020). Some discussants suggest the musical should not be viewed at all because of these issues. The hashtag #CancelHamilton was trending on Twitter within two days of its premiere on Disney+ (Zonosa, 2020).

Those who say that *Hamilton: An American Musical* "ignores slavery" or that it condones the practice are overstating their positions. There are a few explicit mentions of slavery. And, to be fair, the references are not positive. For example, in the first song, "Alexander Hamilton," the character of Lafayette/Jefferson describes a common scene showing the inhumanity of slavery: "And every day while slaves were being slaughtered and carted away across the waves" (Miranda and McCarter, 2016, p. 16). Still, many are frustrated the play does not explicitly rebuke slavery. If the play is to maintain any historical accuracy, that rebuke is not possible: there was not a strong push for abolition when the country was founded. The new Constitution assumed and embraced slavery, "counting each enslaved individual as three-fifths of a person for the purposes of taxation and representation in Congress and guaranteeing the right to repossess any 'person held to service or labor'"—an obvious euphemism for slavery. But analysis of the Laurens Interlude challenges the claim that the show condones or is complicit in accepting slavery. This investigation lays bare that the show acknowledges that Hamilton could have opted to fight for abolition. But, instead, he and the other Founding

Fathers turned their backs on abolition. They opted, instead, to build a country while embracing, or at least ignoring, the practices of slavery. The central focus for the country was to be liberated from England while simultaneously ignoring the liberation of slaves.

This examination of *Hamilton* shows that US independence was led by Founding Fathers who were both visionaries and yet blind. They made selfish and tragic choices that impacted millions of lives and hundreds of years of history. They consciously created the country on the backs of humans who they determined were "property." It is hard to overstate the inhumanity of such decisions. The character flaws do not mean that we should turn our backs on what they did, but rather, that we should see and discuss our history as layered and problematic. This narrative analysis of the Laurens Interlude contributes to the conversation about how slavery influenced our history and how it is presented in *Hamilton: An American Musical*. Far from ignoring the topic, the Laurens Interlude functions as a clear indictment of Hamilton's callous silence to ignore Laurens's dream and to be complicit in ensuring that slavery would be a foundation of the country. This exploration reveals a stark and real reaction that many revolutionaries had to the topic of slavery: silence. Audiences who see and pay attention to the interactions between Hamilton and Laurens cannot help but feel uncomfortable, sad, and disillusioned about the ways that Laurens's voice and vision were ignored.

Suggesting that we silence *Hamilton*, as argued in connection with the #CancelHamilton trend, is ironic. Hamilton silenced Laurens's dream of emancipation by ignoring slavery. This should be acknowledged and discussed. This scene provides critical audiences with some language and understanding to discuss and evaluate the flawed foundation of the country. Miranda encourages the conversation, and in a tweet in the midst of the #CancelHamilton discussion, he wrote, "All the criticisms are valid. . . . Did my best. It's all fair game" (Miranda, July 6, 2020). Rhetorical criticism is one way that we can continue to expose and understand the layers of messages in *Hamilton: An American Musical*. Analysis, conversation, and action are starting points for creating social change.

REFERENCES

Aristotle. (1984). *The Poetics of Aristotle*. Translated by Ingram Bywater. New York: Modern College Edition.

Badger, E. (2018). "Like It or Not, Historians Agree Slavery Caused U.S. Civil War." *Pacific Standard*, May 2, 2018. https://psmag.com/education/of-course-the-civil-war-was-about-slavery-26265.

cassiopeia. (2020). "The Laurens Interlude (Tomorrow There'll Be More of Us)." YouTube, July 5, 2020. https://www.youtube.com/watch?v=vC9tHIoKjQI.

Darsey, J. (2009). "Barack Obama and America's Journey." *Southern Communication Journal* 74, no.1, 88–103.

Dickinson, G., B. L. Ott, and E. Aoki. (2005). "Memory and Myth at the Buffalo Bill Museum." *Western Journal of Communication* 69, no. 2, 85–108.

Farrell, T. B. (1985). "Narrative in Natural Discourse: On Conversation and Rhetoric." *Journal of Communication* 35, no. 4, 109–27.

Fisher, W. J. (1987). *Human Communication as Narration: Toward a Philosophy of Reason, Value, and Action.* Columbia: University of South Carolina Press.

Foss, S. K. (1989). *Rhetorical Criticism: Exploration and Practice.* Prospect Heights, IL: Waveland Press.

Foss, S. K. (2017). *Rhetorical Criticism: Exploration and Practice,* 5th ed. Long Grove, IL: Waveland Press.

Gribas, J., Z. Gershberg, J. DiSanza, and N. J. Legge. (2017). "Finding Story in Unexpected Places: Branding and the Role of Narrative in the Study of Communication." In *Narrative, Identity, and Academic Community in Higher Education,* edited by B. Atteberry, J. Gribas, M. K. McBeth, P. Sivitz, and K. Turley-Ames, 91–110. New York: Routledge.

Hart, R., S. Daughton, and R. LaVally. (2018). *Modern Rhetorical Criticism,* 4th ed. New York: Routledge.

Hein, E. (2020). "How to Watch 'Hamilton' on Disney Plus." Insider, July 6, 2020. https://www.businessinsider.com/how-to-watch-hamilton-movie.

History.com Editors. (2009). "Slavery in America." History.com, November 12, 2009. https://www.history.com/topics/black-history/slavery.

Igoe, K. J. (2020). "The 'Cancel *Hamilton*' Backlash Explained." *Marie Claire,* July 9, 2020. https://www.marieclaire.com/culture/a33261974/hamilton-canceled-explained-lin-manual-miranda/.

Kelly, M. (2019). "America's Most Influential Founding Fathers." ThoughtCo.Com, May 23, 2019. https://www.thoughtco.com/top-founding-fathers-104878.

Kettler, S. (2020). "The Founding Fathers: What Were They Really Like?" Biography.com, June 18, 2020. https://www.biography.com/news/founding-fathers-quotes-facts.

Lewis, W. F. (1987). "Telling America's Story: Narrative Form and the Reagan Presidency." *Quarterly Journal of Speech* 73, no. 3, 280–302.

Loewen, J. W. (2011). "Five Myths about Why the South Seceded." *Washington Post,* February 26, 2011. https://www.washingtonpost.com/outlook/five-myths-about-why-the-south-seceded/2011/01/03/ABHr6jD_story.html.

Mello, D. (2020). "*Hamilton*: 10 Differences Between the Disney Plus Recording and the Original Broadway Soundtrack," ScreenRant, July 5, 2020. https://screenrant.com/hamilton-differences-disney-plus-broadway-soundtrack/.

Miranda, L. [@Lin_Manuel]. (2020). "We couldn't give you the scream at the End of Blow Us All Away. I knew you'd see It. Needed you to see it. #hamilton-musical." [Tweet]. Twitter, July 4, 2020. https://twitter.com/Lin_Manuel/status/1279224528686714880.

Miranda, L. [@Lin_Manuel]. (2020). "Appreciate you so much, @brokeymcpoverty. All criticisms are valid. The sheer tonnage of complexities and failings of these people I couldn't get. Or wrestled with but cut. I took 6 years and fit as much as I could in a 2.5 hour musical. Did my best. It's all fair game." [Tweet]. Twitter, July 6, 2020. https://twitter.com/Lin_Manuel/status/1280120414279290881.

Miranda, L., and J. McCarter. (2016). *Hamilton: The Revolution.* New York: Grand Central Publishing.

Peterson, C. (2020). "Cancel *Hamilton*: A Worthy Discussion or Cancel Culture Disruption?" *OnStage Blog.* https://www.onstageblog.com/editorials/cancel-hamilton.

Romano, A. (2020). "Why *Hamilton* Is as Frustrating as It Is Brilliant—and Impossible to Pin Down," Vox, July 3, 2020. https://www.vox.com/culture/21305967/hamilton-debate-controversy-historical-accuracy-explained.

Seeger, M., and T. Sellnow. (2016). *Narratives of Crisis: Telling Stories of Ruin and Renewal.* Stanford, CA: Stanford University Press.

Sellnow, D. (2018). *The Rhetorical Power of Popular Culture: Considering Mediated Texts*, 3rd ed. Thousand Oaks, CA: Sage Publications.

Warnick, B. (1987). "The Narrative Paradigm: Another Story." *Quarterly Journal of Speech* 73, no. 2, 172–82.

Zonosa, L. (2020). "With 'Hamilton' Now a Movie, an Old Debate Reignites about Who Tells Its Story," *Los Angeles Times*, July 10, 2020. https://www.latimes.com/entertainment-arts/movies/story/2020-07-10/hamilton-movie-critics-lin-manuel-miranda.

Chapter 4

Da Da Da Dat Da

The Rhetorical Construction of Hamilton's Mad Monarch

Sarah Mayberry Scott

There is no doubt that King George III is a villain in American history, remembered as a tyrannical king whose mental illness earned him the moniker "the mad monarch." Despite being a villain in the American consciousness, King George never once set foot onto American soil, and he never actually met Alexander Hamilton. It is curious then why King George appears—and arguably steals the show—in the musical *Hamilton*. Lin-Manuel Miranda, the show's creator, claimed bringing King George into the musical robs the revolution of its inevitability (Miranda and McCarter, 2016, p. 127). While *Hamilton* has a run time of almost three hours, the king appears onstage for a total of less than ten minutes. Yet those minutes are some of the most memorable of the entire production. The character of the king provides immense entertainment with earworm catchy tunes, memorable lyrics, and the satisfying comedic timing of Jonathan Groff, who pioneered the role of the king on Broadway.

The character of King George rhetorically shapes the way the king is remembered in the public imagination. "*Hamilton* infuses American history with current politics, using a soundtrack of American popular music and one of the most inventive librettos ever written," wrote Churchwell (2016, para. 2). *Hamilton* uses contemporary musical stylings, quick-witted turns-of-phrase, and critical racial casting to provide commentary on current political concerns and controversies. The result is a production where "layered references compound meaning like interest: *Hamilton* is metatheatrical, metahistorical, metaphoric" (Churchwell, 2016, para. 5). For this reason, looking at the king from a disability perspective can reveal present-day understandings of what it means to be disabled. While Miranda does not explicitly mention the king's disability, he is definitely still providing commentary on it. King George's mental health plays a central role in his character in *Hamilton*.

Many claims have been made about the disabilities of King George III. While Black (2006) noted in the biography he wrote about King George III that little is known about the king's first ten years of life, others claim that the king had a learning disability and did not learn to read until he was eleven years old (Revolutionary War, 2020). Christie asserted that biographers have described the king as "not very sagacious" (2016, qtd. on p. 209) and that he had a "fundamental simplicity of character" (p. 210). Christie, however, also explained that the king had a "strong streak of intellectual curiosity" (2016, p. 210), and while the king was "no scholar himself" (2016, p. 210), he was widely read and well informed. For almost forty years, the prevailing belief about the king's later illnesses was that he developed porphyria, an inherited blood disorder. This diagnosis was advanced by a mother-and-son psychiatric team, Macalpine and Hunter (1966). In the early 2000s, however, this research was shown to be faulty, and the porphyria theory is now widely discredited (Peters and Beveridge, 2010). Current research suggests that the king experienced bouts of acute mania, and he probably had what would now be diagnosed as bipolar disorder (Peters, 2011). In 1811, the king was declared insane (Wigington, 2019) and spent the last years of his life in seclusion, experiencing acute mania and severe dementia until his death in 1820 (Wigington, 2019).

The character of King George III is a worthy role for rhetorical investigation. Since he was once one of the most powerful rulers in the world, King George has often been the source of scholarly inquiry. This chapter expands existing research by studying the king's character in the popular Broadway musical, *Hamilton*. To that end, this chapter is guided by the following research question: How does the character of King George III in *Hamilton* rhetorically construct contemporary understandings of the "mad monarch"? To answer this question, I conducted a close reading analysis at the intersections of disability studies and sound studies. In doing so, I argue that the character of King George III often adheres to and reinforces stereotypes of individuals with mental illness.

The rest of this chapter proceeds in three parts. First, I provide a review of literature that sets up the theoretical and methodological considerations for this project. Second, I identify the four themes that my close reading analysis revealed, and I provide a discussion of each of the four themes. Lastly, I present some conclusions and consider some limitations and implications of this study.

THEY SAY

Disability studies brings forward the body as a site of rhetorical production and therefore worthy of rhetorical investigation. Disability studies advances disability as more than a medical diagnosis but rather a "political and cultural identity" (Dolmage, 2014, p. 19) whereby the disabled body "is not a discrete object but rather a set of social relations" (Davis, 1995, p. 11). Dolmage claimed that rhetoric has long "ignored the body" (2014, p. 5) and that rhetoric must be recognized as the "circulation of discourse through the body" (2014, p. 5). It is imperative, then, that disability rhetoric attend to the body: the ways bodies move, walk, talk, sound, and exist in conjunction with the communication the body produces. Hawhee advanced the idea that bodily movements "do not recede into the background but work in tandem with wordy movements" (2009, p. 115). When we talk about bodies and the rhetoric those bodies produce, we must talk about aspects such as "sensation, touch, texture, affect, materiality, performativity, movement, gesture, habits, entrainment, biology, physiology, rhythm, and performance" (Hawhee, 2009, p. 5). In *Hamilton*, bodies move and interact as they perform onstage. Therefore, analysis must consider the embodied performances of the actors as they occur in that space. It is equally as important to frame the study of King George III from a disability studies perspective, since the king has become infamous for his "madness." Yet the exploration of King George in *Hamilton* is incomplete without consideration of the sounds of Jonathan Groff's King George character. The sounds a body produces are an often-overlooked part of the embodied experience. The emerging field of sound studies seeks to rectify this oversight.

Sound studies expands the texts critics have available for analysis by arguing for the persuasive power of sound. Sound studies takes sound "as its analytic point of departure or arrival" (Sterne, 2012, p. 2) in the study of a variety of sonic phenomena—radio, media, performances, and voices, often from the intersection of sound and race, gender, or dis/ability. While sound studies does not limit its scope to music, music is a fruitful place for the study of sound/s. Attali argued that music is a mirror of society (1985, p. 4) and that "music is not innocent" (p. 5). Instead, "music is prophetic," and "social organization echoes it" (Attali, 1985, p. 5). Sound carries with it rhetorical weight. Irvine and Kirkpatrick (1972) offered theoretical considerations for understanding the musical form in the rhetorical exchange. For Irvine and Kirkpatrick, a "music artist's activity is rhetorical," the musical form is "capable of generating rhetorical impact," and "the musical form changes the rhetorical message from its normal discursive state" (1972, p. 273). Sellnow and Sellnow (2001) acknowledged that the rhetorical power of music cannot be ascertained by lyrics alone. Similarly, Goodale asserted, "Voices and noises produce meaning beyond words" (2011, p. 4) and that sound/music carries rhetorical force. Goodale (2011) wrote that a rhetorical critic could learn to *read sounds* using techniques, like close reading, that critics conventionally use to interpret the rhetoricity of words and images.

For the rhetorician, close reading or textual criticism is a "mindful, disciplined reading of an object with a view to deeper understandings of its meanings" (Brummett, 2010, p. 9). According to Leff, close reading "in the most basic sense of the term, is a way into a subject" (2016, p. 237). For rhetoricians, *close listening* expands the possibilities of close reading as a method. Close listening as method is advanced by Bernstein (1998) in the interpretation of poetry, which utilizes audio recordings in addition to the printed words to aid and enhance the critic's interpretation. Bernstein (1998) also acknowledged that close listening may produce meanings that are different from or even contradict explanations provided by reading the text exclusively. Blum (1992), a musicologist, argued for analysis that occurs at the crossroads of close listening and close reading. This intersection is of particular utility to rhetoricians who have been trained in the skills and techniques of the close reading of texts. Close reading has limitations. By opening up our methodological understanding to the listening *and* viewing of a text, critics are able to provide a more nuanced reading—one that does not ignore the body, the voice, or the cultural implications that accompany both. In this way, critics can conduct a close reading of a performance in the same way they might close-read a printed text.

To that end, this chapter conducts a close listening/reading analysis of the role and performance of King George III in the musical *Hamilton*. This criticism will draw from Jonathan Groff's performance as King George III in the *Hamilton* production that is currently available on Disney+. While I acknowledge that different performers may inspire various *reads* of the king's character, Groff's performance is one that is easily accessible on Disney+ and is most recognizable as part of the original Broadway cast on the *Hamilton* recording. My close reading analysis will combine aspects of visuals, sounds, and lyrics to provide a more comprehensive reading of Groff's performance. While *Hamilton*'s continued popularity ensures much will be written about the musical and its characters, to my knowledge, there has been no examination of the character of King George III from a disability perspective. While rhetoric has a long history of erasing disability, this chapter attempts to guard against such erasure and add to rhetoric by centering disability as a central part of this study.

CUZ YOU'RE MY FAVORITE SUBJECT[S]

In a close reading analysis of King George III's character in *Hamilton*, four themes emerge. First, the King's songs highlight both the *manic and depressive* arc of his story and his disability in *Hamilton*. The second theme is *violence*, which is supported by the use of violent threats in the king's songs. The king's threats are entertaining, farcical even, and are met with roaring laughter, which brings me to the third theme: the king serves as *comedic relief* in *Hamilton*. Here the music, lyrics, and Groff's performance construct the king's appearances as amusing, perhaps even absurd, and always hilarious. Finally, the fourth theme that emerges is the *simplicity* of the king's songs that stands in sharp contrast to the quick-witted, fast-paced rap and hip-hop songs of many of the other characters.

I'm So Blue

The three songs of King George III call attention to the narrative arc of the king's bipolar disorder by foregrounding both his manic and depressive states. In this section, I will discuss each of the king's three songs to show the manic/depressive progression through the musical. Additionally, I will show how elements such as spitting, laughing, speed, and tone speak to the differing moods of the monarch. I will begin with a discussion of "You'll Be Back."

"You'll Be Back" is the sixth song in *Hamilton* and the audience's first introduction to King George III. While most of the other characters were introduced in the musical's top song, "Alexander Hamilton," the king's appearance is a surprise to first-time viewers and a welcome delight to long-time cast recording listeners. As the music for "You'll Be Back" begins, Groff saunters to center stage, cloaked in full royal regalia, including a mantle, powdered wig, crown, and scepter. Groff is alone on the stage, his eyes glossed over, his face emotionless. As Groff begins to sing, "You say / The price of my love's not a price that you're willing to pay," (Miranda and McCarter, 2016, p. 57) the slower tempo might seem to indicate the king is feeling down, but we quickly learn that he's toying with us. The king asks, "Why so sad?" (Miranda and McCarter, 2016, p. 57) and makes a quick pouty expression that shows he is having fun at our expense. As Groff sings the lyric, "You'll be back" (Miranda and McCarter, 2016, p. 57), the tempo becomes more upbeat. This is a manic episode for the king, characterized by an abnormally upbeat mood and increased agitation. The song coincides in time with the king's first known bout with mental illness in 1765, near the start of the American Revolution (Wigington, 2019).

In "You'll Be Back," the king is typically confident and upbeat. He feels secure that his subjects will return to him, as evidenced by the song's title and lyrics. Even when the king threatens violence, his tone is playful, making his threats all the more menacing. In two places the king continues a line for longer than expected. In the lyric, "You say our love is draining and you can't go on" (Miranda and McCarter, 2016, p. 57), the "on" continues for a full three seconds, in a high pitch, while Groff stands singing in an exaggerated pose with his eyes closed. While this may speak to the thoughts of an autocratic ruler, it also emphasizes the king's acute mania characteristics, where he was known to speak continuously until he would lose his voice (Wigington, 2019). When the king belts out, "And no don't change the subject" (Miranda and McCarter, 2016, p. 57), he is furious, and spit flies from his mouth. While it is not known if the spitting was intentional (Gualtieri, 2020), King George was known at times to anger easily and to talk until he "foamed at the mouth" (Wigington, 2019, para. 12). In the next line, however, the king is once again in a cheerful disposition, and by the time the king sings the famous refrain, "Da da da dat da" (Miranda and McCarter, 2016, p. 127), he is dancing—a little shimmy of the shoulders that indicates a lighthearted or playful attitude. Finally, in "You'll Be Back," not only is the king's mania reinforced to the audience, but the trajectory of his mental illness is foreshadowed with the line, "Now you're making me mad"—particularly interesting because of the double entendre of "mad" (Miranda and McCarter, 2016, p. 57).

The king's second song, "What Comes Next?" comes on the heels of "Yorktown"—the battle (and song) that end the Revolutionary War. "We see King George, glum" (stage directions, Miranda and McCarter, 2016, p. 127) entering the stage, looking confused and slightly on edge, wearing royal regalia but without the mantle this time. "What Comes Next?" is slower and more somber than the king's previous appearance. This song is indicative of the king's depressed state. The king had many bouts of "mania and misery" (Pearce, 2017, p. 197) throughout his life, "punctuated by 'madness' and remission" (Pearce, 2017, p. 198). The song's tempo and pace alert viewers to the change in mood, and the king confesses explicitly, "I'm so blue" (Miranda and McCarter, 2016, p. 127). While this lyric is supposed to be amusing—the king stomps his foot, and the stage lighting turns to blue—the king is revealing his emotional state here. There is no dancing or laughing in this song. Even the king's refrain, "Da da da dat da dat da da da" (Miranda and McCarter, 2016, p. 127), is more subdued and much shorter than in our previous encounter with the king. As the king's song ends with, "You're on your own" (Miranda and McCarter, 2016, p. 127), Groff throws up his hands out of exasperation and walks off the stage—a divergence from his cocky optimism expressed in "You'll Be Back."

The king's final song, "I Know Him," begins as melancholy as the previous song. King George is once again slow to enter center stage and is solemn in manner. The tempo and pace match that of "What Comes Next?" until a soldier interrupts his song and whispers in the king's ear. This is the first time the king interacts intentionally with another character onstage. The sentinel is reporting to King George that John Adams will be the next president of the new United States. It is at this point the king's mood begins to shift. At first, King George seems confused, asking, "John Adams?!" (Miranda and McCarter, 2016, p. 218). But his spirits begin to lift as he realizes the inferiority of his new opponent. With the very next lines, Groff begins to strut across the stage as the tempo quickens. By the time the classic refrain occurs, Groff is in good spirits, moving swiftly to stage right where he releases a crazed laugh that sounds both manic and maniacal, while jumping up and down and clapping his hands. The king is now in a state of acute mania, where he remains for the rest of the show.

While the audience does not hear from the king again (except for a few lines as part of the chorus), the king appears in two more songs in *Hamilton*. In both songs the king is euphoric—a characteristic of mania. During "The Adams Administration," King George sits on a stool, stage right, while Burr introduces the audience to the years of Adams's presidency in his typical narrator style. While Burr is singing, King George begins dancing in his chair, a move that seems wildly bizarre given the nature of the song. His jubilant demeanor denotes the king's continued manic state that "came on intermittently in his life, and as he aged . . . became permanent" (Ross, 2020, para. 6). King George appears in one final scene, during "The Reynolds Pamphlet." At the beginning of the song King George is at the top of the stairs, stage right, reading the Reynolds Pamphlet. Approximately halfway through the song, without any easily identifiable reason, King George descends the stairs, fanning himself with the pamphlet, and proceeds to dance his way across the stage. The king then exits stage left and is not seen again. These two appearances highlight the king's continued state of mania that persisted until he was declared insane in 1811 (Wigington, 2019).

I Will Kill Your Friends and Family

The second theme, violence, serves as evidence of the king's "madness" and reinforces the stereotype that individuals with mental illness are violent and dangerous. Violence is present through declarations of ownership and through statements threatening or lauding violent actions. While critics have noted that the character of King George III "seems more like a jealous ex-boyfriend than a king of a world super-power" (Ross, 2020, para. 1), the aggressive lyrics and actions go well beyond the nature of a scorned lover and suggest mental instability. In this section, I will discuss how the king's claims of ownership and threats of violence frame the king not as a jealous ex-boyfriend but rather as a malevolent leader.

In two of the king's three songs, there are pronouncements of ownership. The king is declaring his right to the land and people of the new colonies and deploys possessive language to reinforce this belief. In "What Comes Next?" the theme of possession continues when the king states, "You were mine to subdue" (Miranda and McCarter, 2016, p. 127). These lyrics cast King George III as the abuser in an abusive relationship, which is heightened by the use of violent threats.

Violence is present in all three of the king's songs, establishing the king as a domineering tyrant. In "You'll Be Back," the king uses explicit warnings, including the promise to "kill your friends and family to remind you of my love" (Miranda and McCarter, 2016, p. 57). In "What Comes Next?" the king's claim to ownership, "You were mine to subdue" (Miranda and McCarter, 2016, p. 127), suggests "subduing" through any means necessary, including violence. And, finally, in "I Know Him" the king finds immense joy in the idea of violence. "They will tear each other into pieces. / Jesus Christ this will be fun!" (Miranda and McCarter, 2016, p. 218). While these lyrics suggest the king was a cruel and malicious oppressor, contemporary historians have challenged that impression.

A read of the king's lyrics, devoid of the embodied performance, shows that King George III is portrayed as a merciless tyrant in *Hamilton* through the use of oppressive and violent language. However, there is not much evidence to suggest that this is an accurate depiction of the king. "Many scholars today view [King George III] as a well-intentioned ruler who found himself in unfortunate circumstances, forced to deal with a significant shift in the global political landscape," Ross writes (2020, para. 7). Black (2006) claims that the king's character was inspired by an "inner conviction that drew on a strong personal piety and clear sense of morality" (p. 114). The king had strong religious beliefs that informed his decision-making and his relationships. He was "the first Hanover king not to take a mistress" ("King George III," n.d. para. 4) and enjoyed a "close and stable marriage that was different from that of many eighteenth-century monarchs" (Black, 2006, p. 118). The king, however, had inherited the debts of the costly Seven Years' War. Three years into his reign, the king was able to end the war, but the financial damage had been done. "This instability was one of the major reasons George III taxed the American colonies so heavily: he wasn't purposely selfish or evil, but he needed money for his country" (Ross, 2020, para. 5). The king's threats, then, may speak more to his perceived madness than to his ruling style.

While *Hamilton* never discusses the king's disabilities outright, there are insinuations of mental illness underpinning the disability myth that individuals with mental illness are violent and dangerous. Ross states, "Groff's performance raises suspicions of mental instability" (2020, para. 5). "They will tear each other into pieces. Jesus Christ this will be fun!" can also be interpreted as an implication of mental illness (Ross, 2020, para. 5). The king's menacing nature is only enhanced by how infrequently Groff blinks. During each of the king's songs, Groff blinks only five to seven times. The average human blinks fifteen to twenty times per minute (Healthline, 2017). This low-blinking technique was used also by Anthony Hopkins in his famous portrayal of Hannibal Lecter in the film *Silence of the Lambs*. Hopkins claimed the lack of blinking kept the audience mesmerized and made the character seem more unnerving ("Anthony Hopkins Doesn't Blink," n.d.). For Groff, the low amount of blinking works similarly—it keeps the audience mesmerized while also feeling like there is something slightly unsettling about the king.

These violent remarks and unsettling behavior from the king reinforce the notion that people with disabilities, especially people who experience emotional distress, are sinister or evil (Barnes, 1992). Longmore claims that one of the most persistent stereotypes of disability in popular entertainment is the "association of disability with malevolence" (1985, p. 32). Corrigan and Watson note that film and print media perpetuate the idea that "people with mental illness are homicidal maniacs who need to be feared" (2020, para. 7) despite the fact that "psychological research shows there is no clear link between mental illness and violence" (American Psychological Association, 2015, para. 1). The king's exuberance at the thought of violence, "They will tear each other into pieces," evidenced by his gleeful laughter and cheerful tone, alludes to a person experiencing psychosis, where the behavior exhibited is wildly inappropriate to the situation at hand (Miranda and McCarter, 2016, p. 127). The lyrics, despite being quite brutal and vicious, are not read as such to the audience of *Hamilton*. Instead, they are quite comical exactly because they are irrational and delusory—manifestations of the king's mental instability—which is just that: funny.

Awesome. Wow.

Third, King George III provides *Hamilton* with comic relief. The audience is meant to understand the king as mentally unstable and, therefore, comical. Groff plays the king as a sardonic tyrant who is out of touch with the colonists and often out of touch with reality. The king appears in full colorful regalia, creating an obvious delineation between his and the rest of the characters' stark costumes. The king appears onstage most often alone, making it evident that he is speaking to the audience from across the ocean, not in the same location as the other characters. When the king first appears, he ambles onto the stage, a move that is repeated for all three of his songs. The king is never in a hurry, and his entrances are slow and calculated, indicating that this character is different from the rest of the characters. In this section, I will show how Groff uses facial expressions, tone, gestures, and bodily movements for comedic effect, but that much of the hilarity of the King George character is wrapped up in the idea that the king is going insane.

The king's exaggerated style matches his extravagant attire and often seems pantomimic. "The visual of the character is so extreme that it's like switching languages in the middle of a paragraph" (Brian d'Arcy James qtd. in Tishgart, 2016, para 12). Groff sometimes uses facial expressions to intensify a moment. For example, in "You'll Be Back," the king sings, "You say our love is draining and you can't go on" (Miranda and McCarter, 2016, p. 57). Groff closes his eyes and wrinkles his nose and mouth as he holds the "on" for four beats—an overemphasized moment that enhances the comedic effect. Other times, Groff uses tone to create humor. For instance, in "What Comes Next?" Groff responds to "You're on your own" with "Awesome. Wow." delivered in a sarcastic and jeering style that elicits chuckles from the audience. Groff also uses gestures, such as in "I Know Him," when he uses air quotes with the word "country" to indicate his disapproval of the colonists. And finally, Groff uses bodily movements to enhance comedic effect. This is perhaps most evident in the king's appearances in "The Adams Administration" and in "The Reynolds Pamphlet" as the king applauds, jumps, and dances onstage, spurring laughter from the audience.

It is almost impossible to talk about Groff's performance without referencing the king's "madness." The king's mental illness is a well-known historical fact and, therefore, seems to be inevitable in the performance of the king as a character. Ableist metaphors are abundant in the reviews and accolades Groff received for his performance of King George III. For instance, fans tweeted comments like, "That #groffsauce maniacal, King George cackle is the best!" (Kira, 2020) and "#Groffsauce really brings the crazy" (P Cheng, 2020). It becomes difficult to describe Groff's performance without using ableist terms such as insane, crazy, maniacal, and mad. This association, however, is not accidental. Andrew Rannells (who briefly replaced Groff in the role) said of playing King George, "It's so fun to have this entire arc of someone going insane . . . you get to show the most erratic side of this guy" (qtd. in Tishgart, 2016, para. 13). Groff stated, "My favorite part is subtly tapping into the madness. . . . I hold that madness underneath all of it, and find ways to change it ever so slightly. . . . You feel like at any moment, [the king's] going to flip his shit" (qtd. in Tishgart, 2016, para 14). What fans and actors are tapping into here is the audience expectation for how a character with mental illness should act—and it will be hilarious. This, however, speaks to long-held assumptions about people with mental illness and the tropes of disability in popular culture.

People with mental disorders are often portrayed as comical, and King George III does not escape this stereotype. Levers (2001) identified twelve contemporary stereotypes of individuals with mental illness in American film, one of which is that of the comic figure. This stereotype has deep roots; "In Rome, it was not unusual for the wealthy to keep a person with a physical or mental disability, often referred to as a 'fool,' for their amusement. Later royal courts commonly kept 'fools' or 'court jesters' as playthings" (Minnesota Governor's Council on Developmental Disabilities, 2021, para. 1). Well into the twenty-first century, the trope of mental disability as comedic prevails, and individuals with mental illness are still objectified by being used as sources of entertainment. Maybe laughing at King George does not feel wrong because he is coming to us from a position of privilege—he is not a pitiable character but a rich and powerful man. The king is also the antagonist of the story, one of whom most of history has treated as a cruel and oppressive tyrant; perhaps we feel vindicated in getting to laugh at his expense. But none of these justifications does anything to negate the stereotype, because in *Hamilton* we feel emboldened and encouraged to laugh at the king's "madness."

Da Da Da Dat Da

The last theme that emerges from the reading of King George III in *Hamilton* is that of simplicity, which not only infantilizes the king but also speaks to the lack of depth and discernment often stereotypically associated with people with disabilities. This theme is shown through the use of short, simple words and phrasing, the musical styling of the king's songs, and the famous refrain, "Da Da Da Dat Da." In this section, I argue that the theme of simplicity reflects what we know about the king's disabilities and infantilizes him because of them.

The king's songs are arguably the simplest songs in *Hamilton*. This does not mean that the king's three songs are completely vapid. In "You'll Be Back," King George uses the word "subject" to mean more than one thing in consecutive sentences: "And no don't change the subject, / Cuz you're my favorite subject." Here "subject" is used as two different nouns—the topic being discussed and someone under the king's authority. (Miranda and McCarter, 2016, p. 57). This "clever turn of phrase," however, is not particularly subtle, as the king uses the phrase and, as Miranda and McCarter claim, "beats it into the ground" (2016, p. 57).

The king's songs have a slower cadence than many of the other songs in *Hamilton*, making King George's songs memorable, easy to sing along with, and exceedingly catchy. Williams identifies five elements of a song that make the song potentially addictive (some would call these songs earworms): surprise, predictability, rhythmic repetition, melodic potency, and listener receptiveness (Earls, 2016, para. 3). The king's songs rank highly on this scale, partly due to the musical styling that became the king's trademark. "You'll Be Back," "What Comes Next?," and "I Know Him," Miranda says, were inspired by the Beatles, and the king's songs reflect the Beatles' Britpop style (Churchwell, 2016, para. 6). Jarck argues that the king's British-inspired songs sound older "because the King is stuck in the past while the revolutionary colonists are singing in the much cooler and newer hip hop style" (2018, para. 4), reminding the audience that the king is an interloper in Hamilton's story (McCarthy, 2015).

By far the most memorable feature of the king's songs is the chorus. "Da da da da dat da da dat da da da ya da" may very well be some of the most recognizable lyrics in all of *Hamilton*. The king's songs and popular chorus are "sung in a very childish tone" (Khatri, 2018, para. 2), ensuring the audience never sees him as a real threat to the revolutionaries. Together, the simplicity of the king's songs and the well-known chorus point to the disability history of King George III.

Rentoumi, Peters, Conlin, and Garrard (2017) argue linguistic analysis of the king's many writings support the theory that the king had bipolar disorder. By comparing the king's writings during mentally healthy times to times of mania, the scholars were able to show that during manic episodes, the king showed "a reduced vocabulary, with fewer distinct word types, but also a tendency to greater redundancy and predictability" (Rentoumi et al., 2017). These same traits are the cornerstone of the king's songs in *Hamilton*—simplicity of vocabulary compared to other characters and a high level of redundancy, "Da da da dat da dat da da" (Miranda and McCarter, 2016, p. 127). The king's lyrics, then, are representative of his mental and cognitive states during his manic episodes, but the lyrics also reveal something more insidious. The childlike tone of the king's voice paired with his tantrum-like attitude, and the simplicity of the lyrics infantilize King George. We do not take the king seriously, and his appearances read more like laughable, embarrassing outbursts from a nephew at Thanksgiving dinner than proclamations from a noble sovereign. A more generous reading could suggest the childlike portrayal of King George makes him appear vulnerable, but the problem with that reading is that as the only known disabled character in *Hamilton*, depicting the king as unsophisticated and simple deepens an already implicit bias often held in relation to people with disabilities. Robey, Beckley, and Kirschner contend that not only did their research participants relate disability to negatively connoted words, they were also more likely to "associate disability-related words with childhood or with child-like features" (2006, p. 451) and that "persons who hold implicit associations of disability with words connoting childhood also have some tendency to express infantilizing attitudes" (p. 452). Wilson, Nairn, Coverdale, and Panapa (1999) found in their analysis of depictions of mental illness in prime-time dramas that individuals with mental illness were often portrayed as simple/childlike. Characters with mental illness "lack comprehension and performance of everyday adult roles, appearing lost and confused. Typical actions include speaking in grammatically simple sentences, in a childish voice, and breaking into children's songs" (Wilson et al., 1999, p. 234). I contend that the king's "da da da" chorus is his childish tune, sealing our understanding of the king as a petulant child, incapable of sophisticated thought, and more of a caricature than a king.

WHAT COMES NEXT

Themes of mania and depression, violence, comedic relief, and simplicity framed the character of King George III as a man who was going insane before our eyes, doing little to change the ongoing legacy of the king as the "mad monarch." While the king is the antagonist of the story, he is not a villain because he is simply too absurd to be taken seriously. This analysis contributes to the field of rhetoric by providing critical insights for how a rhetorical imagination helps us understand the life and legacy of King George III. This study also adds to the growing body of research that attends to the embodied performance of disabled characters and how the performance of disabled characters can deepen or challenge our understandings of disability and disabled bodies. This analysis also provides opportunities for continued research. For instance, while not the focus of this study, the character of King George is always played by a White actor. While many scholars are discussing race in relation to the casting of *Hamilton*, it is also important to investigate how the Whiteness of the king's character affects rhetorical readings. Another area, important to mention, is the casting of a disabled character in a production. I would be remiss if I did not note the continued objection from the disability community of nondisabled people playing a character with a disability. Called *cripping up* or *disability drag*, the concept of a nondisabled person playing a person with a disability is equivalent to a White person donning blackface. The calls for authentic casting are strong from the disability community and disability advocates. It will be interesting and important to see how *Hamilton* does or does not meet those calls with future casting choices.

The character of King George III, despite his songs' simple word choices and catchy melodies, is not straightforward. The king is complicated and complex: he was a young king, thrown into an ongoing war with tremendous financial burden. The king also had a mental illness that, at times, made ruling more difficult. The king, as portrayed in *Hamilton*, is full of contradictions. He is a paradox; one we are never supposed to fully understand. However, these contradictions are underscored by the king's mental illness. The audience recognizes the king as mentally unstable and, therefore, views all of his future actions through that lens: as occurring because of his mental illness. This flattens the king to a one-dimensional character, one who is going mad, and all subsequent acts are in service to that narrative. The king serves as comic relief, and we learn to recognize the manifestations of his disability as hilarious, there for our entertainment. While Groff's performance of King George III is captivating and enjoyable, rhetoric and disability studies must always push against damaging stereotypes and myths of disability. Ultimately, when we ask, "Who tells your story?" rhetoricians must attend to the stories of disabled persons—these stories have revolutionary power, if we only take the time to see it.

REFERENCES

American Psychological Association. (2015). "Speaking of Psychology: Dispelling the Myth of Violence and Mental Illness." https://www.apa.org/research/action/speaking-of-psychology/dispelling-myth.

"Anthony Hopkins Doesn't Blink during *Silence of the Lambs*." (n.d.). Unreal Facts. https://unrealfacts.com/anthony-hopkins-doesnt-blink-silence-lambs/.

Attali, J. (1985). *Noise: The Political Economy of Music*, vol. 16. Manchester: Manchester University Press.

Barnes, C. (1992). "Disabling Imagery and the Media." *British Council of Organisations of Disabled People*. Ryburn Publishing. https://disability-studies.leeds.ac.uk/wp-content/uploads/sites/40/library/Barnes-disabling-imagery.pdf.

Bernstein, C., ed. (1998). *Close Listening: Poetry and the Performed Word*. New York: Oxford University Press.

Black, J. (2006). *George III: America's Last King*. New Haven, CT: Yale University Press.

Blum, S. (1992). "In Defense of Close Reading and Close Listening." *Current Musicology*, 41–54. https://doi.org/10.7916/D8HM577T.

Brummett, B. (2010). *Techniques of Close Reading*. Los Angeles: Sage Publications.

Christie, I. R. (1986). "George III and the Historians—Thirty Years On." *History* 71, no. 232, 205–21.

Churchwell, S. (2016). "Why *Hamilton* Is Making Musical History." *The Guardian*, November 5, 2016. https://www.theguardian.com/stage/2016/nov/05/why-hamilton-is-making-musical-history.

Corrigan, P. W., and A. C. Watson. (2002). "Understanding the Impact of Stigma on People with Mental Illness." *World Psychiatry* 1, no. 1, 16–20. https://www.ncbi.nlm.nih.gov/pmc/articles/PMC1489832/#B19.

Davis, L. J. (1995). *Enforcing Normalcy: Disability, Deafness, and the Body*. London and New York: Verso.

Dolmage, J. T. (2014). *Disability Rhetoric*. Syracuse, NY: Syracuse University Press.

Earls, J. (2016). "Scientists Name the Ultimate Earworm and Explain What Makes Songs Addictive." NME, September 2, 2016. https://www.nme.com/news/music/queen-1203599.

Goodale, G. (2011). *Sonic Persuasion: Reading Sound in the Recorded Age*, vol. 30. Urbana: University of Illinois Press.

Gualtieri, J. (2020). "OK, Jonathan Groff, What's with the Spit?" Distractify, July 8, 2011. https://www.distractify.com/p/why-does-the-king-spit-in-hamilton.

Hawhee, D. (2009). *Moving Bodies: Kenneth Burke at the Edges of Language*. Columbia: University of South Carolina Press.

Healthline. (2017, Sept. 2). "How Many Times Do You Blink in a Day?" Healthline, September 2, 2017. https://www.healthline.com/health/how-many-times-do-you-blink-a-day#less-frequent-blinking.

Irvine, J. R., and W. G. Kirkpatrick (1972). "The Musical Form in Rhetorical Exchange: Theoretical Considerations." *Quarterly Journal of Speech* 58, no. 3, 272–84. https://doi.org/10.1080/00335637209383124.

Jarck, M. (2018). "Why Is There a Beatles Song in *Hamilton*?" Palaces Out of Paragraphs, June 12, 2018. https://sites.gatech.edu/1102hamilton/2018/06/12/why-is-there-a-beatles-song-in-hamilton.

Kail, T., dir. (2020). *Hamilton* [Film]. Walt Disney Studios.

Khatri, A. (2018). "How Tone of Voice Affects Characters and Audiences in *Hamilton*." Palaces Out of Paragraphs, May 29, 2018. https://sites.gatech.edu/1102hamilton/2018/05/29/how-tone-of-voice-affects-characters-and-audiences-in-hamilton/.

"King George III." (n.d.) *PBS: American Experience*. https://www.pbs.org/wgbh/americanexperience/features/adams-king-george-III/.

Kira [@kiwi71281]. (2020, July 3). "That #groffsauce maniacal, King George cackle is the best!" #hamilfilm [Tweet]. Twitter. https://twitter.com/kiwi71281/status/1279217568398614534?s=21.

Leff, M. C. (2016). "Things Made by Words: Reflections on Textual Criticism." In *Rethinking Rhetorical Theory: Criticism, and Pedagogy: The Living Art of Michael C. Leff*, edited by Antonio de Velasco, John Angus Campbell, and David Henry, 291–306. East Lansing: Michigan State University Press.

Levers, L. L. (2001). "Representations of Psychiatric Disability in Fifty Years of Hollywood Film: An Ethnographic Content Analysis." *Theory and Science* 2, no. 2. http://theoryandscience.icaap.org/content/vol1002.002/lopezlevers.html.

Longmore, P. K. (1985). "Screening Stereotypes: Images of Disabled People." *Social Policy* 16, no. 1, 31–37. http://people.tamu.edu/~dscott/340/U7%20Readings/6%20-%201985%20Longmore%20Screening%20Stereotypes.pdf.

McCarthy, E. (2015). "26 Things You Might Not Have Known about *Hamilton*." Mental Floss, November 17, 2015. https://www.mentalfloss.com/article/71222/20-things-you-might-not-have-known-about-hamilton.

Macalpine, I., and R. Hunter. (1966). "The 'Insanity' of King George 3d: A Classic Case of Porphyria." *British Medical Journal* 1, no. 5479, 65. https://doi.org/10.1136/bmj.1.5479.65.

Minnesota Governor's Council on Developmental Disabilities. (2021). *Parallels in Time: A History of Developmental Disabilities.* Minnesota Governor's Council on Developmental Disabilities. https://mn.gov/mnddc/parallels/one/4.html.

Miranda, L. M., and J. McCarter. (2016). *Hamilton: The Revolution.* New York: Grand Central Publishing.

P Cheng [@mdrivel]. (2020). "#Groffsauce really brings the crazy #hamilfilm, #hamiltonwatchparty" [Tweet]. Twitter, July 3, 2020. https://twitter.com/mdrivel/status/1279204561119408129?s=21.

Pearce, J. M. (2017). "The Role of Dr. Francis Willis in the Madness of George III." *European Neurology* 78, nos. 3–4, 196–99. https://doi.org/10.1159/000479815.

Peters, T. (2011). "King George III, Bipolar Disorder, Porphyria and Lessons for Historians." *Clinical Medicine* 22 no. 3, 261–64. https://doi.org/10.7861/clinmedicine.11-3-261.

Peters, T. J., and A. Beveridge. (2010). "The Blindness, Deafness and Madness of King George III: Psychiatric Interactions." *Journal of the Royal College of Physicians of Edinburgh* 40, no. 1, 81–85. https://doi.org/10.4997/jrcpe.2010.116.

Rentoumi, V., T. Peters, J. Conlin, and P. Garrard. (2017). "The Acute Mania of King George III: A Computational Linguistic Analysis." *PLoS One* 12, no. 3. https://doi.org/10.1371/journal.pone.0171626.

Revolutionary War. (2020, March 4). "King George III." https://www.revolutionary-war.net/king-george-iii.

Robey, K. L., L. Beckley, and M. Kirschner. (2006). "Implicit Infantilizing Attitudes about Disability." *Journal of Developmental and Physical Disabilities* 18, no. 4, 441–53. https://doi.org/10.1007/s10882-006-9027-3.

Ross, B. (2020). "*Hamilton*: What the Musical Changes about the Real King George III." ScreenRant, July 25, 2020. https://screenrant.com/hamilton-musical-king-george-changes-differences-missing.

Sellnow, D., and T. Sellnow. (2001). "The 'Illusion of Life' Rhetorical Perspective: An Integrated Approach to the Study of Music as Communication." *Critical Studies in Media Communication* 18, no. 4, 395–415. https://doi.org/10.1080/07393180128090.

Sterne, J., ed. (2012). "Introduction." *The Sound Studies Reader.* New York: Routledge.

Tishgart, S. (2016, Jan. 14). "Brian d'Arcy James, Jonathan Groff, and Andrew Rannells on Playing *Hamilton* Fan Favorite King George III." Vulture, January 24, 2016. https://www.vulture.com/2016/01/hamilton-king-george-brian-darcy-james-jonathan-groff-andrew-rannells.html.

Wigington, P. (2019). "King George III: British Ruler during the American Revolution." ThoughtCo, January 7, 2019. https://www.thoughtco.com/king-george-iii-biography-4178933.

Wilson, C., R. Nairn, J. Coverdale, and A. Panapa. (1999). "Mental Illness Depictions in Prime-Time Drama: Identifying the Discursive Resources." *Australian and New Zealand Journal of Psychiatry* 33, no. 2, 232–39. https://doi.org/10.1046/j.1440-1614.1999.00543.x.

SECTION II

Revelations about Race

Chapter 5

Casting as a Rhetorical Act

Color-Purposeful Casting and Hamilton's Anti-White Casting Call

Ailea G. Merriam-Pigg

I remember the first time a musical truly confused me. I was watching *Side Show*, a musical about conjoined twins from the 1920s/1930s, and I did not understand how Violet, one of the conjoined twins starring in the show, could be so cruel to Jake, a man in love with her. When Jake professes his love, Violet declares, "I couldn't bear what they would say if I loved you that way." Jake responds back, "If I can see past your affliction, why can't you see past mine?" (Krieger, 1997). What affliction? What was wrong with Jake? Why couldn't Violet love this man who so clearly loved and cared for her? As I later discovered, Violet could not bring herself to openly love Jake, a man described as being "from the inky jungles of the darkest continent" (Krieger, 1997), specifically due to the deeply ingrained segregation and racism of this time. So why was I confused? The Jake in the production I saw was White.

The first time I saw *Hamilton*, however, was a different story. Who tells your story? In the case of this musical, the story is largely told by a diverse cast, primarily made up of non-White individuals. Hamilton was originally played by a man of Puerto Rican descent, Lin-Manuel Miranda. The other male central characters, including George Washington, were played by African American men. The ensemble included people from a number of backgrounds, from White to Black to Latinx to Asian, but only featured one White actor in a lead role, King George. For a casual viewer, the original Broadway debut of *Hamilton* appears to rely on colorblind casting, which decenters Whiteness to create a diverse cast of characters. However, rather than colorblind casting, which has been denounced for reifying systemic racist practices (see Banks, 2013; Carr, 1997; Catanese, 2011; Hornby, 1989; Parker, 2014; and Wilson, 1997), *Hamilton* employs a strategic casting style which, as repeated by multiple members of the cast, including Miranda, is meant to tell the "story about America then, told by America now" (Miranda and McCarter, 2016, p. 33). This color-purposeful casting strategy reveals the rhetoricity of casting in entertainment.

And yet, the producers of *Hamilton* were accused of being racist and discriminatory in their hiring practices due to an "anti-White" casting call. In March 2016, *Hamilton* placed a casting call for "NON-WHITE" (capitalization original to call) men and women for current and future productions of the show. The show was preparing to start touring productions and so was hiring for both lead and ensemble roles, on and off Broadway. However, the language of the call, "NON-WHITE" in particular, set off a viral firestorm of news articles and posts, claiming that *Hamilton* had put out a racist casting call. Civil rights attorney Randolph McLaughlin questioned the legality of the call, stating "What if they put an ad out that said, 'Whites only need apply?' Why, African-Americans, Latinos, Asians would be outraged." McLaughlin continued:

> You cannot advertise showing that you have a preference for one racial group over another. As an artistic question—sure, he can cast whomever he wants to cast, but he has to give every actor eligible for the role an opportunity to try. (Emery, 2016)

Although the producers of *Hamilton* stated the advertisement was approved by Actor's Equity, the union stated they would not have approved such language. Maria Somma, the Equity spokesperson, said, "The *Hamilton* call on their website is inconsistent with Equity's policy. All of our calls have the following language: 'Performers of all ethnic and racial backgrounds are encouraged to attend'" (Emery, 2016). *Hamilton* rewrote the casting call to include that all people were welcome to audition but also stated:

> It is essential to the storytelling of *Hamilton* that the principal roles—which were written for non-white characters (excepting King George)—be performed by non-white actors. This adheres to the accepted practice that certain characteristics in certain roles constitute a "bona fide occupational qualification" that is legal. This also follows in the tradition of many shows that call for race, ethnicity or age specific casting, whether it's *The Color Purple* or *Porgy and Bess* or *Matilda*.

Though the casting issue was resolved quickly, it was reintroduced to the political sphere after the cast addressed then vice president–elect Mike Pence when he went to see the show in late 2016. The cast expressed their fears that the Trump/Pence administration would not "defend us and uphold our inalienable rights" and urged Pence and the administration he represented to do so. These rights include those for people of color, of non-male gender, and of the LGBT community. Then president-elect Donald Trump tweeted about the speech, claiming it was harassment and that performers should not use their literal stage presence to be political. Partisan news outlets took up Trump's tweet and compared it with the "non-White" casting call from March, implying that *Hamilton*'s producers and cast were hypocritical to ask for equal treatment when they did not support equality. Show producer Jeffrey Seller was confronted about the apparent casting call violation and disclosed that *Hamilton* encourages diversity but that it was legitimate to issue a non-White casting call. In his words, "I stand by it and believe it to be legal" (Emery, 2016).

Although this casting call was for non-White performers, I have labeled it the "anti-White" casting call because that is how it was perceived in the media. Randolph McLaughlin equated the casting call to racist advertisements from the 1960s and prior, which requested only Whites apply. Trump and partisan news outlets in support of Trump equated the casting call with racism, implying *Hamilton* is not a show dedicated to diversity. Even the Actor's Equity Union stated that the call did not align with its ideals of encouraging actors of all backgrounds to audition. However, Actor's Equity seemingly ignored the fact that this ideal was put in place to increase roles for women, racial minorities, and disabled persons in theater. In fact, this is the origin of colorblind casting practices.

The notion of colorblind casting was primarily adopted in the 1980s as part of the Actors' Equity Association's Non-Traditional Casting Project (Parker, 2014). According to Davis and Newman (cited in Catanese, 2011), nontraditional casting is "the casting of ethnic, female, or disabled actors in roles where race, ethnicity, gender, or physical capability are not necessary to the characters' or play's development" (p. 12). This casting practice was necessary because, as the founder of the Non-Traditional Casting Project, Harry Newman, stated, "A four-year study . . . completed in January 1986 revealed that over 90 percent of all professional theatre produced in this country—from stock and dinner theatre to the avant-garde to Broadway—was staged with all-Caucasian casts" (cited in Banks, 2013, p. 2). These dedications to diversity were never meant to increase roles for White people, who to this day make up the majority of theater performers.

Each of the arguments against *Hamilton*'s non-White casting call is made from a place of neoliberal colorblind ideology. These arguments claim that by not encouraging Whites to apply right alongside non-Whites, by creating a casting call for only non-Whites, *Hamilton* is being racist, not equal. This ignores the fact that Whiteness is still centered in theater. In the last five years, excepting 2019, there has only been one musical nominated for Best Musical at the Tony Awards that featured predominantly non-White casts. From 2015 to 2021, only four musicals that featured predominantly non-White casts, including *Hamilton*, were nominated for Best Musical at the Tony Awards (*Hamilton*, *Hadestown*, *Ain't Too Proud*, and *Tina*). *Hadestown*, a retelling of the Greek myth of Orpheus, is the first musical nominated since *Hamilton* to reconceptualize a traditionally White-centered tale for a non-White cast (Persephone, the Fates, Eurydice, and the narrator Hermes most notably are originated by Black/Indigenous/other people of color performers) and the first primarily person-of-color show to win Best Musical since *Hamilton*.

The systemic centering of Whiteness is still present in theater, despite efforts since the 1980s to become more inclusive. Although theater has become more inclusive, it is nowhere near equal, so calls that *Hamilton* is not being fair in its casting are calls to recenter Whiteness, just as colorblind casting has moved from its original goal of creating space for BIPOC to allowing White people to be cast in ethnic roles. Think of Jake played by a White man, the example that opened this chapter, or Kristin Chenoweth, the blonde who originated the role of Glinda in *Wicked*, being cast in a production of *The King and I* as Tuptim, a Burmese slave (Suskin, 2013). Colorblind casting, once intended to move performance to more equitable practices, was altered to allow White people to fill up even more space. These arguments against *Hamilton*'s casting call and practices reaffirm this White-centered practice of colorblind ideology.

Furthermore, this argument seems to be mired in an expectation of what *Hamilton* should be, not what it is. As stated by the producers, *Hamilton* was specifically created for non-White actors, excepting King George. No one would bat an eye at a non-White casting call for *The Color Purple* or *Porgy and Bess*, but *Hamilton*, since it is a show about the founding of the United States of America, a tale of predominantly White men, causes people to protest non-White casting calls. The importance of the actors being non-White is forgotten in the place of audience expectation. To those against the non-White casting call, these historical figures were White (debatable on the part of Hamilton) and therefore excluding Whites is inherently wrong and not allowing appropriate casting for the roles.

However, this ignores the mantra from the cast that this is the story of America then told by America now. It is just as much the story of who we currently are as a nation as it is about who we were at our birth. Similar shows, shows like *1776*, were originally cast with primarily White men (there are two female roles in *1776*) and eventually adapted for nontraditional casts, such as all-female productions. However, *Hamilton* was created with the intention of having a nontraditional cast from the beginning, to better connect the United States' past to its present. Although Lin-Manuel Miranda wanted to be accurate in his historic depictions of the story and consulted Ron Chernow (the author of the book that inspired Miranda), the race of the primary characters, outside of King George and, debatably, Alexander Hamilton, was never supposed to be historically accurate. Chernow was surprised by the move but eventually understood that the voices of non-White people were the best suited to tell the story of *Hamilton* that Miranda had created, since the tale was just as much a telling of the founding of the nation as it was an ode to the history of hip-hop and to the contemporary makeup of the United States (Miranda and McCarter, 2016).

Although White hip-hop artists and rappers, such as Eminem, do exist, the music genre was created by Black people for Black people. This show is about the marginalized (then revolutionary colonists/now Black/Indigenous/ other people of color) rising up against their oppressor (then the tyrant King George/now White privilege and systemic racism). Having a predominantly White cast performing songs inspired by hip-hop inspired would be disingenuous to the history of the genre and would not have made for nearly as compelling a performance. As wonderful as performers like Alex Brightman, Aaron Tveit, and other White men are, their performances would have fallen flat. They would not have been the correct casting choice for this show. Their casting would not be persuasive to the audience. Casting, after all, is a rhetorical act.

CASTING AS A RHETORICAL ACT

According to Conquergood, "Culture is transacted through performance" (1989, p. 83). Performance has long been considered a form of communication through which culture is articulated and spread. In 1975, Richard Bauman wrote, "It is part of the essence of performance that it offers to the participants a special enhancement of experience, bringing with it a heightened intensity of communicative interaction which binds the audience to the performer in a way that is specific to performance as a mode of communication" (p. 43), both solidifying performance as a "mode of communication" and showing it to be something more; a rhetorical space.

The space of performance, like many spaces of rhetorical discourse, can be a space of conflict. "Because it is public, performance is a site of struggle where competing interests interact, and different viewpoints and voices get articulated," Conquergood wrote (1989, p. 84). The theater may be a space where existing ideas are reaffirmed, but it has traditionally been a space of challenging and progressing ideas, through the art of performance. For instance, the first musical recognized as such was *Show Boat*, first performed on Broadway in 1927. The story is based on a novel by the same name and follows the lives of the workers of a Mississippi River showboat. This includes Black workers ("Ol' Man River") and an illegally married couple of mixed race ("Can't Help Lovin' Dat Man"). Therefore, the performative space of musical theater originated with tales of interracial conflict. However, rather than fully reaffirming the laws of segregation of the time, the show casts doubt on the legitimacy of these laws, portraying the mixed-race couple as victims rather than degenerates. Thus, the performative space of musical theater originated with progressive tales meant to challenge the status quo of American culture.

According to Conquergood, "[Turner] advances performance theory by pushing beyond 'culture as performance' to the potential of performance as a way of knowing, a hermeneutics for intercultural understanding" (1989, p. 85). It is not enough to say that performance is a reflection of culture. Rather, performance is a way of pushing at the borders of culture(s) to increase understanding of the other. While performance may be utilized to demonize the other and solidify borders, it is usually a space of transition and change. Donald Trump's objection to the speech of *Hamilton*'s cast to Mike Pence reifies the power of the performative space as persuasive and transformative. By telling them not to use their platform to be political, he acknowledges the power of that platform to persuade audiences (in this case, against his personal interests).

Performance may be seen as a liminal space for both the performer and audience. According to Heuman and Gonzalez, "A liminal space is a transitional space; it is a period of in-between-ness that may result in affirmation of one's current identity or the adoption of a new identity" (2018, p. 338). Performers must live in the liminal space, both affirming their own identities while adopting new ones and often having their own identities altered through their roles. Lin-Manuel Miranda wrote numerous times in *Hamilton: The Revolution*, the book about the musical's creation, on how he identified with Hamilton in different ways (Miranda and McCarter, 2016). Through this identification, Miranda was able to slip into the role of Hamilton, living in the liminal space as both himself and the Founding Father.

The audience must also live in the liminal space. The audience is tasked with taking in a performance and, just as with a persuasive speech, must choose whether to reaffirm their identity or allow themselves to be changed by the performance. While the performance is occurring, however, the potentiality of both outcomes is not solidified until the performers take their last bows and the house lights come up. With *Hamilton*, the choice to cast BIPOC performers as the leading roles allowed BIPOC audience members (in many cases, children) to identify with these historical figures (Miranda and McCarter, 2016). Black students, who have largely only heard their ancestors' contributions to US history in terms of slavery (which is often glossed over) and the Civil Rights Movement, were suddenly feeling a connection to the powerful originators of our country. This connection is further solidified by the casting of a White man as the antagonist and oppressive force. While it is debatable whether BIPOC youth identifying with Founding Fathers, by and large slave owners and flawed men, is a positive outcome, this identification phenomenon nevertheless illustrates the power of casting (and representation) in performance.

If performance is rhetorical by nature, it must follow that casting is also rhetorical. Casting, or the choosing of certain performers for specific roles or shows, is a process found from the smallest community theaters to the largest Broadway productions (and in other spaces of entertainment). According to Vatz, "To the audience, events become meaningful only through their linguistic depiction" (1973, p. 157). However, this does not hold true for the space of performance. If linguistic depiction was all that was required for events to become meaningful, I would not have been confused when Violet rejected a White Jake in *Side Show*. Context is important in all aspects of rhetoric. The line "I have a dream that my four little children will one day live in a nation where they will not be judged by the color of their skin, but by the content of their character" would not have been as impactful if delivered by a White man instead of Martin Luther King Jr. Context, therefore, enriches our understanding of linguistic depictions, especially within the performative space. According to Raka Shome:

> Space is not merely a backdrop, though, against which the communication of cultural politics occurs. Rather, it needs to be recognized as a central component in that communication. It functions as a technology—a means and medium—of power that is socially constituted through material relations that enable the communication of specific politics. (2003, p. 40)

In other words, the performative space is a sphere of influence in which people open themselves to being persuaded through the actions of the performers. By its very nature, therefore, performance (and casting) is couched in persuasion. Performers must go in front of a casting board and, through their audition, attempt to persuade the board that they are the best fit for a role. The casting board, simultaneously, must decide not only who is the best at persuading them but which performer is likely to be the most persuasive to an audience. Once roles are assigned and rehearsals begin, actors work to establish their characters and immerse themselves in their roles. It is a bad actor, a bad persuader, who merely steps forward to say their lines and then steps back into the role of their true identity. For a properly persuasive performance, the actors must take on their roles through every moment onstage, maintaining the immersive experience for the audience and enriching their own interactions with the other performers.

The shows we perform and the people we choose to perform them are rhetorical acts. According to Bauman, "The emergent quality of performance resides in the interplay between communicative resources, individual competence, and the goals of the participants, within the context of particular situations" (1975, p. 38). Though my own experiences with community theater have often shown a lack of thought about inclusive casting (the White Jake being one of many examples that comes to mind), the casting practices of *Hamilton* specifically target this White hegemony. *Hamilton* decenters Whiteness through its employment of what I am calling *color-purposeful casting*.

Hamilton's Color-Purposeful Casting

Hamilton employs a strategic casting style which is meant to tell the "story about America then, told by America now" (Miranda and McCarter, 2016, p. 33). When I saw *Hamilton*, I interpreted this color-purposeful casting choice as a new way to represent the diversity and race relations of the eighteenth century. It can be difficult sometimes to remember that White is not a race but a way to conglomerate power. Not all who are seen as White now were White in the eighteenth century. Those who practice Judaism, the Irish, and the Polish are all examples of groups who are now considered White who were once persecuted and kept out of the group of dominant power. "Fears of floods of immigrant hordes extended to southern and eastern European immigrants, who quickly became, in the public imagination, both unassimilable and undesirable," Flores wrote (2003, p. 368). By casting racial minorities, especially Black and Latinx performers, in roles seen as traditionally White, *Hamilton* is both able to dismantle the White race myth and connect the story of "America then" to the story of "America now."

This casting is different from other forms of nontraditional casting that came before it. While *Hamilton*'s casting is neither a form of societal casting or cross-cultural casting—as it neither casts marginalized performers in roles they would already play nor does it completely transplant the setting of the musical to a different context—it is also not conceptual casting or (color) blind casting. Blind casting is premised in the neoliberal notion of colorblindness and requires that all actors be considered for a role no matter their marginalized status. As previously mentioned, this seemingly equitable casting practice has been used to reaffirm the White center. Conceptual casting seems the closest to the casting practice employed by *Hamilton*, since it is premised on the notion of a marginalized actor being cast in a role to give it greater resonance. However, *Hamilton*'s casting is not conceptual. This casting practice assumes that a marginalized performer is taking on a role to "give it greater resonance." Implied by the *greater* is the *than before*. This casting practice assumes that marginalized performers are taking over a role from a White, non-marginalized person, rather than originating the role. *Hamilton*, on the other hand, was written with the intent of marginalized performers playing the primary roles from the start. Therefore, while conceptual casting still centers Whiteness, even in its attempts to increase roles for marginalized performers, *Hamilton* partakes in a casting practice that is *color-purposeful*.

Color-purposeful casting forces audiences not only to consider how the Founding Fathers were different from each other but also to focus on how Hamilton's immigrant status set him apart from the other Founding Fathers. According to Miranda and the cast, choosing to cast non-White performers was utilized to tell the story of America then through a representation of the diversity in America today. This take is popular and, though most audiences seeing *Hamilton* are still White and affluent, Miranda and the cast have worked to increase accessibility to lower-income and racial minority students by partnering with the Theater Development Fund. Teachers have utilized the musical to connect their students with American history and the arts (Miranda and McCarter, 2016).

These students see themselves in the musical. According to Ginger Bartkoski Meagher of the Theater Development Fund, "It's theater telling them a story about themselves, a story that they didn't know" (Miranda and McCarter, 2016, p. 157). Casting all White men for these parts, therefore, would have collapsed this difference and erased the important message regarding immigrants for contemporary audiences, especially for young marginalized people. Though subtle, this color-purposeful casting moves our society toward rethinking our history as a country as not just a history of the White-powerful but as a history encompassing the multitudes of American identities. According to Miranda, each night, one line received so much applause it drowned out the next lines, whether audiences were predominantly White or featured students seeing the show through the Theater Development Fund. No matter how many musical bars they put in between this line and the next, the audience still drowned out the next words (Miranda and McCarter, 2016). The line that always received this reaction was "Immigrants: We get the job done" ("Yorktown"). Audiences connect this line about immigrants then to both immigrants and racial minorities now, seeing a message in the musical that immigrants strengthen the United States.

And the message of *Hamilton* is undoubtedly political in nature, even without considering its resonance with the founding of the United States. The musical, in general, is concerned with the question of legacy. Alexander Hamilton, surrounded by death and abandonment since he was young, born as a bastard with seemingly no prospects, is obsessed with the legacy that he will leave. In the opening song, Hamilton introduces himself and says, "There's a million things I haven't done / But just you wait, just you wait . . ." ("Alexander Hamilton"). Approximately halfway through the song, the tempo increases. According to Miranda, "We double the tempo here because Hamilton's found his way out: He's going to double down on his education, and make himself undeniable" (Miranda and McCarter, 2016, p. 17). Both the lyrics provided and the quote from Miranda showcase how Hamilton is obsessed with working hard and leaving something behind. The entire song "My Shot" is Hamilton declaring that he will take every opportunity to become something great, something memorable. Hamilton says that this is the movement "Where all the hungriest brothers with something to prove went" ("My Shot"), counting himself among the hungry for a chance to prove themselves. The song starts with Hamilton calling out Aaron Burr for not taking a stand. When Hamilton is asked who he is and what he's going to do, Hamilton declares, "I am not throwing away my shot" ("My Shot"), making it clear that he will seize his opportunity to cement his legacy. In fact, most of the songs Hamilton sings are concerned with his legacy. While his wife, Eliza, tells him, "We don't need a legacy" ("That Would Be Enough"), Alexander is obsessed with the concept of a legacy until the moment he dies in a duel with Burr. In the moment before he shoots, Hamilton performs a rapped soliloquy where he reflects on what a legacy is, beginning with "If I throw away my shot, is this how you remember me?" and stating that a legacy is "planting seeds in a garden you never get to see" ("The World Was Wide Enough"). Hamilton decides to shoot in the air, claiming his time is up and asking that Eliza take her time before joining him in the afterlife. Hamilton finishes his soliloquy by returning to a lyric from "The Story of Tonight," a song that Hamilton and his friends sang in Act I about their place in the upcoming revolution. Instead of one of the lyrics focused on their potential death or glory, Hamilton reiterates a simple call to "Raise a glass to freedom" ("The Story of Tonight"). Hamilton's concern with legacy is not just his own legacy but that of the United States. The audience is not just seeing a man concerned with how he will be remembered but a man concerned with his country's future. Hamilton was an orphan immigrant of questionable racial background and he was able to become the first treasury secretary of the United States and a man respected enough that his opinion is considered the deciding factor in the presidential race between Thomas Jefferson, a man he despised, and Aaron Burr, his friend.

There is a clear political message about the role of immigrants to the metaphorical health of the United States. It is not just that this one immigrant was able to excel; it is that immigrants, in general, "get the job done." The show has a clear message, then, concerning both how people (and the nation) will be remembered and how the country's political heads should conceive of immigrants. While Rob Asen emphasizes the role of discourse in contemporary citizenship (2004), here we see a performative invitational rhetoric (Foss and Griffin, 1995) that is very much couched in performers and creators enacting their citizenship (and BIPOC status) to create meaningful conversation. They are utilizing the liminal space of the theater to push at the boundaries of society and question the status quo. They are being, as all theater is, rhetorical.

SO WHO TELLS YOUR STORY?

Casting and performance are rhetorical.

> As Harry Elam aptly suggests: The discourse on race . . . [has] been intricately linked to issues of theater and performance. Definitions of race, like the processes of theater, fundamentally depend on the relationship between the unseen and seen, between the visibly marked and unmarked, between the "real" and the illusionary. (qtd. in Johnson, 2003, p. 105)

Color-purposeful casting, like that seen in *Hamilton*, allows for the relationship between performance and rhetoric to be better articulated and explored.

Previous nontraditional casting practices have been criticized for their role in further empowering the White hegemony (Banks, 2013, p. 1). While color-purposeful casting is not necessarily the solution to these concerns, it is a new step toward productive change in theater. In 2019, *Hadestown* followed *Hamilton* in earning the Best Musical Tony Award with a color-purposeful cast. Prior to *Hamilton*, the last primarily BIPOC cast to win the award was *Memphis* (2010), the story of a White disc jockey who brought Black music to White radio. Notably, while *Memphis* heavily relies on a Black cast, it tells the story of another White man, another White savior. With color-purposeful casting, notions of these White-affirming traditions, even our White-affirming history, are challenged. In 2022, the legacy of *Hamilton* continues to make the space of theater more inclusive, with all six Best Musical nominees featuring historically marginalized groups (Black, Queer, Jewish, woman) in their plots and four with BIPOC actors in 50 percent or more lead/featured roles (*A Strange Loop, MJ, Paradise Square, Six*).

Hamilton says the story of the United States as a nation belongs to the immigrants, Black, Latinx, Asian, and the other marginalized. The musical ends with Hamilton's wife Eliza's work in commemorating and keeping alive the work of her husband and the other founders, speaking out against slavery, and establishing "the first private orphanage in New York City" ("Who Lives, Who Dies, Who Tells Your Story"). Eliza becomes Alexander's legacy and, in doing so, shifts the musical's protagonist to a woman. So the story belongs to women, immigrants, people of color, and other marginalized people. Who tells your story? It is all of us.

REFERENCES

Asen, R. (2004). "A Discourse Theory of Citizenship." *Quarterly Journal of Speech* 90, no. 2, 189–211.

Banks, D. (2013). "The Welcome Table: Casting for an Integrated Society." *Theatre Topics* 23, no. 1, 1–18.

Bauman, R. (1975). "Verbal Art as Performance 1." *American Anthropologist* 7, no. 2, 290–311.

BroadwayInHD. (2016). "70th Annual Tony Awards 'Hamilton'" [Video]. YouTube, October 15, 2016. https://www.youtube.com/watch?v=b5VqyCQV1Tg.

Carr, L. G. (1997). *"Colorblind" Racism.* Thousand Oaks, CA: Sage Publications.

Catanese, B. W. (2011). *The Problem of the Color[blind]: Racial Transgression and the Politics of Black Performance.* Ann Arbor: University of Michigan Press.

Conquergood, D. (1989). "Poetics, Play, Process, and Power: The Performative Turn in Anthropology." *Text and Performance Quarterly* 9, no. 1, 82–88.

Emery, D. (2016). "Producers of 'Hamilton' Issued 'Non-White' Casting Call." *Snopes*, November 21, 2016. https://www.snopes.com/fact-check/hamilton-non-white-casting-call/.

Flores, L. A. (2003). "Constructing Rhetorical Borders: Peons, Illegal Aliens, and Competing Narratives of Immigration." *Critical Studies in Media Communication* 20, no. 4, 362–87.

Foss, S. K., and C. L. Griffin. (1995). "Beyond Persuasion: A Proposal for an Invitational Rhetoric." *Communications Monographs* 62, no. 1, 2–18.

Heuman, A., and A. González. (2018). "Trump's Essentialist Border Rhetoric: Racial Identities and Dangerous Liminalities." *Journal of Intercultural Communication Research* 47, no. 4, 326–42.

Hornby, R. (1989). "Interracial Casting." *Hudson Review* 42, no. 3, 459–66.

Johnson, E. P. (2003). "Race, Ethnicity, and Performance." Special issue, *Text and Performance Quarterly* 23, no. 2.

Krieger, H. (1997). *Side Show* [Album]. Masterworks Broadway.

Miranda, L. M., and J. McCarter. (2016). *Hamilton: The Revolution.* London: Hachette UK.

Parker, H. (2014). "Let's Do Color-Inclusive, Not Color-Blind, Casting." *Southern Theatre* 55, no. 4.

Shome, R. (2003). "Space Matters: The Power and Practice of Space." *Communication Theory* 13, no. 1, 39–56.

Suskin, S. (2013). "How Kristin Chenoweth Embraced Tuptim, Marian, Rosabella, Flora, Johanna, Dolly, and Other Dames." *Playbill*, February 19, 2013. https://www.playbill.com/article/how-kristin-chenoweth-embraced-tuptim-marian-rosabella-flora-johanna-dolly-and-other-dames-com-202658.

Vatz, R. E. (1973). "The Myth of the Rhetorical Situation." *Philosophy and Rhetoric*, 154–61.
Wilson, A. (1997). "The Ground on Which I Stand." *Callaloo* 20, no. 3, 493–503.

Chapter 6

Hamilton's Revolutionary Aesthetic

Race, Hip-Hop, and the American Style

Luke Winslow and Jonathan Veal

When *Hamilton* appeared on Broadway, it changed "the language of musicals" with an aesthetic style never before seen on the stage (Brantley, 2015). Lin-Manuel Miranda drew from the artistic work and legacy of hip-hop and R&B musicians ranging from Notorious B.I.G. to Drake (Wickman, 2015). The juxtaposition between a popular Broadway musical and an artistic genre associated with criminality (McCann, 2017) was wildly popular, including with the mostly White people attending Broadway plays (Demby, 2016).

The narrative of the musical follows Alexander Hamilton, a young man who describes himself as "just like my country . . . young, scrappy and hungry" (Miranda, 2015c) as he embarks to New York during the American Revolution in search of opportunity. Early in his adventures, Hamilton comes across the man who is to become his rival, Aaron Burr, who admonishes him to be less outspoken and keep his ideas to himself—to "talk less, smile more" (Miranda, 2015b). Ignoring Burr's advice, Hamilton distinguishes himself on the battlefield and as a lawyer but manages to make enemies due to his quick temper and controversial political positions. After promoting his vision of American federalism, his political career was cut short when his opponents leaked details regarding an extramarital affair. Hamilton later challenges Burr to a duel and is shot dead. Not only did *Hamilton* take the Tony Award for Best Musical, the production went home with eleven Tony wins, only one shy of the record set by *The Producers* ("'Hamilton' Wins 11 Tony Awards," 2016).

Scholars of communication and rhetoric perform some of their most valuable critical work on social contradictions, paradoxes, and conundrums. In this case, *Hamilton* resonated with an audience harboring historical connections to the underlying suspicion and discrimination still haunting American society in the form of anti-Black racism. Nearly 80 percent of White Americans maintain anti-Black bias, according to Hardin and Banaji (2013). In subsequent years since *Hamilton*'s release, the antagonisms between America's political apparatus and its Black population have reached new intensities. Racial strife was visible in 2015 as the wave of protests following the death of Michael Brown in Ferguson, Missouri, cast a shadow on the final year of Obama's presidency. It was clear that the underlying racial tensions of America's past had not been smoothed over by the election of America's first Black president, nor by the widespread acceptance of Black art and culture by White America. As a consequence, *Hamilton*'s ability to addresses the antagonisms of historical slavery and the resurgence of White supremacy activities is of great political and practical interest.

In the musical, Alexander Hamilton is simultaneously depicted as being against slavery and as a merchant who made his living selling sugar and tea—products produced on plantations. He is further described as being close with the slaveholder George Washington. This ambiguity notwithstanding, the production's far more impactful contribution was the musical's challenge to the aesthetic associations existing in the American unconscious regarding Black identity. In this chapter, we explore how the aesthetic presentations of Blackness found in *Hamilton* reconcile the aesthetic images of anti-Black disgust circulating in American culture. We begin by discussing aesthetics and frame analysis as critical analytical tools. We then look at how *Hamilton* makes use of its style to frame its conflict and story in a way that moves to reconcile its audience with hip-hop style, before finally considering the potential and limitations that *Hamilton*'s aesthetic presentations create.

AESTHETIC REVELATION

To suggest that *Hamilton* had a distinct rhetorical style is to align an inquiry into *Hamilton*'s broad appeal with a body of literature linking the aesthetic dimensions of public presentation to how we make and transmit meaning, organize our social worlds, and influence those around us. Individually, the aesthetic functions as a powerful heuristic that reduces confusion and connects mystery with the symbolic cues that allow us to navigate the complex rhetorical dimensions of our lives. Socially, the aesthetic allows our unique communicative performances to be read by others, interpreted by others, and used by others to position ourselves within a social order—often beneath the critical radar. Our aesthetic performances function as a socially held language (Brummett, 2008; Hariman, 1995). As with any language, symbolic influence can be arbitrary but also widely available and understood. In the language of the aesthetic, for instance, identity markers are signified as referential tools that, consciously or not, allow us to make important judgments about others based on stylistic presentation. Aesthetics influence social formation by telling us who we are in relation to others. Malcolm Barnard provides an example by pointing out that clothing does not merely reflect social organization but also constitutes important class relations (1996). Robert Hariman described aesthetic style as a tool activating the subject (1995). Like a shell we wear on our backs, our aesthetic style tells a consistent story about our identity. Because there is often internal coherence, the aesthetic allows us to make important judgments about ourselves and others based on these public presentations. This is especially prevalent as the aesthetic helps an audience read off socially useful information about gender, race, and class. The aesthetic is not only read and noticed by others but is also used to call individuals into coherent audiences, publics, and communities.

Hamilton's aesthetics intrigues and challenges its audience by presenting styles drawn from hip-hop culture. In *Hamilton*'s first number, various characters introduce their roles by performing a short verse. Hip-hop groups such as N.W.A., A Tribe Called Quest, and Wu-Tang Clan used this formula for many of their most memorable tracks. These verses contrasted with the chorus of the track, which sounds far more like the familiar style found in Broadway musicals. The audience is being exposed to lyrics and performances that are part of hip-hop style even as the more traditional elements remind the audience of the familiar. When Alexander Hamilton is struggling to survive as a young man in New York, he delivers the line, "Only nineteen but my mind is older" (Miranda, 2015c) to describe the maturity he had to develop making his own way as an orphan and outsider. This line is a direct allusion to the song "Shook Ones Part II" by Mobb Deep, where the rapper Prodigy delivered the line, "I'm only 19, but my mind is old" (Mobb Deep, 1995) to describe his rapid maturation caused by the daily violence he had experienced. It is unlikely that *Hamilton*'s audience is familiar with Prodigy's work. However, even though Broadway audiences may not understand why certain lines and use of rhyme feel authentic, these presentations of hip-hop style are unmistakable to even the most casual observer of the genre.

As a rhetorical device, a single rhyme, reference, or choreographic choice does not constitute style in the broad sense. Instead, the stylistic dimensions of public presentation must congeal and overlap to construct a uniform identity so that one can assume an aesthetic that reads "surfer," "professor," "Broadway," or "Harlem." It is the community-building nature of the aesthetic that allows a certain way of talking or cut of fabric to act as a cohesive center gathering together diffused identities into collective groups. Put another way, it is through the aesthetic that categories are marked, experiences are organized, values are affirmed, political functions are performed, and people are divided who might otherwise identify with one another (Ewen, 1988; Winslow, 2014). The aesthetic creates and transmits whole sets of interrelated signs and turns them from fractured compositions of various symbols into coherent and concrete communities.

Accordingly, the aesthetic is a potent expression of political struggle. Aesthetics can elicit fear, sympathy, compassion, and hostility, and aesthetics can spur the polity into action (Mitchell, 2005). The aesthetic constructs identities that correlate to social position, class standing, sexual orientation, political leanings, and religious affiliations, allowing individuals to also assume different levels on the social hierarchy. As an overarching label, the aesthetic can account for many of the communicative dimensions of public presentation assisting in the construction and positioning of people within this hierarchy.

Communication and rhetorical scholars have positioned the aesthetic within the interpellation process: although often beyond conscious awareness, individuals do make attributions about social relationships and identity markers like sex, race, class, and political affiliation based on aesthetic representations. While many single parents, regardless of race, struggled to provide for their children and earn a living in the late twentieth century in America, the figure of the Black single mother as a "welfare queen" acted as an object of disgust, covering over the myriad of problems facing American economic and social systems, intensifying a particular type of racism, and resulting in austerity measures allowing politicians to justify creating categories that were considered not deserving of participation in American social programs (Hancock, 2004). This politics of disgust relies on powerful aesthetic images. Black unmarried women with Cadillacs and single mothers living in squalor simultaneously held weight in this welfare myth despite these images' obvious incongruence. It is these aesthetic images that not only divided the American poor along racial lines but also freed the Reagan administration of the burden of having to address the plight of single parents.

The rhetorical potency of aesthetics is largely unacknowledged, capable of functioning hegemonically in a way that gathers consent for an individual or group's genteel oppression. Without being fully aware of it, conventions of aesthetic sensibility are always already at work in our minds, ready to be drawn upon by a rhetor to accomplish an objective—not the least, promoting social affiliations, structuring groups of people into political forces, and teaching individuals how to cohere around similar aesthetic representations (Hariman, 1995; Hebdige, 1979). Ultimately, this literature suggests that a pop culture phenomenon like *Hamilton* can use aesthetics to negotiate a meaningful intermediate space where a fresh alternative identity can be discovered and expressed. The adopted aesthetics of cultural transgressors provides examples of the polysemic nature of aesthetic devices. The marginalized can excorporate aesthetic style into a recurring strategy of empowerment because each choice of costume, each choreographed move, each lyric generates an infinite range of meanings.

This literature also lends insight into the *community-building* function of the aesthetic. Individuals are drawn into communities by their ability to create and transmit aesthetic messages. The intersection of culture, politics, economics, and the aesthetic aligns with a rhetorical climate where messages do not target referential audiences, but rather, serve a constitutive function carving out audiences that do not yet exist. The aesthetic calls into being audience, publics, and groups of people. The aesthetic allows a certain way of walking or cut of fabric to pull together diffused identities into collective groups. Material and real audiences are created out of these scattered communities by encoded shared meanings that recognize a distinction between "us" and "them."

The subjective nature of aesthetic rationales prompts a nuanced and nimble account of the relationship between sender and receiver. In other words, the aesthetic works within existing frameworks in the minds of the audience. The aesthetic does not work *on* audiences but *with* audiences. Audiences are not blank slates through which aesthetic rationales are imposed. Instead, audiences are hailed by aesthetic symbol systems within zones of intersubjectivity in which cultural and social expectations—developed over a lifetime of seeing and responding to various styles—are used to navigate the social dimensions of their lives. The aesthetic can change minds, present new ways of seeing the world, change memories and imaginations, and impose new criteria and new desires in relation to the mental orientation of an audience (Asen, 2002). The aesthetic is akin to a language because we examine the signs, artifacts, and meanings produced by a rhetor by noticing and responding to the meaning grounded in the culture, setting, and environment behind the text (Brummett, 2008).

It would not be accurate to say communication and rhetorical scholars have neglected aesthetics. But unfortunately, communication and rhetorical studies are marked by a history of prioritizing expositional, explicit influence attempts over aesthetics. For 2,500 years, the canon of rhetorical studies focused more on verbal messages, and it defined aesthetics as an affectively trivial pursuit, limited in range and weak in comparison to a rhetor's expositional arguments. However, these limitations highlight flawed referential assumptions about the nature of the audience. Because the audience was thought to be passive and assumed, the rhetor was charged with discovering the available means of persuasion and deploying those instruments on the audience in a way that accomplished the rhetor's objectives. Consequently, a primary focus of traditional rhetorical training was the development of inventions, proofs, and arguments that appealed to the logic and reason of the audience, whose standards of evaluation were already in place. For most of our discipline's history, the result was intellectually limited scholarship that neglected the power of aesthetics, paid scant attention to the stylistic capabilities of rhetorical messages, and lacked a contemporary rationale and methodology for the study of aesthetics (Vivian, 2002). Hariman (1995) criticized this tendency, pointing out that we have yet to produce a strong account of what most politicians, teachers, salespersons, and consumers know intuitively: accessing competence, skill, and affinity engages conventions of persuasion activated by deeper stylistic and aesthetic reactions.

There is some dated literature on unique rhetorical styles categorizing different racial and ethnic identity formations (Kochman, 1980; Labov, 1969). Black American rhetorical style has been found to be more emotionally intense, dynamic, and demonstrative. Black Americans tend to be more comfortable adopting an argumentative style, and Black males tend to boast more about talents and abilities than other races and ethnicities. Kochman suggested that Black Americans tend to talk louder, with more emotional force, animation, vitality, and expressiveness. In contrast, a White rhetorical style tends to be more modest, subdued, and emotionally restrained. White style tends to be more detached and unemotional, understating talents and abilities (Kochman, 1980).

Some research has been done on the intersectionality of these different identity markers and how style changes in accordance. For example, Michaels found that White children adopt a rhetorical style that is more tightly organized, topic-oriented, linear, and lexically cohesive, with a higher degree of topical cohesion (1981). Black children tend to adopt a rhetorical style that features more topic-associating, consisting of a series of implicitly associated personal anecdotes and fewer explicit statements of the overall theme or point, meaning the thematic focus is rarely overtly stated but instead inferred from the series of anecdotes.

In sum, the extant literature on the aesthetic and sense making highlights a useful critical tool for understanding *Hamilton*'s rhetorical potency. But before we begin a closer textual analysis, we want to further illustrate the value of this discrete critical tool by linking the aesthetic with frame analysis.

AESTHETIC FRAME ANALYSIS

Frame analysis offers a valuable critical tool for exploring the relationship among aesthetics, meaning making, and influence. According to Stephen

Reese (2007), a *frame* is a socially shared organizing principle that works symbolically to shape democratic discourse and influence public opinion by creating and promoting particular vocabularies. Television news coverage illustrates the value of frame analysis. Assignment editors and reporters make decisions about how to report the news. Media consumers want to know what happened, why, and what should be done about it. Assignment editors and journalists will want to answer those questions in a way that resonates with the cognitive schema already in place in the minds of their audience. The frame is the socially shared organizing principle that informs how media coverage can fulfill the audience's need to make sense of these news events in a way that aligns with their existing orientations.

Frames function heuristically as a cognitive shortcut for efficient sense making. This shortcut function can be compared to how you might remember a new phone number: your brain may have trouble recalling all ten digits of a phone number. It has a much easier time recalling two sets of three digits and one set of four, as in 206-254-1037. Likewise, frames turn fragmented symbolic resources into coherent organizing schema and transform complex political, social, cultural, and economic issues into coherent thought structures. But unlike a phone number, frames do not merely produce a neutral account of the world. There is no objective truth that a frame can illuminate. Frames are always imposing a specific logic on an audience and foreclosing alternatives perspectives in subtle and taken-for-granted ways. Frames shape public opinion through the persuasive use of symbols, and in many cases, end up influencing legislative and public policy decisions. And yet, frame analysis belies associations to a top-down, totalizing, and manipulative conception of media consumption. Like aesthetics, frames are not targeted at a referential, static, and passive audience. The power of a frame is not derived from its capacity to shape discourse mindlessly, totally, and completely. Like aesthetics, frames do not work *on* audiences; frames work *with* audiences. Frames encourage a particular interpretive lens, but because frames are contingent and dynamic, they must derive their appeal from existing cultural narratives, symbolic traditions, and social orientations. The contingent and dynamic nature of framing opens up fresh lines of inquiry for aesthetic analysis.

As a critical tool, aesthetic frame analysis is concerned with identifying a set of systematic, generalizable principles that illuminate the relationship among symbolic influence, cognitive heuristics, and political power. Because frames are revealed in symbolic expressions, the critic can begin by looking for specific aesthetic vocabularies. In the next section, for example, we identify and catalog both the verbal and visual aesthetic dimensions converging to constitute a coherent community drawn together by *Hamilton*. A variety of symbolic resources are considered as the text coheres in Lin-Manuel Miranda's journal, *Hamilton* production meetings, critical reaction, and social media posts. Not every symbolic resource resonates, and not every symbol affirms the frame. The symbols that resonate are reproduced by the public in a way that confirms the resonance of a particular interpretive lens. As a result, the critic watches for consistency, durability, and lasting power. When symbols cohere strongly enough, and for long enough, they can lift an isolated event, issue, or person into a larger narrative.

Frames are produced by a series of strategic decisions made by rhetors—artists, producers, and journalists. Those decisions position an abstract event, issue, or person into a concrete schema in a way that is designed to resonate with an audience. When done well, those decisions resonate with the public in a way that will ensure a large audience. The frame reveals the rhetor's perspective on what will attract an audience. By choosing to highlight *this* character or plotline and not *that* one, rhetors can influence what outlook is affirmed by first dictating how reality is defined. Thus, the critic also attends to absences and silences—to what is said and unsaid.

HAMILTON'S AESTHETIC REVOLUTION

Hamilton's stylistic choices aligned with the familiar form of musicals from which to challenge existing framings of Black style, reinventing them in ways that resonated with White audiences. The first way *Hamilton* accomplished its project is through its framing of success. *Hamilton* eschewed conventional White framings to focus on a style of success coming from a long tradition of hip-hop performers. The opening track made it clear that Hamilton's rise from obscurity and poverty was due to his work ethic and intelligence. In the opening number the chorus asserts, "For someone less astute, / he would've been dead or destitute." The American identity is linked to a unique Protestant work ethic that still endures in our culture into the modern era (Giorgi and Marsh, 1990). *Hamilton* reframed the Protestant work ethic in the context of "the hustle." Consider this wording when Hamilton's efforts to educate himself are described in the first track as "scammin' for every book he can get his hands on" (Miranda, 2015a). Usually, we would not associate a word such as "scam" with a desire for knowledge and studiousness. However, scammin' is intentionally associated with self-advancement and ambition in *Hamilton*. Throughout the production, Hamilton's actions are described in terms that emphasize his industriousness, his unwillingness to follow conventions, and his distrust of authority. Hip-hop MCs have long boasted of their ability to rise above their peers due to hard work, but not through an adherence to legal or social norms. Consider how Jay-Z, for example, joined together his illegal past with his legitimate present in the lyric, "I sold kilos of coke, I'm guessin' I can sell CDs" (Jay-Z, 2005).

Jay-Z is in many ways synonymous with New York's hip-hop style. Much of this style's allure stems from a rags-to-riches narrative reflected in the Protestant work ethic—but more concerned with resourcefulness than following the rules. Miranda borrowed from the aesthetic image of the "hustler" as a rhetorical technique resonating with Broadway audiences. But by associating these characteristics with the protagonist, *Hamilton* disturbed the neat categories often allowing Americans to associate White performances of industriousness as positive while viewing the same performances negatively in associating with Black life and culture at the same time. The "hustler" reconciles the gaps among Broadway, colonial America, and contemporary music, in other words. Consider the importance of New York. The city was central to Alexander Hamilton's biography. Manhattan is the home of Broadway, and the Bronx was the birthplace of hip-hop. New York functions in the musical as a binding element, allowing for a cohesive fusion of these styles. New York is, therefore, cast as a place of opportunity and uncertainty. At the end of the first track, a gospel chorus asserts, "In New York you can be a new man." But by the third track, Hamilton is struggling to survive in New York, telling the audience that although the "New York City streets get colder" he remains focused on shouldering "ev'ry burden, ev'ry disadvantage" of his challenging conditions (Miranda, 2015c). Hamilton's experience mirrors that of East Coast rappers who saw New York as both a site of opportunity and a place of poverty and desperation. Nas (1994) had the famous line: "Dwellin' in the Rotten Apple, you get tackled, or caught by the devil's lasso," while Jay-Z described New York as "the melting pot" full of "corners where we sellin' rock" (Jay-Z, 2009). Like Nas and Jay-Z, Hamilton manages to thrive in New York due to his ambition and hustle. The long and varied legacy of New York City provides a wealth of aesthetic sounds and images that *Hamilton* melded into a production allowing for a largely White audience to appreciate an underprivileged outsider who is looking for a chance to get ahead.

In addition to resourcefulness and ambition, Alexander Hamilton has an excited temper. *Hamilton* framed violence by drawing from the style of polemics and aggressive rhetoric found in rap music. Representations of Black violence are dependent on strong visual and aesthetic elements. In particular, disproportionate representation of Black people as criminals in the media possesses a positive correlation to the public perception of Blacks as uniquely violent (Dixon, 2008). *Hamilton* reframed violence by setting it in contexts familiar to its audience. Alexander Hamilton—the historical figure—did wish for a war to prove himself and advance his position in the world. In the play, Hamilton sings of wishing for a war, knowing that war "was the only way to" rise up. He also expresses comfort in a destiny in which he either rises up or "dies on the battlefield in glory" (Miranda, 2015b).

Hamilton inspires audiences to sympathize with his ambition by blending aesthetic elements of Black style in the lyrics and music with a visual aesthetic grounded in colonial dress and scenery. The costume design for the production featured accurate re-creations of certain elements of eighteenth-century dress (Miranda and McCarter, 2016). The plan for the costume design was, "period from the neck down and modern from the neck up," according to costume designer Paul Tazewell (Pacheco, 2016). The background actors are dressed in an off-white, making room for the vivid colors used in the waistcoats and dresses of the main characters. *Hamilton* allowed the audience to view representations of Black violence in the safe context of colonial revolutionary struggle. Even though the actors are not of European descent, their cause is rooted in a struggle acceptable to American viewers.

Along with costuming, the dance choreography provided a soothing frame for the Broadway audience. While the choreography and dance owe much to hip-hop, many of the performer's movements were inspired more by nineteenth-century impressionism than contemporary dance. Choreographer Andy Blankenbuehler commented, "Audiences usually focus on vocalists in musicals. The audience doesn't look at the surroundings but they can feel the framing device that informs what they're looking at" (Smart, 2016). The fluid choreography complements and softens certain aspects of the actors performances—and accentuates others. During the number "My Shot," even as Hamilton and the other main characters thump their chests at the thought of battle, the supporting dancers fluidly whirl around them, as if sanctifying their cause. Because the violent style of the revolutionaries was contextualized in a revolutionary cause seen by the audience as just, *Hamilton* maintained the freedom to explore violence in an acceptable manner.

Reframing violence through a juxtaposition of European and Black style is repeated in representations of dueling. Hypermasculine, violent hip-hop discourse has appealed to young White men since the early 1990s. Much of the music and narratives found in hip-hop were stripped of much of their depth and commodified to market to a wider audience (Watts, 1997; Jeffries, 2014). Consequently, many people today associate hip-hop with endorsements of Black violence. The anxiety among many older Americans related to the aesthetic image of the rapper-as-gangster comes from this commodified and sensationalized framing. For this reason, one of the ways *Hamilton* approached violence is through the intermediated lens of dueling.

In the course of the production, Alexander Hamilton engages in two duels, the second ending his life. The stylistic presentation of these duels drew heavily on hip-hop influences. The track "Ten Duel Commandments" is a direct reference to Biggie Smalls's song, "The Ten Crack Commandments."

Like Biggie, Hamilton died of a gunshot wound, and while Broadway audience may not be familiar with Biggie's work, the audience is invited to enjoy the stylistic portrayal of violence in a setting that does not excite the feelings of anxiety often associated with violence in hip-hop music. "Ten Duel Commandments" also educates the audience on the proper conduct in a duel. Each commandment corresponds to a particular custom when preparing to duel, just as each commandment in the original Biggie Smalls track corresponded to a particular strategy for selling drugs. But here *Hamilton* managed to integrate the practices of dueling and gang violence by exposing their shared underlying adherence to codes of honor and performances of violent masculinity.

This same process of relating Black style to a setting familiar to the audience is repeated in the two "Cabinet Battles." These two rap battles take the form of disputes between Hamilton and Jefferson in George Washington's cabinet. The formal setting provides cover for Hamilton and Jefferson to throw insults and accusations at each other. In these battles, *Hamilton* explored issues that are commonly discussed in hip-hop through a frame of governmental procedure. In the cabinet battles, the assembled members are seated in a semicircle, cheering on Hamilton's and Jefferson's best lines. Governmental procedures and rap battles both require a strict adherence to proper form. In each cabinet battle, George Washington acts as moderator—or hype man—as he asks the two sides to debate an issue. In the first battle, Jefferson, who gets the first word, argues against a federal taxation system. Before dropping the mic, one of his most biting remarks attacks Hamilton's self-sufficiency: "In Virginia, we plant seeds in the ground. We create. You just wanna move our money around." Jefferson is going straight for Hamilton's status as a self-made man. Contemporary Black culture and the colonial period are united here by similar discourses regarding masculinity and independence. *Hamilton* is aware of how honor and dignity act to move both cultures and allows audiences to view one through the frame of the other. Jefferson's comment represents southern sentiments during the nation's founding while also offering a cutting personal attack on Hamilton. Quick-witted Hamilton has a reply: "A civics lesson from a slaver," he remarks, before reminding Jefferson, "Your debts are paid cuz you don't pay for labor" (Miranda, 2015d).

After Hamilton's response, the two men almost come to blows, and the rap battle concludes—but not before Hamilton puts forth the most cogent critique of slavery in the entire production. While Hamilton attacks Jefferson's reliance on slavery, he does so on the grounds of attacking Jefferson's self-sufficiency. Rather than a rights-based condemnation, Hamilton taunts slavers like Jefferson for their unmanly reliance on others' industriousness. And yet, one of the limitations of *Hamilton*'s approach is that while the aesthetic is represented mostly by Black Americans, they self-describe as British, some own slaves and, in Hamilton's case, work as merchants who trade goods produced by slave labor. While *Hamilton* worked to undermine the aesthetic prejudices existing among its audience, it did so at the expense of smoothing over other aspects of the narrative.

CONCLUSION

Hamilton grew into a cultural icon for a variety of reasons. It is the critic's methodological imperative to put forth enough evidence to explain why. Our analysis suggests that *Hamilton* was successful because it was *cognitively efficient*. By that we mean *Hamilton* resonated with preexisting mental pathways connecting similar plotlines and characters in a larger American story. These mental associations were easier to access and, therefore, became the widely accepted affective heuristic used to narrow the American public's understanding of our complicated history and challenging historical moment.

Additionally, the inclusion of Black stylistic elements was novel for a successful Broadway musical. Black style opened an opportunity to provide the audience with some understanding of historical marginalized identities through a reframing of their struggles and culture in terms digestible even for those unfamiliar with the origins of Black style. Of course, there is a chance the Broadway audience missed the references to hip-hop, and there is no guarantee bigoted viewers will lose their apprehension and disgust when viewing Black style removed from *Hamilton*'s safe context. But by applying an aesthetic frame analysis to *Hamilton*, we hope this chapter demonstrates both the advantages and limitations of using aesthetics to engender new understandings of historically marginalized cultures.

Future research should continue to develop fresh critical tools to explore intractable social challenges, especially as historic centers of power are contested. Power concedes nothing without a demand. By having so much control over how issues, events, and people are framed, elites often construct a reality that contradicts the fundamentals of a healthy democracy. As a theoretical, methodological, and critical tool, an aesthetic frame analysis offers scholars a powerful way to illuminate sense-making processes that prop up unjust hierarchies of power. More specifically, future research can employ the tools of aesthetic frame analysis to explore how exposure to marginalized styles impacts the impressions and judgments audiences have toward social others.

REFERENCES

Asen, R. (2002). *Visions of Poverty: Welfare Policy and Political Imagination*. East Lansing: Michigan State University Press.
Barnard, M. (1996). *Fashion as Communication*. London: Routledge.
Brantley, B. (2015). "Review: 'Hamilton,' Young Rebels Changing History and Theater." *New York Times*, August 6, 2015. https://www.nytimes.com/2015/08/07/theater/review-hamilton-young-rebels-changing-history-and-theater.html.
Brummett, B. (2008). *A Rhetoric of Style*. Carbondale: Southern Illinois University Press.
Delgado, R., and J. Stefancic. (2017). *Critical Race Theory: An Introduction*. New York: New York University Press.
Demby, G. (2016). "Watching a Brown 'Hamilton' with a White Audience." NPR, March 8, 2016. http://www.npr.org/sections/codeswitch/2016/03/08/469539715/a-brown-hamilton-a-White-audience.
Entman, R. (1993)." Framing: Toward Clarification of a Fractured Paradigm." *Journal of Communication* 43, no. 4, 51–58.
Entman, R. (2004). *Projections of Power: Framing News, Public Opinion, and U.S. Foreign Policy*. Chicago: University of Chicago Press.
Dixon, T. L. (2008). "Who Is the Victim Here? The Psychological Effects of Overrepresenting White Victims and Black Perpetrators on Television News." *Journalism* 9, no. 5, 582–605.
Ewen, S. (1988). *All Consuming Images: The Politics of Style in Contemporary Culture*. New York: Basic Books.
"'Hamilton' Wins 11 Tony Awards on a Night That Balances Sympathy with Perseverance." (2016). *Los Angeles Times*, June 12, 2016. http://www.latimes.com/entertainment/la-et-cm-tony-awards-live-updates-is-hamilton-the-top-broadway-musical-1465771651-htmlstory.html.
Hancock, A. M. (2004). *The Politics of Disgust: The Public Identity of the Welfare Queen*. New York: New York University Press.
Hardin, C. D., and M. R. Banaji. (2013). "The Nature of Implicit Prejudice: Implications for Personal and Public Policy." In *The Behavioral Foundations of Public Policy*, edited by E. Shafir, 13–32. Princeton, NJ: Princeton University Press.
Hariman, R. (1995). *Political Style: The Artistry of Power*. Chicago: University of Chicago Press.
Hebdige, D. (1979). *Subculture: The Meaning of Style*. London: Methuen.
Giorgi, L., and C. Marsh. (1990). "The Protestant Work Ethic as a Cultural Phenomenon." *European Journal of Social Psychology* 20, no. 6, 499–517.
Jay-Z. (2005). "Diamonds from Sierra Leone (Remix)." *Late Registration*. New York: Def Jam.
Jay-Z. (2009). "Empire State of Mind." *The Blueprint 3*. New York: Roc The Mic Studios.
Jeffries, M. (2014). "Hip-Hop Urbanism Old and New." *International Journal of Urban and Regional Research* 38, no. 2, 706–15.

Kochman, T. (1980). *Black and White Styles in Conflict*. Chicago: University of Chicago Press.

Labov, W. (1969). The Logic of Non-standard English," *Georgetown Monographs on Language and Linguistics* 22, no. 1, 1–31. https://repository.library.georgetown.edu/bitstream/handle/10822/555462/GURT_1969.pdf.

Lewis, S. C., and S. D. Reese. (2009). "What Is the War on Terror? Framing through the Eyes of Journalists." *Journalism and Mass Communication Quarterly* 86, no. 1, 85–102.

McCann, B. J. (2017). *The Mark of Criminality: Rhetoric, Race, and Gangsta Rap in the War-on-Crime Era*. Tuscaloosa: University of Alabama Press.

Michaels, S. (1981). "'Sharing Time': Children's Narrative Styles and Differential Access to Literacy." *Language in Society* 10, no. 3, 423–42. http://www.jstor.org/stable/4167263.

Miranda, L. (2015a). "Alexander Hamilton." *Hamilton*. Avatar Studios.

Miranda, L. (2015b). "Aaron Burr, Sir." *Hamilton*. Avatar Studios.

Miranda, L. (2015c). "My Shot." *Hamilton*. Avatar Studios.

Miranda, L. (2015d). "Cabinet Battle #1." *Hamilton*. Avatar Studios.

Miranda, L. M., and J. McCarter. (2016). *Hamilton: The Revolution*. London: Hachette UK.

Mitchell, W. J. T. (2005). *What Do Pictures Want? The Lives and Loves of Images*. Chicago: University of Chicago Press.

Mobb Deep. (1995). "Shook Ones (Part II)." *The Infamous*. New York: RCA.

Nas. (1994). "The World Is Yours." *Illmatic*. New York: Columbia.

Pacheco, P. (2016). "'Hamilton' Costume Designer on How He Streamlined 18th Century Looks for a 21st Century Show." *Los Angeles Times*, June 11, 2016. https://www.latimes.com/entertainment/arts/la-et-cm-paul-tazewell-hamilton-costumes-20160610-snap-htmlstory.html.

Reese, S. D. (2007). "The Framing Project: A Bridging Model for Media Research Revisited." *Journal of Communication* 57, no. 1, 148–154. doi:10.1111/j.1460-2466.2006.00334.

Reese, S. D., and S. C. Lewis. (2009). "Framing the War on Terror: The Internalization of Policy in the US Press." *Journalism* 10, no. 6, 777–97. doi:10.1177/1464884909344480.

Reese, S. D., O. H. Gandy, and A. E. Grant, eds. (2001). *Framing Public Life: Perspectives on Media and Understanding Our World*. Mahwah, NJ: Lawrence Erlbaum.

Smart, J. (2016). "Inside the Choreographic Storytelling of *Hamilton*." *Backstage*, last updated October 1, 2020. https://www.backstage.com/magazine/article/inside-choreographic-storytelling-hamilton-6542/.

Vivian, B. (2002). "Style, Rhetoric, and Postmodern Culture." *Philosophy and Rhetoric* 35, 223–42.

Watts, E. K. (1997). "An Exploration of Spectacular Consumption: Gangsta Rap as Cultural Commodity." *Communication Studies* 48, no. 1, 42–58.

Wickman, F. (2015). "All the Hip-Hop References in *Hamilton*: A Track-by-Track Guide." *Browbeat* (blog), September 24, 2015. http://www.slate.com/

blogs/browbeat/2015/09/24/hamilton_s_hip_hop_references_all_the_rap_and_r_b_allusions_in_lin_manuel.html.

Winslow, L. A. (2014). "The Imaged Other: Style and Substance in the Rhetoric of Joel Osteen." *Southern Communication Journal* 79, no. 3.

Chapter 7

Hamilton, Social Revolution, and the Black Lives Matter Movement

Caleb George Hubbard

Hamilton is a Broadway musical loosely based on the life of Alexander Hamilton, his fight against social injustice, and his pursuit of freedom. This spirit of the early United States continues as a pillar of a country still fighting for social justice. The musical visibly centers this theme of disassembling injustices and contending for freedom; in the words of Miranda's titular character: "I've seen injustice in the world and I've corrected it" (Miranda and Kail, 2020). Throughout the production, Hamilton and company witness an array of injustices. Lin-Manuel Miranda, writer/star of *Hamilton*, understood that resisting oppression is an ongoing process requiring continual attention. He demonstrates through *Hamilton* that many obstacles to equality that plagued the nation long ago persist today.

Hamilton was a story about America in the late 1700s through the early 1800s, but the production first came to off-Broadway in 2015 (Miranda and McCarter, 2016). Soon *Hamilton* became a must-see on a large Broadway stage. At the same time that *Hamilton* was selling out and winning awards, a social movement that came to be known as Black Lives Matter (BLM) was taking shape. BLM took to many places, through social media and street protest, to spotlight current injustices within a nation which continues to uphold White privilege by propagating both literal and symbolic attacks on Black individuals and culture.

Quotes from *Hamilton* started to emerge from self-described BLM associates as the two phenomena simultaneously gained traction (Capewell, 2017). When interviewed regarding *Hamilton* quotes in BLM social media, *Hamilton* members expressed their support for those standing up against racial inequality. Individual affiliates of *Hamilton* spoke in support of BLM in interviews, social media, and other public avenues. Miranda (2020a) himself publicly stated that *Hamilton* is a story that clearly shows the support of BLM, even though Miranda did not create the story of *Hamilton* with BLM in mind. While most of the narrative was created before BLM, Miranda was pleased to see his art applied toward messages about social change. Miranda shared, "Sometimes the right person tells the right story at the right moment, and through a combination of luck and design, a creative expression gains a new force" (Miranda and McCarter, 2016).

My argument in this chapter is that the *Hamilton* narrative has significant overlap with the values of the BLM movement and has been rhetorically deployed to resist contemporary racial inequity. The chapter is organized by first looking at a brief history of BLM and laying out important themes produced by the movement. The next section examines how *Hamilton* has been used within BLM, especially reviewing comments the stars of *Hamilton* made about social inequity. Additionally, I lay out how fans and supporters of BLM used *Hamilton* within their social protest. Finally, the chapter concludes with a deconstruction of themes within *Hamilton*'s content in conjunction with those evident in the BLM movement. The last section will observe that *Hamilton* is a story of the American Revolution, and similarly, BLM is attempting a new kind of revolution in the name of freedom. In *Hamilton*, a question is raised: "Do we not fight for freedom?" Ultimately, I argue that BLM continues the work of fighting for liberty hundreds of years later.

BLACK LIVES MATTER

The year 2020 was marked by a series of momentous historical events. At the same time as the COVID-19 global pandemic, Donald Trump was running for a second term as US president, and numerous concerns about racism arose around his administration (Pengelly, 2020). The Trump administration's racial callousness seemed to enable further those who would commit overtly racist violence, resulting in several significant protests from BLM—especially events surrounding the murders of George Floyd and Breonna Taylor (Deliso, 2020; Oppel and Taylor, 2020). But it was seven years earlier, in 2013, that BLM began in earnest after Trayvon Martin was murdered in Sanford, Florida. Martin was a Black, seventeen-year-old high school student who was shot by a neighborhood watch volunteer, George Zimmerman. The watchman was placed on trial for slaying Martin, but he was soon acquitted of the second-degree murder charges (Alvarez and Buckley, 2013). Shortly following the trial, #BlackLivesMatter started gaining momentum on social media. BLM was created by Alicia Garza, Ayọ Tometi (formerly known as Opal Tometi), and Patrisse Cullors in response to the injustice around

Trayvon Martin's death (Lebron, 2017). BLM's mission is "to eradicate white supremacy and build local power to intervene in violence inflicted on Black communities by the state and vigilantes" (Garza, Cullors, and Tometi, 2020). In addition, the creators wanted BLM to seek to find the beauty that centers around Black joy. In the following sections, I spotlight themes that have been studied and identified in BLM posts and events.

The first theme is identification and understanding of privilege. BLM attempts to make privilege transparent and provide education regarding privilege throughout the United States. Privilege ranges from naturally given privilege (e.g., race or sex) to privilege of power (e.g., political office). Privilege is fueled by ideological association. As Carney (2016) explained, White privilege does not always correspond to appearing Caucasian. Within the Trayvon Martin case, Martin's killer, Zimmerman, is visibly Latinx, thus illustrating "the way that whiteness as an ideology does not necessarily correspond to white bodies" (Carney, 2016, p. 187).

Accordingly, a significant factor in the creation of BLM was the pervasiveness of police brutality and misuse of law enforcement power. Even though BLM was created in 2013, mainly in response to Martin's murder, BLM focuses on a broader and historical array of racist problems within America. Even so, BLM focused on police brutality, which is a long-standing issue in the United States. For instance, Black communities have a history of being targeted by transparently inequitable policies through political leadership, such as the "War on Drugs" in the 1980s. Compared to White individuals, Black citizens are incarcerated at a rate of six to one (Taylor, 2016). Further, Taylor (2016) has described how White men with a criminal record are equally likely to get hired as Black men without a criminal record.

Those who hold positions of privilege create policies written to benefit those who are privileged, thereby structuring the means to withstand their own power. Regardless of someone's political privilege, virtually everyone in the United States acts in a manner that [re]affirms supremacist agendas through habit and socialization (Carney, 2016). BLM attempts to address and change both inequitable policies and mundane habits unevenly distributing power to certain parties.

Another theme in BLM texts is equality and its inherent opposite, inequality. Part of America's long-standing history of inequality is the nation's foundation built on slavery and the systematic treatment of Black individuals as less than White individuals. This history includes the horrific fact that there have been times in which Black lives were *legally* equaled to three-fifths of a person. American citizens have since then adjusted some of these issues; however, there are countless examples of inequality in US history even beyond the transatlantic slave trade, which continues to plague the country (Edwards and Harris, 2015).

Inequality in the United States is also not solely about race but rather a plethora of intersecting matters of identity (e.g., gender and sexual orientation). One of BLM's stated goals is to pursue equality for all people regardless of their identities. The BLM movement is full of young minority leaders, many of whom are women and/or queer, demanding a systemic change emphasizing BLM's commitment to seeking equity for all peoples (Ransby, 2018).

The final theme emerging from BLM is taking action. BLM attempts to motivate individuals to take action further against and speak up to those in power (Lebron, 2017). BLM depends upon action from all people. They recognize that some people may be blinded to inequality, and potential complacency in propagating structures of inequality, by invisible privilege. BLM calls for people to reflect on their privileges in the hope that they will speak up against unjust policies. The warrant is that keeping silent functionally maintains the system that has the historical force of privileging White citizens at the expense of Black lives (Garza, Cullors, and Tometi, 2020). After all, BLM's aims are more than symbolic. "While discourse is crucial," Carney writes, "the goal should not be to merely 'win' an argument but to encourage people to fundamentally change structures of oppression that permeate our lives" (2016, p. 186).

Starting in 2013, BLM has called attention to the mechanisms of inequality by oscillating between communication via media and physical protests. BLM saw a recent resurgence after the deaths of Floyd and Taylor, at which time the content of *Hamilton* began to intermingle with BLM messaging. For instance, in an interview with Kelly Ripa and Ryan Seacrest, *Hamilton* star Renée Elise Goldsberry described her time at a BLM protest. She discussed how society has encountered protest and social movements before, but current protests are subject to unique constraints, such as protesting with masks on amid the COVID-19 pandemic. She stated that she feels the current iterations of BLM are different in that "it's the risking your life, for something" (2020c). While protest against powerful systems and agents has always included risk, Goldsberry acknowledges the increased challenge of existential threat beyond the ire of one's neighbors. Additionally, Goldsberry is not the only *Hamilton* star (or the only user of the *Hamilton* production) who has been quoted by or shown support for BLM. *Hamilton* has been applied in multiple ways by both fans and celebrities, to connect concepts from the musical to the objectives of BLM, which will be discussed in further detail in the next section.

HAMILTON

Hamilton tells the story of the American Revolution. To many, the Broadway production exceeds a passive viewing of history and raises awareness about its narrative's continuous and iterative tropes. The cast members view *Hamilton* as a story about fighting for freedom, which parallels the goals of BLM. Producers also seem to share this view, given that *Hamilton* was released on the Disney+ streaming service at a particular moment where millions of viewers could "take a look at *Hamilton*, as America looks at itself" amid an election season (Roberts, 2020).

Hamilton Cast Support of BLM

Hamilton shifted the traditional story of the White US Founding Fathers. Leslie Odom Jr., Tony Award winner for the role of Aaron Burr, stated that *Hamilton* "is the people who were shut out of the story, now taking ownership of the narrative" (Odom, 2020). Within the same interview, Christopher Jackson, who played George Washington, told a story of how his grandmother said he could be anything when he grew up. He continued to explain how his grandmother, somewhat paradoxically, could have never imagined a Black president. During the Obama administration, Jackson, a Black man, was able to play the role of the first president of the United States, marking one way in which *Hamilton* progressively stepped outside the narrow lens of shared history. Goldsberry (2020a) expressed similar interests by highlighting the roles of Black people and women in the birth of the nation. Although *Hamilton* shows the faults of its characters, it also shows that White men were not solely responsible for the formation of the United States. Cast members have publicly stated that *Hamilton* was designed to showcase the talent of minorities and give a platform to those who typically lack social amplification of their voice (Miranda and McCarter, 2016). Miranda has spoken in support of BLM in addition to using his personal celebrity status as a platform to speak in favor of the BLM movement (Holmes, 2020; Miranda, 2020a, 2020b). Even so, his voice for racial justice, like that of the whole cast, did seem strangely absent regarding BLM activities for a lengthy period of time, leading up to later supportive comments for the movement and garnering public backlash.

In May 2020, the official *Hamilton* Twitter account tweeted about BLM. Miranda (2020d) used a video to speak about the support *Hamilton* received from BLM. Miranda discussed how *Hamilton* attempted to speak about many social issues, but he also recognized the "moral failure" of not speaking about

BLM through *Hamilton* outlets sooner. In addition, Miranda gave a call to action to the listeners:

> Hamilton doesn't exist without the Black and Brown artists who created and revolutionized, and changed the world through the culture, music, and language of hip-hop. Literally, the idea of the show doesn't exist without the brilliant Black and Brown artists in our cast, crew, and production team who breathe life into this story every time it's performed . . . it's up to us and words and deeds to stand up for our fellow citizens. It's up to us to do the work to be better allies and have each other's backs.

Along that same thread, the *Hamilton* producer shared his thoughts through the official *Hamilton* account:

> I'm not a politician. I'm not an activist. I'm not an expert. I'm a theater producer. But what I realize today is, most importantly I'm an American citizen, and silence equals complicity, and I apologize for my silence thus far (Seller, 2020).

Even though *Hamilton* failed to publicly speak for BLM for some time, the cast of *Hamilton* did individually speak in favor of the social movement. Many cast members used their association with *Hamilton*'s platform beyond their personal social accounts to make connections between the show and current social issues regarding race and ethnicity. Phillipa Soo (2020a), who played Eliza Hamilton, felt that *Hamilton* shows people what it is like to stand up and be an advocate, and what it means to fight for freedom. In an interview with *Deadline*, Soo (2020b) spoke about *Hamilton* moving to Disney+ and the current political climate:

> There's a lot of progress that has been made, but I think there's many things that we just have not dealt with. We're tired, and we're fed up, and this administration has literally squeezed the patience out of us . . . We have to stand up and fight against that—and revolution is necessary. Change is necessary. I hope the show asks people to change and, at the same time, inspire people.

Hamilton created a new space for people to take a public stance for freedom and equity. Cast members spoke out through interviews and participated in social protests. Goldsberry (2020b) stated in an interview with *PeopleTV* that *Hamilton* "was a movement. I believe that it will continue to be." She not only discussed *Hamilton* in the interview but also the importance of BLM. In another discussion on *LIVE with Kelly and Ryan*, Goldsberry (2020c) described differences in the thoughts and goals of the current BLM movement as compared to its roots:

The pain that we have felt is not new . . . what is new is this feeling that everyone is searching themselves for how they are complicit . . . everyone is asking themselves, what do I need to do to make the change.

As many cast members recognized, conversations about race and inequality can be difficult. Still, *Hamilton* acted as a communicative catalyst to trigger that conversation for many people who were exploring concepts of power and privilege for the first time. Daveed Diggs, who played Lafayette and Jefferson, said, "Art is and should be a part of the conversation of what is going on in the world around" (2020). *Hamilton* represents more than a Broadway play to many of the artists and audience members, and according to Okieriete Onaodowan, who played Mulligan and Madison, *Hamilton* partially operated as a platform helping BLM "seek out understanding and support" (2020). Both Diggs and Onaodowan have demonstrated their support of BLM through interviews and their own public accounts, including an interview with Robin Roberts (2020) in which Diggs and Onaodowan are both wearing BLM shirts showing support for the movement.

By showcasing support for BLM in public spaces, *Hamilton* stars might connect with newer audiences. There are still individuals who have their first contact with a Black individual through media, such as film or television (Smith and Davis, 2015). Although it may seem strange to some, *Hamilton* going to Disney+ is a moment where many people were exposed to a large group of people of color for the first time. Research has shown that visual media showcases opportunities to learn and understand history, including adding to the ongoing conversation about race (Loewen, 1991; Smith and Davis, 2015), which speaks to the importance of studying how popular texts like *Hamilton* interact with political discourse. In sum, *Hamilton* has opened many doors for discussion about race in the United States. In addition to the cast of the *Hamilton* production itself, *Hamilton* fans have used the show's spectacle within their support of BLM.

Hamilton Fan Support of BLM

Not only did the cast and crew leverage *Hamilton* in their efforts toward social change but fans across the country used the Broadway show to help propel their own work toward a more equitable future. *Hamilton*, an American Revolution story, is thereby brought back into the public sphere for new, contemporary micro-revolutions.

During the social protest, people took pictures of their *Hamilton*-inspired posters and started to tag Lin-Manuel Miranda, including quotes from *Hamilton* on their protest signs (Capewell, 2017). One mash-up quote read, "We hold these truths to be self-evident, that all men are created equal, but when I meet Donald Trump, I'm gonna compel him to include ALL women in the sequel. Let's work" (Michelle, 2017). Some signs used quotes to inspire consideration for how the story of the present historical moment will be written, such as "History has its eyes on you" (Manuell, 2017), while other signs called out to fellow citizens, such as "If you stand for nothing, what'll you fall for?" (Hall, 2017). But *Hamilton* quotes were not the only aspect of the show used by fans within BLM. While wearing a *Hamilton* shirt, Wayne Felton II (2020) rapped the lyrics to "My Shot," showing images and making connections to icons associated with BLM, such as Floyd and Taylor. Tweets like this were not only seen by Felton's Twitter fans but were retweeted by more prominent names, such as Jimmy Fallon and Lin-Manuel Miranda.

Even though many people saw *Hamilton* as a productive tool within BLM, there were also those who opposed such usages (Morales, 2020). One main factor of opposition, from both liberals and conservatives, was the fact that Alexander Hamilton, along with other Founding Fathers, owned and traded slaves. Miranda wrote a few sections within *Hamilton* that directly discussed the issue of slavery (as discussed in more depth in the next section); however, soon after *Hamilton* hit Disney+, the hashtag #CancelHamilton started to trend (Gordon, 2020). Notably, many of the articles produced to cover #CancelHamilton were generated by outlets like the *New York Post* (Markowicz, 2020), a known conservative tabloid, and many of the individuals who called for *Hamilton*'s cancellation opposed BLM. For example, Megyn Kelly (2020a), a previous Fox News reporter, and Nick Adams (2020a), an author endorsed by Donald Trump, both criticized the musical. This conveys that many of the people and organizations who opposed *Hamilton* have also, almost paradoxically, challenged and opposed BLM (Adams, 2020b; Kelly, 2020b).

Hamilton has been both supported and opposed as related to topics of race, gender, and equality. A primary observation of this chapter is that many fans of the Broadway production have simultaneously shown their support for both BLM and *Hamilton*. Additionally, *Hamilton* is known for being a storyline that places minorities center stage. The stars of *Hamilton* have spoken out in favor of BLM while creating connections between *Hamilton* and BLM. It is then pertinent to consider what aspects of *Hamilton*'s content overlap with the values and goals of BLM.

BLM IN *HAMILTON* ANALYSIS

The following section analyzes *Hamilton* by providing portrayals of problematic social structures and the ways they are mirrored in the present social environment, thereby uncovering how the musical's narrative content becomes accessible to contemporary movements like BLM.

Hamilton Debates on Inequality

A drive of *Hamilton* is the emphasis on a diverse cast of characters with intersecting positionalities that have been historically silenced or otherwise underserved, especially immigrants and women. The resultant narrative impact is likely to inspire reflections on issues of inequality. Several of these issues, with a focus on links between *Hamilton* and current social concerns, will be highlighted below.

Hamilton and colleagues owning slaves is a topic over which *Hamilton* has received backlash. This problem is a central warrant for #CancelHamilton. This topic is, in fact, brought up in *Hamilton* itself. Miranda included narrative segments featuring debates about slavery throughout the play. The dialogue about slavery is evident in the first song, during Lafayette's line in the introduction, "Every day while slaves were being slaughtered and carted away across the waves" (Miranda and Kail, 2020). Slavery was an ongoing topic of discussion within the production. In the first act, John Laurens's primary goal is to gain freedom for revolutionaries and enslaved Black Americans alike. Laurens believed that no one can be free until "those in bondage have the same rights as you and me" (Miranda and Kail, 2020). Furthermore, Laurens has a dream to create the first fully Black battalion. In *Hamilton*'s final song, slavery is again brought into the forefront of conversation. Eliza Hamilton talks about what she does in the memory of her late husband and states, "I speak out against slavery" (Miranda and Kail, 2020). From the first song in the production, the concept of slavery is discussed and remains an ongoing theme until the end of the show. Even as the production concludes, Eliza is still speaking out against slavery. The implication is that the problem was not resolved by the end of the period covered by the play and that issues around slavery continue.

Even though slavery was formally abolished over a century ago, progressive critics continue to note the ongoing structuring of slave systems in the prison industrial complex and other capitalist trappings. Perhaps the most apparent ongoing concern lies with the issue of viewing one life as more important than another. This problem is one of the main starting points of BLM. Similar to BLM's contention that lives should be valued equally across all peoples, *Hamilton* focuses on the idea that voices should be equally valued for all people as well.

Hamilton also forwards the concept that minorities have historically been forced to speak louder than others to get their opinions into public conversation. Early in *Hamilton*, Miranda and cast (Miranda, 2020c) discussed the idea of inequality: "Away across the waves, he [Hamilton] struggled and kept his guard up." Miranda and McCarter (2016) have explained that the foregoing line quoted from the play displayed ways in which Hamilton's life paralleled those who struggle with traumatic events associated with a struggle against inequality. Traumatic events, such as watching a video of someone with visual similarities die as he states, "I can't breathe," which occurred with George Floyd's death, tragically continue. However traumatic Hamilton's childhood was, the character maintained his ability to "shoulder ev'ry burden, ev'ry disadvantage [he] learned to manage" (Miranda and Kail, 2020). Although the line may seem unsympathetic when ripped from its full context, the lyric is situated such that, far from endorsing a necessity of suffering, it communicates the optimism for a better future that spared Hamilton a great deal of pain: a future that, in part, is due to the support of his community; a community that many individuals do not have.

Similarly, BLM messages often highlight how Black individuals are treated differently due to skin color. In the summer of 2020, BLM took to the streets in protest of the unjust murders of Floyd and Taylor. Like Fox News' Tucker Carlson, many people vocally stood out against BLM protests, saying that the group should protest differently (Mazza, 2020). However, when football player Colin Kaepernick decided to peacefully protest against inequity for Black citizens years earlier by taking a knee during the national anthem, he was told not to protest that way (Bailey, 2020). It seems that no matter what method of protest is adopted by Black citizens, it is not welcome; thus, they disappointingly have to "holler just to be heard" (Miranda and Kail, 2020). From the perspective of BLM, there is no "good way" to protest and speak up according to those in power. In this way, a contemporary tension between silence and amplification mirror historical marginalizations reflected in *Hamilton*.

Miranda's play shows how fighting can make for social change, but it also endorses an array of tools for voice, agency, and struggle against oppression. A large part of what Hamilton's character does to gain agency is writing. Burr suggested that Hamilton "wants to fight, not write" (Miranda and Kail, 2020), but Hamilton opted to manage Washington's journal during the revolution. After the war ended, Hamilton writes "essays against slavery," "documents to defend the Constitution," and "creates his own form of government" (Miranda and Kail, 2020). Hamilton's mind and creativity lived on through his words. In this way, *Hamilton* shows that there are multiple viable options for making sustainable social change, but it takes diverse talents and creativity to achieve such social progress.

Additionally, BLM and *Hamilton* do not seek social change for only one group. Hamilton and Lafayette expressed "immigrants: we get the job done" (Miranda and Kail, 2020). The Schuyler sisters pointed out that "all men are created equal" (Miranda and Kail, 2020) but compel others "to include women in the sequel." In a similar fashion, BLM has raised awareness not only about Black lives (Garza, Cullors, and Tometi, 2020) but about those of other minority groups (e.g., trans lives) who are seeking "the same rights as you and me" (Miranda and Kail, 2020).

A current example linking to this issue is that, even though the Biden administration has the most diverse cabinet thus far in American history, research still finds that it does not truly reflect the demographics of the larger American population (Prasad, 2021). BLM aims for a nation where everyone is equitably represented and has an equal seat at the table. As portrayed in *Hamilton*, excluding people from the "room where it happens" (Miranda and Kail, 2020) also occurred. Odom (2020) and Diggs (2020) have raised the questions of how to best ensure fair representation for all peoples such that everyone can be in the room. Both have also mentioned noticeable positive changes for amplification of minority voices in recent years, even though they hope for even more opportunities for underrepresented communities in the future.

As a means of creating such positive social change, BLM has also focused public messaging on issues surrounding the concept of privilege. Alexander Hamilton does not see eye to eye with numerous people within the story. Burr and Hamilton, for instance, disagreed throughout the play, ultimately leading to the duel where Burr kills Hamilton. Those disagreements might be attributed to divergent perspectives produced by differing intersections of privilege. Early on, Burr told Hamilton, "Don't let them know what you're against or what you're for . . . fools who run their mouths off wind up dead" (Miranda and Kail, 2020). Hamilton countered by asking, "If you stand for nothing, Burr, what'll you fall for?" (Miranda and Kail, 2020). These lyrics exemplify the characters' differing views on the revolution, even as Burr fought alongside Hamilton.

Burr stood for similar ideas as Hamilton yet told his peers to be quiet. As a parallel in today's society, Black people are regularly socialized in particular scripts for how to interact with people in power differently than White people, such as police officers (Carney, 2016). Burr is saying that to be successful, you have to work the system. His position of changing systems from within contrasts with Hamilton's belief in revolution. Burr contended that minorities have to understand the unspoken norms and work around them. In other words, you can be successful as long as you remain under the radar. Conversely, Hamilton finds that staying under the radar means the people in power will always remain in power. Trying to change who is in positions of power is more reflective of Hamilton's goals and also seems to parallel the aims of the BLM movement.

Burr and Hamilton disagree constantly throughout the storyline. Hamilton is fighting for what he thinks is right, and Burr is afraid to back "the wrong horse" (Miranda and Kail, 2020). Hamilton cannot understand why Burr is sitting back and waiting for things to happen; however, one piece of information that Burr does not disclose to Hamilton concerns his family's wealth. When Hamilton and Burr first meet, Hamilton asks Burr how he finished college so early. Burr tells him it was his parents' wish before they died. But what Burr does not discuss is that his father was the president of the college Burr attended (Miranda and McCarter, 2016). Burr had the connection and social privilege that allowed him to graduate early—completing college only accrued new types of privilege for Burr at the time.

Miranda (2016) crafted both characters similarly when it comes to strength and wit, but the paths the two characters take are significantly different. Burr is given more assistance and opportunities to be successful based on his social status and formal training. Even so, Hamilton rises to success against the odds by means of loyalty, collaboration, and persuasive letter writing. Hamilton's success could be accredited to Hamilton having to work "non-stop" (Miranda and Kail, 2020) to be perceived with status equitable to Burr's position (albeit different). Burr represents that of "naturally given" power in which certain privilege is passed on by means of status at one's birth. With this symbolism in mind, audiences can further analyze Burr and Hamilton's discussion for the need for revolution. A difference in their perspectives is that Burr was in a place of greater social power than Hamilton and has moments where he is unsure if speaking up is needed. Indeed, Burr may have felt that the stakes were higher given his status-related advantages. This tension reflects those also discussed by BLM, as the movement not only endeavors to showcase the need for change but urges people to stand up and fight. Like many individuals in today's society, Burr sees the need for social change but does not always want to stand up. Hamilton, like many within BLM, demands that Burr not only see the need for change but also use his place of power to facilitate change. Even though Burr and Hamilton had divergent methods for forward progress, they still fought on the same side.

Hamilton includes arguments between those who are on opposite sides of the issue. One other disagreement to be highlighted is that of Hamilton and Samuel Seabury. Seabury's character only is within one song, but the theatrical moment mirrors dilemmas associated with different types and degrees of privileged. Seabury's opposes the revolution, singing, "Heed not the rabble who scream revolution; they have not your interest at heart" (Miranda and Kail, 2020). The character choice for Seabury's casting was one of lighter skin, thereby showcasing the social privilege Seabury had in that social context and implying how he so overlooked the suffering of others. This is akin to many people today who express disagreement with BLM. Many White people speak of equality but do not understand the core of certain social problems because they have not experienced the problems themselves to understand their nuances. Today, those suspicious of BLM tend to be people who echo Seabury, worried that "chaos and bloodshed are not a solution" (Miranda and Kail, 2020). *Hamilton* shows the audience that change may be messy, and those who are not facing the issues and those who do not need the change are regularly ignorant of the movement's driving force. Thus, they see no need for a revolution.

As Seabury goes on to speak against the revolution, Hamilton jumps in to counter Seabury's claims. The audience hears two opposing sides to the argument. Hamilton is quick to point out that people might not want chaos and bloodshed, but chaos and bloodshed are already happening, much like the exigency of BLM regarding unfair incarcerations and regular killing of unarmed Black individuals. Hamilton points out how Seabury is speaking of this possible future that might arise from standing up, but Hamilton quickly reminds everyone about "all that we've lost" (Miranda and Kail, 2020). Seabury represents many Americans who speak of equality but do not see the need for upsetting the status quo because they ignore the bloodshed that is already occurring among those in different social positions. These critics have lives that have given them rights and privileges to which they have grown accustomed, and speaking up can threaten their privilege.

Further, equal opportunity is a crucial value sought by BLM. As another parallel within *Hamilton*, the play shows a group of characters who are looking for their chance—who are "not throwing away [their] shot" (Miranda and Kail, 2020). Alexander Hamilton understood that he was poor and that he had little status from which to draw the formal power for change. He told his future wife about this inequity when he was thinking back on his life. He understood that he would need to stand up and fight for the changes envisioned. But Hamilton was not the only character seeking to improve the conditions of their life. *Hamilton* highlights multiple stories of people in different places and how the revolution variously enabled social privilege. Hercules Mulligan contended that the revolution was his "chance to socially advance, instead of sewin' some pants" (Miranda and Kail, 2020), similar to many individuals within BLM who are seeking a better life for themselves and the others around them.

Hamilton Manifests How to Stand Up and Fight

Hamilton has a clear position in favor of standing up for what you believe in. Not only was Hamilton himself fighting for what was right but characters like Laurens and Washington fought for others who were unable to stand up. Miranda (2016) discussed that concept by saying, "Those who stand for nothing fall for anything." This lyric type was based on the wording Miranda discovered throughout Alexander Hamilton's original writings. *Hamilton*, therefore, exhibits how specific modes of injustice may extend from social status and shows that more individuals need to "take an honest stand" (Miranda and Kail, 2020).

Given that the first act of *Hamilton* is based around the American Revolution, the storyline has a clear connection to fighting for what one believes is correct. Likewise, BLM attempts to create social change by standing for their beliefs, which generates clear ground for the associations BLM social media users and protesters have made between their own mission and the narrative content of *Hamilton*. Additionally, *Hamilton* displays an array of alternate methods of standing up. Eliza Hamilton's character, for example, offers the chance to consider fresh perspectives on standing up and taking action. In a different context early on in the play, Eliza says, "Look around, look around at how lucky we are to be alive right now" (Miranda and Kail, 2020). Eliza recognized that she was living in a time of change, and she was excited by that change. However, when Eliza sees her future husband for the first time, she is "tryin' to catch your [Alexander Hamilton's] eye from the side of the ballroom" (Miranda and Kail, 2020). It was not until Angelica took action that Eliza's life started to change. The theme is extended later in the show as Eliza reminded Hamilton about the greatness he had accomplished so far in life—an encouragement not to despair in the face of continued obstacles. She sang, "Look at where you are, look at where you started. The fact that you're alive is a miracle. Just stay alive, that would be enough," (Miranda and Kail, 2020). Eliza was telling Hamilton to remember the good things in life, but at the same time, Hamilton is showcasing the importance of attempts to make change. The show communicates value for both perspectives and challenges the audience to strive for a balanced position between acting toward change and optimism for the future.

Eliza is a supportive wife and mother, but that is the extent to which she is characterized in the play for a long time. After Hamilton goes public with his extramarital affair, Eliza claims that she will remove herself from Hamilton's narrative. It is not until Hamilton dies that Eliza places herself back into the story and boasts of a long list of incredible social changes. Within *Hamilton*, Eliza displays that nothing gets done without action. Eliza spent her whole life helping others (Soo, 2020a), and once she started taking action, she made changes for the better, such as creating an orphanage and speaking out against slavery. *Hamilton*, therefore, shows that people must both seek out future change and showcases how a "revolution is messy but now is the time to stand" (Miranda and Kail, 2020). This messiness continues in the present day, but groups such as BLM have embraced these challenges, even if by necessity, in an active attempt to make a positive change.

CONCLUSION

This chapter focused on how *Hamilton*'s narrative content addressed concepts related to social change overlapping with BLM. This overlap has been illuminated by the fact that BLM members have regularly used *Hamilton* images and quotes within their social activity. The Broadway production has clearly generated a unique platform for BLM. Additionally, the cast of *Hamilton* has supported BLM while using *Hamilton* as the communicative vehicle. The cast members and fans alike have drawn inspiration to "rise up" and "tell your brother that he's gotta rise up" from the musical (Miranda and Kail, 2020). *Hamilton* is a starting point for exploring comparisons between issues from the nation's founding and similar issues of inequality present in the modern day, thereby inspiring audiences to take part in a project that helps move America forward in new and exciting ways.

Finally, *Hamilton* does not provide insight in a void but shows what it means to be an advocate (Soo, 2020a). The audience of the show is charged with the responsibility to create a better and more equitable America (Diggs, 2020). An exemplary of this tradition is that BLM attempts to hold the country accountable for the current culture: a culture that is formed by the social foundations built by US forefathers.

BLM has utilized aspects of *Hamilton* that connect art, popular culture, and political change. These connections continue in a grand tradition of art being used to inspire social change, such as *Rent* highlighting social issues around the AIDS epidemic. Even though art seeking to create social awareness is a concept that has been around for centuries, *Hamilton*'s connection to BLM is a unique case. *Hamilton* was not necessarily generated with the overt purpose to make social change, but many members of BLM have employed *Hamilton* content as a vehicle to inspire change. With the case of *Hamilton*, fans, creators, and stars used the show to forward social advocacy. Further research needs to explore the in-depth ways fans deploy pop culture toward social purposes.

This chapter, while acknowledging that art and pop culture are not always geared toward social change, finds optimism in the notion that fans may grab onto concepts within popular culture and connect them to political and social advocacy. Further research of this kind is critical for understanding contemporary social environments. Embracing popular culture, including social media content, as an integral part of these environments also enables exploration of possibilities such as those demonstrated by BLM's use of media to expand and connect with others. These means of connection suggest that popular creators and their content, like Miranda and *Hamilton*, can link to large fan bases and leverage their bonds toward civic action.

The story of Alexander Hamilton happened centuries ago, and yet its themes reverberate today through the work of Miranda and others. Cast members and fans of *Hamilton* know that even though things might be getting better in some ways, "the war is not done" (Miranda and Kail, 2020) until each life is seen as equally important and all have a place "in the room where it happens." BLM has drawn on these *Hamilton* themes in an effort toward social revolution and equality for all.

REFERENCES

Adams, N. (2020a). "Alexander Hamilton bought and traded slaves. Is @broadway-com going to cancel one of the top-grossing shows of all time?" Twitter, July 2, 2020. https://twitter.com/nickadamsinusa/status/1278743322308329474.

Adams, N. (2020b). "RT: Black Lives Matter is a fraud organization!" Twitter, June 29, 2020. https://twitter.com/nickadamsinusa/status/1277647121483804672.

Alvarez, L., and C. Buckley. (2013). "Zimmerman Is Acquitted in Trayvon Martin Killing." *New York Times*, July 14, 2013. https://www.nytimes.com/2013/07/14/us/george-zimmerman-verdict-trayvon-martin.html.

Bailey, A. (2020). "On This Day Four Years Ago, Colin Kaepernick Began His Peaceful Protest during the National Anthem." *USA Today*, August 26, 2020. https://www.usatoday.com/story/sports/nfl/2020/08/26/colin-kaepernick-started-protesting-day-2016/3440690001/.

Capewell, J. (2017). "Protesters Are Using 'Hamilton' Lyrics to Defend Rights across the Country." Huffpost, February 1, 2017. https://www.huffpost.com/entry/hamilton-lyrics-make-pretty-good-muslim-ban-protest-signs_n_58920abce4b02772c4ea8582.

Carney, N. (2016). "All Lives Matter, but So Does Race: Black Lives Matter and the Evolving Role of Social Media." *Humanity and Society* 40, no 2. https://doi.org/doi.org/10.1177/0160597616643868.

Deliso, M. (2020). "Timeline: The Impact of George Floyd's Death in Minneapolis and Beyond." ABC News, June 10, 2020. https://abcnews.go.com/US/timeline-impact-george-floyds-death-minneapolis/story?id=70999322.

Diggs, D. (2020). *Hamilton: History Has Its Eyes on You.* (Roberts, R.) Disney+.

Edwards, S. B., and Duchess Harris. (2015). *Black Lives Matter*. Minneapolis, MN: ABDO.

Felton, W., II. (2020). "I took the words of @Lin_Manuel and his #hamiltonmusical to talk about what's happening right now. #blacklivesmatter #GeorgeFloyd #BreonnaTaylor." Twitter, June 7, 2020. https://twitter.com/waynefeltonii/status/1269751653558870027.

Garza, A., P. Cullors, and O. Tometi. (2020). "HerStory." Black Lives Matter. https://blacklivesmatter.com/herstory/.

Goldsberry, R. (2020a). *Hamilton: History Has Its Eyes on You.* (Roberts, R.) Disney+.

Goldsberry, R. E. (2020b). "Hamilton's Renée Elise Goldsberry on What Protesters Have in Common with the Founding Fathers." *Entertainment*, July 11, 2020. https://ew.com/theater/hamilton-renee-elise-goldsberry-protesters-founding-fathers/.

Goldsberry, R. E. (2020c). "Renée Elise Goldsberry Protested with Her Family in New York." *LIVE with Kelly and Ryan*, July 3, 2020. https://www.youtube.com/watch?v=-K7ObNUx4h4.

Gordon, J. (2020). "#CancelHamilton Sweeps the Internet with Calls for the Musical to be AXED After Its Debut on Disney+ Over Criticism of the Founding Father for His Role in Slave Trade." *Daily Mail*, July 6, 2020. https://www.dailymail.co.uk/news/article-8492387/Backlash-Hamilton-musical-revisionist-history-days-debuted-Disney-amid-BLM-protests.html.

Hall, L. (2017). "This was mine on Monday in Columbus Ohio!" Twitter, February 1, 2017. https://twitter.com/leahhall27/status/826804509871587329.

Holmes, H. (2020). "Lin-Manuel Miranda and Black Lives Matter Leaders Are Working on the Future of 'Hamilton.'" *Observer*, June 22, 2020. https://observer.com/2020/06/lin-manuel-miranda-hamilton-black-lives-matter/.

Jackson, C. (2020). *Hamilton: History Has Its Eyes on You*. (Roberts, R.) Disney+.

Kelly, M. (2020a). "Can Hamilton—A show that celebrates America and her founders—Survive cancel culture?" Twitter, July 3, 2020. https://twitter.com/megynkelly/status/1278967141274996736.

Kelly, M. (2020b). "Megyn Kelly: Black Lives Matter and MeToo Have Been Co-Opted By Activists." *The Carlos Watson Show*, December 5, 2020. https://www.youtube.com/watch?v=EPa3iC0KzgA.

Lebron, C. J. (2017). *The Making of Black Lives Matter: A Brief History of an Idea*. New York: Oxford University Press.

Loewen, J. W. (1991). "Teaching Race Relations from Feature Films." *Teaching Sociology* 19, no. 1, 82. https://doi.org/10.2307/1317580.

Manuell, L. (2017). "History has its eyes on you." Twitter, February 1, 2017. https://twitter.com/lynnmanuell/status/826749633963638784.

Markowicz, K. (2020). "The 'Cancel' Crowd Should Be Gunning for 'Hamilton.'" *New York Post*, July 2, 2020. https://nypost.com/2020/07/02/the-cancel-crowd-should-be-gunning-for-hamilton/.

Mazza, E. (2020). "Tucker Carlson Dials Up Fear Factor in Ugly New Attack on Black Lives Matter." *Huffpost*, June 16, 2020. https://www.huffpost.com/entry/tucker-carlson-black-lives-matter-fear_n_5ee82c49c5b6b735a6481735.

Michelle. (2017). "@Lin_Manuel #Hamilton protest sign in San Francisco! So many kids sang the lyrics when they saw it! #NoBanNoWall #WomensMarch." Twitter, February 1, 2017. https://twitter.com/Emmieinthecity/status/826714153607794689.

Miranda, L.-M. (2020a). "Black lives matter. If you are feeling helpless, here's a starter of actionable items. God keep you safe." Twitter, May 30, 2020. https://twitter.com/lin_manuel/status/1266782619364208642.

Miranda, L.-M. (2020b). "Donating and adding the Louisville Community Bail Fund to the list below. Https://actionnetwork.org/fundraising/louisville-community-bail-fund/ . . . If you cannot donate, amplify/volunteer. If you are heartsick over racism and injustice, let it manifest action, work towards justice, however you can manage.

God keep you safe." Twitter, May 29, 2020. https://twitter.com/Lin_Manuel/status/1266391183770750976.

Miranda, L.-M. (2020c). *Hamilton: History Has Its Eyes on You*. (Roberts, R.) Disney+.

Miranda, L.-M. (2020d). "We stand on the side of justice. Black Lives Matter. Take action now in the links below. #BlackLivesMatter [@HamiltonMusical]." Twitter, May 30, 2020. https://twitter.com/hamiltonmusical/status/1266941365277114368.

Miranda, L.-M., and T. Kail. (2020). *Hamilton*. Disney+.

Miranda, L.-M., and J. McCarter. (2016). *Hamilton: The Revolution*. New York: Grand Central Publishing.

Morales, E. (2020). "The Problem with the 'Hamilton' Movie." CNN, July 7, 2020. https://www.cnn.com/2020/07/05/opinions/hamilton-movie-mixed-messages-black-lives-matter-morales/index.html.

Odom, Leslie, Jr. (2020). *Hamilton: History Has Its Eyes on You*. (Roberts, R.) Disney+.

Onaodowan, O. (2020). *Hamilton: History Has Its Eyes on You*. (Roberts, R.) Disney+.

Oppel, R. A., and D. B. Taylor. (2020). "Here's What You Need to Know about Breonna Taylor's Death." *New York Times*, August 13, 2020. https://www.nytimes.com/article/breonna-taylor-police.html.

Pengelly, M. (2020). "Trump Equates Support for Confederate Flag with Black Lives Matter." *The Guardian*, July 19, 2020. https://www.theguardian.com/world/2020/jul/19/donald-trump-confederate-flag-black-lives-matter-fox-news-sunday.

Prasad, R. (2021). "Biden Cabinet: Does This Diverse Team Better Reflect America?" BBC News, January 25, 2021. https://www.bbc.com/news/world-us-canada-55080344.

Ransby, B. (2018). *Making All Black Lives Matter*. Oakland: University of California Press.

Roberts, R. (2020). *Hamilton: History Has Its Eyes on You*. (Roberts, R.) Disney+.

Seller, J. (2020). "We stand on the side of justice. Black Lives Matter. Take action now in the links below. #BlackLivesMatter." Twitter, May 30, 2020. https://twitter.com/HamiltonMusical/status/1266941366908706816.

Smith, D. C., and J. J. Davis. (2015). "No Filter: Counter-Storytelling and The Help." In *Films as Rhetorical Texts: Cultivating Discussion about Race, Racism, and Race Relations*, edited by Janice D. Hamlet, 107–16. Lanham, MD: Lexington Books.

Soo, P. (2020a). *Hamilton: History Has Its Eyes on You*. (Roberts, R.) Disney+.

Soo, P. (2020b). "Phillipa Soo Talks How 'Hamilton' Is a Mirror to the Current Social and Cultural Movement." *Deadline*, July 2, 2020. https://deadline.com/2020/07/phillipa-soo-hamilton-musical-disney-plus-diversity-representation-inclusion-1202975124/.

Taylor, K. Y. (2016). *From #BlackLivesMatter to Black Liberation*. Chicago: Haymarket Books.

SECTION III

Revelations about Sociopolitical Issues

Chapter 8

Immigrants

Getting the Job Done, Then and Now

Judith P. Roberts

Immigration has not always been a heated political issue. Immigrants from Europe and Africa assisted in the creation of the United States. They fought in the Revolutionary War to gain freedom from England. They introduced the Articles of Confederation, which, over a number of years, evolved into the Constitution. They created a culture of Americana, which is evident across the fifty states today. But over time, immigrants and those seeking asylum within the geographic and political borders of the United States have found themselves facing scrutiny and danger in the land of opportunity. This has brought about policies from presidential administrations as well as artistic endeavors seeking to revolutionize immigration once again. As former president Donald Trump sought to cast a negative light on immigrants, *Hamilton* sought to counter that rhetoric and turn the world upside down. Though *Hamilton* opened in 2015, the year before Trump was elected, even then, the then presidential candidate was spewing anti-immigrant rhetoric on his campaign trail. It is obvious with his election that some of his remarks resonated with his voting constituents—but not everyone in the country. A parallel comparison can be seen in *Hamilton* with immigrants, such as Hamilton and Lafayette, sometimes being seen in a favorable light but then not as beloved in other parts of the musical. The most memorable lines, however, do shed a positive light on immigrants. *Hamilton* often shows admiration to immigrants and praises how they care for this country. Alexander Hamilton himself is commended as an immigrant from the Caribbean islands, and his determination to create a new nation with equal rights is lauded throughout the production, such as when Hamilton and John Laurens sing about not being able to be free until slavery is ended. Particularly in the song "Yorktown (The World

Turned Upside Down)," the Hamilton and Lafayette characters emphasize the resilience and bravery of immigrants by singing the line, "Immigrants: we get the job done." However, just as it is an issue today, the view of immigrants remains varied. In *Hamilton*, even, this can be seen when Hamilton is confronted with his amorous misdeeds and his opponents indicate that Hamilton ought to return to the country of his birth.

This chapter will look at how *Hamilton*, with its casting and with its lines, encourages voters of today to start a new revolution—to fight for immigrants' rights by reminding them that many of our heroes of the American Revolution were immigrants themselves—and just like now, immigrants had to fight for their place and their new home. The chapter will look at the cognitive behavioral theory to explore how voters view immigrants and political policies in *Hamilton* and how even now citizens are speaking out in protests and rallies and with their vote. Lin-Manuel Miranda may have written the lyrics to "Yorktown" that reminded Americans of their own immigration status as revolutionists, but the production of *Hamilton* is only the spark that is turning the world upside down.

However, as *Hamilton* was riveting audiences and critics alike with pro-immigration rhetoric, another discussion on immigration was beginning in New York City. Donald Trump, star of the NBC show *The Apprentice* and hotel developer, announced that he would run for president in the same year *Hamilton* first premiered at the Richard Rodgers Theatre. While always a talking point for politicians, Trump and his campaign team elevated immigration during the 2016 presidential election. As Trump began his campaign, his rhetoric against immigrants and immigration policy immediately resonated with his emerging base of supporters. From the moment he announced his candidacy, Trump started berating immigrants, speaking against Mexico for sending "rapists" to the United States. He claimed he would build a wall between the United States and Mexico and that Mexico would pay for it. This was no doubt seen as a way to keep undocumented workers from entering the country in attempts to find jobs and, in many cases, safety. He said he wanted to send away all undocumented immigrants but bring the "good" ones back legally (no clarification was given on who would be considered "good" nor who would determine the goodness of an undocumented immigrant). He claimed he would triple the number of immigration and customs enforcement officers and end birthright citizenship for individuals who were born in the United States. Further, NBC News reported more than one hundred stances that Trump took on immigration during his first White House run, which included the aforementioned rhetoric, as well as stating that Trump's views on immigration were always consistent, Muslims would be unable to immigrate or even visit the United States, and opposing the H-1B program—allowing nonimmigrant visas for specialty occupations (Timm, 2016). All of this only served to strengthen his own voter base, scare many immigrants, and put the possibility of citizenship for a vast number of people into question. Not only that, but it magnified the gap between individuals who supported pro-immigration reform, such as allowing illegal immigrants a chance to become American citizens, and those who did not, such as those who supported Trump's plan to build a wall between the United States and Mexico.

And yet, *Hamilton* thrived within this political context. From the opening song, *Hamilton* sets the stage for immigrants now and in Founding Father Alexander Hamilton's time with the first lyrics introducing the star character as a "bastard orphan son of a whore and a Scotsman." As the song "Alexander Hamilton" progresses, audience members find out Hamilton grew up in the West Indies but made his way to New York to "be a new man." As this worldwide phenomenon hit the Broadway stage August 2015, rumors were already circulating around it, with Lin-Manuel Miranda already making a name for himself and the play. Miranda, who garnered success with a previous musical, *In the Heights*, started hinting about a *Hamilton* musical in 2008. When he mentioned such a concept, it was lauded as a joke, but Miranda proceeded to perform what would eventually become the opening song for *Hamilton* for then president Barack Obama and first lady Michelle Obama at the White House Evening of Poetry, Music, and the Spoken Word. The song, as well as the future musical, was then tentatively titled, *The Hamilton Mixtape*, but whatever the name, it started generating excitement and buzz in the Broadway community. Drafts of the musical continued into 2013, but by February 2015, the play was debuted off-Broadway at the Public Theater to rave reviews. The musical opened to the public in August of that same year in the Richard Rodgers Theatre and would become a smashing success, winning eleven Tony Awards, including Best Musical, and would eventually be filmed and streamed on Disney+ four years later. As the musical opens with lines denoting Hamilton's immigration status, it continues to discuss various immigration and even slavery issues in songs such as "Yorktown," "We Know," and others (Brantley, 2015; George, 2019; Stasio, 2015; Vankin, 2017).

Hamilton became more than just a celebrated historical play—it was a celebrated political play as well. When viewers meet Alexander Hamilton in the play's first song, "Alexander Hamilton," Hamilton is identified by several biographical and ethnic characteristics—not all of them favorable or positive. While his father abandoned his family, Hamilton is called a bastard son of a whore. However, in New York, Hamilton could be a new man—someone of power and influence, just as immigrants for hundreds of years hoped to become. Miranda added to the political foray through a multicultural cast, which added to the multiracial dimensions of the play but also echoed the current American demographics. However, many of Trump's voters were uncomfortable with this rhetoric because they felt Trump "related to the discomfort of an older, Whiter generation of Americans who struggled with the changing face (and skin) of the America that *Hamilton* represents" (Arivett, 2020, p. 137). It can come as no surprise that Trump tweeted for his followers to boycott the play after his vice president, Mike Pence, was booed by audience members when he attended a showing of *Hamilton* (Arivett, 2020).

Miranda's decision to cast Hamilton, Lafayette, George Washington, and other historically White men as non-White also brings race to the forefront of the play. America, as Monteiro (2016) stated, has never been a White nation. One of the first men who died in the American Revolution was Crispus Attucks, who was of African and Native American ancestry. Slavery, however, is downplayed in the play except for the aforementioned line and another one in "Cabinet Battle #1" in which Hamilton (played by Miranda) states, "We know who's really doing the planting," indicating Thomas Jefferson's slaves were doing the actual planting of cotton and not Jefferson himself, as Jefferson (played by Daveed Diggs) implied. The song "Yorktown" had one notorious line about immigration that was actually an accidental success. "Immigrants: we get the job done" was a line Miranda added simply because he thought it was funny. However, it became successful, having audiences cheer it night after night, because it resonated with audiences against Trump's anti-immigration rhetoric. As Arivett (2020, p. 136) stated, "The 2015 American audience was already prepared for the themes and content of *Hamilton*, giving the show influence and success that could not have been achieved decades before."

However, a note needs to be added that the original Ron Chernow biography of Alexander Hamilton, which was Miranda's inspiration for the *Hamilton* musical, made mention that while Hamilton was an immigrant from the Caribbean, Hamilton was not an American immigrant, at least not how we think of an American immigrant today (Hogeland, 2018). Few believed in the eighteenth century that the United States would be invigorated by the new ideas and perspectives of outsiders, such as Hamilton. However, in light of immigration today, Hamilton's story is legendary, almost mythical in nature. As noted in the musical, Hamilton was "dropped in the middle of a forgotten spot in the Caribbean by providence, impoverished, in squalor." Hamilton was poverty-stricken. Orphaned. A bastard at birth. Yet he rose from all of his disadvantages and made his contributions clear as a Founding Father, not only during the Revolutionary War but also during the beginning years of the United States. But Hamilton's story is hardly unique to him. As he had to go to work in his teenage years to support himself, so did other Founding Fathers such as Benjamin Franklin and even George Washington.

This chapter would be remiss, however, if notice was not given to the Biden administration's policy changes beginning in 2020. Just as Hamilton focused on immigrants working to create a new country, so is the Biden administration working to increase immigrants' status, safety, and sustainability. As reported by the Associated Press, newly elected Joe Biden started his administration with sweeping changes to immigration. While Trump's policies refused asylum seekers crossing the border, Biden granted temporary legal status to Liberians who fled civil war. While Trump's policies separated children from their families in detention centers, Biden rescinded one of Trump's first executive orders making anyone in the country illegally a priority for deportations. While Trump's policies sought to make it difficult for immigrants to become US citizens, Biden's policies sought to offer a path to citizenship for illegal immigrants (Spagat, 2021; Fox, 2020). However, Biden's ambitious policies faced opposition, as, only days after he signed his new policies, a federal court in Texas suspended Biden's hundred-day moratorium on deportations. Additionally, it was to be expected that the immigration bill would lose some of its power during political debates—akin to "Cabinet Battle #1" and "Cabinet Battle #2" in *Hamilton*. No doubt the animosity that followed Hamilton and Jefferson in the musical and in real life is echoed by the hostility shared between minority leader Mitch McConnell, a Republican from Kentucky who was a strong supporter of Donald Trump until the January 6, 2021, riot on the Capitol building, and Chuck Schumer, a Democrat from New York who helped lead Trump's second impeachment trial.

However, despite Biden's opening moves for immigration reform, seeking to undo many of the harmful immigration policies that the Trump administration enforced, many immigrants fear that the Biden administration will not be able to make the sweeping changes needed before they are deported. Not only did the Texas federal court file a moratorium but the legislature, less than a month into Biden's term, has much to distract it from immigration reform, including coronavirus relief packages and vaccine rollout plans. This leaves children still separated from their families and fears of asylum deportation still a clear and present danger for immigrants (Weissert and Merchant, 2021). Although immigrant deportation was not a policy topic in *Hamilton*, the idea that immigrants could be separated from their parents most definitely was. Throughout the musical, Alexander Hamilton struggles with being an orphan, watching his mother die, and not having his father in his life. He clutches on to Eliza and her family because they offer him the affection of a family he never experienced. As he stated in "Helpless," he was penniless, broke, and had only love and honor to give his new bride. The rhetoric echoed in Hamilton's song to his love can be viewed by all, not just immigrants, who have grown up without a sense of family and the relief that comes in marrying into a family; not only did Hamilton gain a loving spouse but he also gained a family who adored him. Unlike many of the media reports that scholars have studied, Hamilton's rhetoric shows how immigrants being taken away from their families can have lifelong effects.

Based on aforementioned research of rhetoric in lyrics and politics, we can now look at cognitive behavioral theory and apply it to how the writers, actors, and fans of *Hamilton* are using these lyrics from the musical's songs to protest, rally, and let their voice be heard. Cognitive behavioral theory is often seen in the psychological realm, but due to possible trauma that immigration delays, separations, and trials can endure, it is relevant for this inquiry. As noted previously, the Trump administration reflected an anti-immigration outlook. Dobson and Dozois (2001) stated that since cognitive activity can affect behavior (based on their study of young children), cognitive activity can be observed and changed, therefore allowing behavioral modifications through cognitive variation. Cognitive behavioral theory has been studied for decades; in fact, it merges together cognitive theory, which looks at behavioral issues as a result of outside stimuli, and behavioral theory, where therapists focus on recalled and observed experiences rather than the individual's awareness of such experiences (Ellis, 1989; Watson, 1924). Therefore, cognitive behavioral theory is actually the result of these two theories that are distinct but not completely different from one another. As Kendall and Holton (2013) found, cognitive behavioral therapy looks at the bidirectional movements that have been dictated and directed by empirical data and pragmatic necessities, such as what behavioral therapists understand from training to be corrective therapeutic approaches and cognitive therapists' desire to follow a strict methodology of behaviorism. Therefore, looking at both the behavioral and cognitive, internal and external variables can be studied for treatment and understanding to contribute to behavioral change (Kendall and Holton, 2013).

The cognitive behavioral theory (CBT) states that one's cognition can attribute to how one views various life situations. A person's cognitive processes, such as meanings, assumptions, and even the state of the world, are formatted in one's brain due to an individual's life events, which either help or hinder that person's adaptation to the surrounding world. While therapy based on this theory is used to treat a wide range of mental disorders, such as PTSD, depression, and anxiety, when studying this theory academically, one must remember that while people may not recognize specific instances that shaped their life, they can be made aware of them with therapy. In looking at this theory, the media can affect immigrants' status both in public policy and through social inclusion or exclusion. Consider, for instance, the internet as a medium. Individuals may visit various websites and then soon develop an expectation of receiving similar knowledge when they visit the internet again. Individuals who have a positive experience on the internet will expect a similar experience next time. What a person receives from the internet in the past will be what that person expects to receive from that medium in the future (LaRose and Eastin, 2004). Also, with or without conscious knowledge of realizing how one's situations and life experiences have affected one's life, one will react to social and environmental cues based on past occurrences (Gonzalez-Prendes and Resko, 2011). An instance can be seen in looking first at part of Trump's base, who have already been mentioned in this chapter as generally older, generally White, and generally undesiring of change. Brader, Valentino, and Suhay (2008) found that White US citizens are more anxious when they hear media reports about Latinx immigration than any other immigration group, such as from European nations. Stereotypical majority group cues trigger anxiety in this voting bloc of Americans. Researchers have found that this public is likely to be more susceptible to lies and manipulation in relation to Latinx immigration when the media report ties into their anxiety (Brader, Valentino, and Suhay, 2008).

For example, one of the ways immigrants, from the actual lifetime of Alexander Hamilton to now, have had to deal with pejorative rhetoric is through ethnophaulisms—racial and ethnic slurs attributed to immigrants. Due to ethnophaulisms, Mullen and Rice (2003) found that immigrants are excluded from mainstream society because the dominant culture views immigrants in a negative and derogatory manner. Immigrants, simply because of the location of their birth, often face prejudice and social division because of ethnophaulisms. This can be seen in *Hamilton* in the lyrics of Aaron Burr, who derides Hamilton in the first line as an immigrant. We must consider this characterization of Hamilton as a negative, as he includes it with "bastard" and "son of a whore." Communication matters, especially to immigrants. As Kim (1977) noted, communication is crucial to acculturation for immigrants. Immigrants who do not participate as much in the majority or mainstream society will not successfully acculturate into the society. With ethnophaulisms leading to exclusion from the mainstream society, this acculturation cannot occur. The perceptions American citizens have on immigration and immigrants are important in shaping public policy. If ethnophaulisms and a lack of successful immigrant acculturation occur, they will not only be seen as individual issues but as political ones as well. Research across disciplines has shown that group membership, such as with immigration, are often linked in the media with social issues, such as crime and terrorism. Seate and Mastro (2015) found that one inference with practical and theoretical significance is the influence of emotion on policy decision-making, stating:

> Although exposure to immigration threat coverage did not directly impact attitudes toward immigration policy or policy support behaviors, exposure did indirectly impact policy support through feelings of contempt. This result suggests that individuals may be just as likely to support legislation based on the emotions they experience in association with the issue, as they are based on the facts related to the issue. In other words, it appears that as long as individuals experience strong (and negative, in the current media environment) emotions in

association with group-related policy issues (such as immigration), individuals may engage in unsympathetic behaviors to protect what they see as their group's best interest. (p. 818)

It may be unsurprising how media shapes public opinion and policy when it comes to the topic of immigration and immigrants themselves. Research across the globe continuingly suggests that media coverage on immigration contributes to concerns over immigration policy. This has been seen in Germany, where researchers found positive association between daily media updates of migration and immigration and fears expressed by interview participants (Benesch et al., 2019). Media's influence is found in the United States, where the media generally frames immigrants in a negative light, echoing worries of an immigrant "threat" narrative that could contribute to hostile attitudes toward immigrants (Farris and Silber Mohamed, 2018). And, most importantly to this piece of work, it comes up in politicians' speech, such as when Trump used the term "bad *hombres*" to criticize Latinx immigrants while he was campaigning for president in 2016. From Trump's rhetoric and the media's coverage of it, researchers found support for the "bad *hombres*" hypothesis, influencing the public's attitude toward immigration policy (Silber Mohamed and Farris, 2020).

CONCLUSION

The rhetoric of *Hamilton* shows how communication can tie history and the present together. In doing so, immigration reform can be seen as revolutionary in terms of how politics and the arts combine to show force in what can be done when voters are informed, enlightened, and excited. In this case, Miranda has stated that he wanted to tell a story about America's past that is told by America's present. Romano and Bond Potter (2018) stated that the performance uses musical traditions of rap and hip-hop and R&B to show how the Founding Fathers were driven to make a new country out of a ragged, disunited union. From the genres of music to the lyrics and the conscious casting of people of color for the main characters, *Hamilton* is full of artistic study for rhetoric scholars. And as Romano and Bond Potter (2018) said, it deserves the scholarship:

> But *Hamilton* deserves—indeed, it demands, this kind of scholarly attention. With its widespread appeal, the show has the potential to shape how Americans understand the nation's early history for some time to come. And as part of a genre of fictional and nonfictional accounts of the Early Republic . . . *Hamilton* has created a common space for contemporary political debates about partisan

politics, race, multiculturalism, and immigration. Moreover, as a show that has been repeatedly labeled as "revolutionary," *Hamilton* needs to be explored as a historical phenomenon in its own right. (Romano and Potter, 2018, p. 6)

As the musical *Hamilton* inspired audiences with its pro-immigration rhetoric, focusing on the main character, who was an immigrant, we can see how *Hamilton* also encouraged individuals during the ascendancy and presidency of Donald Trump. Immigration policy overall is a controversial topic, and rhetoric of support and disdain can be problematic for immigrants and voters, as seen through the cognitive behavioral theory. Negative media coverage of immigration lends itself to voters and politicians not supporting immigration policy. However, as it was highly lauded, reported, and disseminated through Disney+, *Hamilton* gave immigrants and immigration policy a more positive rhetorical representation.

The United States was founded by immigrants, by revolutionaries who fought against improper taxation and treatment of colonists. People from across the Atlantic Ocean saw the New World as a place with new opportunities and freedoms. While freedom did not come for many during the American Revolution, as the *Hamilton* lyrics resonate, "We will never be free until we end slavery." Slavery for African Americans ended, but equality for all is still a fight we are struggling with today. However, diverse groups and innovative ideas, such as using minority casting in *Hamilton*, can help shed light on problems that are occurring and offer insight on solutions, compromises, and decisions. The anti-immigration rhetoric of Trump and his backers can be countered by *Hamilton*, by realizing that America started as a home for individuals who wanted to live here peacefully and who then turned the world upside down.

This work is ongoing, as the research into the Trump presidency and immigration research related to the cognitive behavioral theory continues. However, with constituents supporting immigration policies through voting and rallies, change can occur. Change is already occurring with the new Biden administration, and as lawmakers debate, rhetoric in the arts, such as in *Hamilton*, can assist with pro-immigration rhetoric in the media and in public policies. As the characters Hamilton and Lafayette state, immigrants *do* get the job done.

REFERENCES

Arivett, E. (2020). "The Timeliness of *Hamilton: An American Musical*." *Popular Culture Studies Journal* 8, no. 2.5, 126–44.

Benesch, C., S. Loretz, D. Stadelmann, and T. Thomas. (2019). "Media Coverage and Immigration Worries: Econometric Evidence." *Journal of Economic Behavior and Organization* 160, 52–67.

Brader, T., N. A. Valentino., and E. Suhay. (2008). "What Triggers Public Opposition to Immigration? Anxiety, Group Cues, and Immigration Threat." *American Journal of Political Science* 52, no. 4, 959–78.

Brantley, B. (2015). "Review: 'Hamilton,' Young Rebels Changing History and Theater." *New York Times*, August 7, 2015. https://www.nytimes.com/2015/08/07/theatre/review/Hamilton--young-rebels-changing-historyand-theater.html.

Dobson, K. S., and D. J. A. Dozois. (2001). "Historical and Philosophical Bases of the Cognitive Behavioral Therapies." In *Handbook of Cognitive-Behavioral Therapies*, 2nd ed., edited by K. S. Dobson. New York: Guilford Press.

Ellis, A. (1989). "Comments on My Critics." In *Inside Rational-Emotive Therapy: A Critical Appraisal of the Theory and Therapy of Albert Ellis*, edited by M. E. Bernard and R. DiGiuseppe. San Diego, CA: Academic Press.

Farris, E. M., and H. Silber Mohamed. (2018). "Picturing Immigration: How the Media Criminalizes Immigrants." *Politics, Groups, and Identities* 6, no. 4, 814–24.

Fox, B. (2020). "Trump Leaves Mark on Immigration Policy, Some of It Lasting." Associated Press News, December 30, 2020. https://apnews.com/article/joe-biden-donald-trump-politics immigration-united-states-a5bfcbea280a468b431a02e82c15a150.

George, D. (2019). "'Hamilton' Timeline: From Miranda's 'Joke' to Obama's White House to Broadway to Chicago." *Chicago Tribune*, April 18, 2019. https://www.chicagotribune.com/entertainment/theater/ct-ae-hamilton-exhibition-timeline-0421-story.html.

Gonzalez-Prendes, A. A., and S. M. Resko. (2011). "Chapter 2: Cognitive Behavior Theory." *Smith College Studies in Social Work* 81, no. 4.

Hogeland, W. (2018). "From Ron Chernow's *Alexander Hamilton* to *Hamilton*: An American Musical." In *Historians on Hamilton: How a Blockbuster Musical Is Restaging America's Past*, edited by R. C. Romano and C. Bond Porter, 17–41. New Brunswick, NJ: Rutgers University Press.

Kendall, P. C., and S. D. Hollon, eds. (2013). *Cognitive-Behavioral Interventions: Theory, Research, and Procedures*, vol. 21. Academic Press.

Kim, Y. Y. (1977). "Communication Patterns of Foreign Immigrants in the Process of Acculturation." *Human Communication Research* 4, no. 1, 66–77.

LaRose, R., and M. S. Eastin. (2004). "A Social Cognitive Theory of Internet Uses and Gratifications: Toward a New Model of Media Attendance." *Journal of Broadcasting and Electronic Media* 48, no. 3, 358–77.

Monteiro, L. D. (2016). Review Essay: "Race-Conscious Casting and the Erasure of the Black Past in Lin-Manuel Miranda's *Hamilton*." *Public Historian* 38, no. 1, 89–98.

Mullen, B., and D. R. Rice. (2003). "Ethnophaulisms and Exclusion: The Behavioral Consequences of Cognitive Representation of Ethnic Immigrant Groups." *Personality and Social Psychology Bulletin* 29, no. 8, 1056–67.

Romano, R. C., and C. Bond Potter. (2018). "Introduction." In *Historians on Hamilton: How a Blockbuster Musical Is Restaging America's Past*, edited by R. C. Romano and C. Bond Potter. New Brunswick, NJ: Rutgers University Press.

Seate, A. A., and D. Mastro. (2015). "Exposure to Immigration in the News: The Impact of Group Level Emotions on Intergroup Behavior." Available at *Communication Research* 44, no. 6 (2017): 817–40.

Silber Mohamed, H., and E. M. Farris. (2020). "'Bad Hombres'? An Examination of Identities in US Media Coverage of Immigration." *Journal of Ethnic and Migration Studies* 46, no. 1, 158–76.

Spagat, E. (2021). "Biden Bets Big on Immigration Changes in Opening Move." Associated Press News, January 20, 2021. https://apnews.com/article/biden-inauguration-joe-biden-mexico immigration-us-news-8d565946dfdec1f365bef-dada879023e.

Stasio, M. (2015). "Off Broadway Review: 'Hamilton' by Lin-Manuel Miranda." *Variety*, February 17, 2015. https://variety.com/2015/legit/reviews/review-hamilton -public-theaterlin-manuel-miranda-1201435257/.

Timm, J. (2016). "The 141 Stances Donald Trump Took during His White House Bid." NBC News, July 26, 2016. https://www.nbcnews.com/politics/2016-election /full-list-donald-trump-s-rapidly-changing-policy-positions-n547801.

Vankin, D. (2017). "A 'Hamilton' Timeline: How a Single Song Grew into a Global Musical Juggernaut." *Los Angeles Times*, August 10, 2017. https://www.latimes .com/entertainment/arts/theater/la-ca-cm-hamilton-history-timeline-20170813 -htmlstory.html.

Watson, J. B. (1924). *Behaviorism*. New York: People's Institute.

Weissert, W., and N. Merchant. (2021). "Immigrants, Activists Worry Biden Won't End Trump Barriers." Associated Press News, February 8, 2021. https://apnews.com/article/joe-biden-el-salvador-coronavirus-pandemic-immigra-tion-michael-pence-dcf280136d3abf820bb1e7418e1e762b.

Chapter 9

The Sphere Where It Happens

Reading Hamilton's Representations of the Public/Private Sphere as Gendered, Restraining, and Revolutionary

Erika M. Thomas

In the summer of 2020, society was adjusting to a new understanding of "public" during the ongoing COVID-19 pandemic. Many people in America grappled with their contentious desire to celebrate Fourth of July publicly despite cancellations of Independence Day events and recommendations to stay home (Wolfson, 2020). That same weekend, Lin-Manuel Miranda's live stage recording of a 2015 *Hamilton* Broadway performance aired on the Disney+ streaming service with 1.8 million households tuning in for the debut (Frankel, 2020). Thus, as the pandemic restrained and changed people's relationships with public, private, and domestic spheres, *Hamilton* generated a public text through its viewership.

However, as notable as the significantly sized audience and circumstances surrounding the musical film's release are, this chapter considers *Hamilton*'s rich subtext and relevant messages that revise the discursive and ontological states of public/private delineation. In this chapter, I conduct a narrative textual analysis of *Hamilton* to interrogate Miranda's commentary and themes on the public and private, the constructions' representations, and their significance in interpreting the film's gender dynamics. Reading through a feminist lens, I will argue that the musical's lyrics, narrative, and visual elements challenge assumptions and gender roles framed according to the public and private/domestic spheres. Initial idealizations of the public/private sphere are eventually exposed as fictional, deficient, and counterproductive to the democratic and accessible values they claim to uphold. Thus, Miranda's *Hamilton* offers a critique of the public/private assumptions rather than accepting them at face value, which communicates a more progressive understanding of the film's gender representations, challenging feminist claims that the film iterates a patriarchal story.

I begin with literature reviews on the public/private sphere theory and gender criticisms relevant to *Hamilton*. Next, I examine discursive messages and representations of the spheres in *Hamilton*'s storyline and illustrate how it both reifies and challenges the traditional assumptions surrounding publicity and its relation to patriarchy.

THE PUBLIC/PRIVATE DICHOTOMY AND FEMINIST CRITIQUES

The theoretical development of "the public" and its relation to democratic communication has remained "ubiquitous in contemporary social theory," especially in Western scholarship (DeLuca and Peeples, 2002, p. 127). These theoretical conceptualizations of the public sphere share significant thematic consistencies. For Dewey (1927), the public necessitates "a certain amount of public discussion" in American democracy and representative government (p. 181). Fearing its loss, Dewey upholds the public as a fundamental ideal vital to communities and continued democracy. Complementary to Dewey's theory, Habermas (1991) provides one of the most influential and pervasive framings of the public and private spheres in Western society and within academic literature (Wahl-Jorgensen, 1999; DeLuca and Peeples, 2002).

For Habermas, the emergence of a bourgeois public sphere developed in a European context of changing trade market economies, initiating and requiring communication of information. It involved "private persons," who "did not 'rule'" but used "the standards of 'reason' as a means to undercut the principles of dominating authority or concentrated power" (Habermas, 1991, p. 28). Persons in public engaged in debates and dialogues in taverns, coffeehouses, and literary societies. Another condition required individuals to have unrestricted freedom of speech when assembling and communicating opinions. It generally involved enlightenment, education, and information gathering from early press so people could discuss and deliberate matters of common good for the population. In Great Britain, for example, the public marked dissipation in censorship, creation of the first representative cabinet, and a perception of flourishing public discourse. Thus, Habermas's bourgeois public sphere became an exemplar construct for "true" democratic governance standing in sharp contrast to the private, intimate, familial sphere, which was not reserved for state governing and rational-critical discourse.

However, Habermas concludes, during the nineteenth century, a social-structural transformation of the public sphere occurred due to state expanded activity and influence from mass media and private interests. Though the public sphere no longer exists as it once did, Habermas ultimately historicizes and reifies an idealization of the public and its emancipatory potential. Wahl-Jorgensen (1999) explains that "the metaphorical nature of the 'public sphere' makes it a heuristic regulative ideal, rather than an orthodox prescription of a particular situation of mediation." (p. 30). It is the yardstick for comparing the ideal communicative and democratic condition.

The public sphere is recognized as powerful and provocative, and it has received criticisms and endorsements in scholarship (DeLuca and Peeples, 2002; Wahl-Jorgensen, 1999). One recurring critique is that the public sphere is patriarchal because it is discursively and politically distinguished from the private, a separation fundamental to Habermas's conception and the public's supposed emancipatory power (McLaughlin, 1998; Calhoun, 1992). Historically, the descriptions exemplify the segregation of certain individuals and topics and represses and relegates other individuals, bodies, and concerns to the private. For this reason, Habermas's public and private spheres are often contested by feminist scholars for failing to acknowledge their gendering and the public's masculine tendencies and assumptions (Calhoun, 1992; Benhabib, 1992; Fraser, 1992; Landes, 1988; Ryan, 1992; Eley, 1992).

Prior to Habermas, bodies politic and the exclusion of groups of people were common in "the realm of the *polis*," or the public (Arendt, 1958). Due to exclusions based on gender, class, and race, Habermas's account only touts its inaccessibility (Fraser, 1992). Further, the public is constructed with masculinist biases, like Rousseau's "ideology of the republican motherhood," which charged women with "agency" as protectors and cultivators of men in homes but "still not accepted in public" (Berg Paup, 2021). Overall, modernist approaches to accessibility and rules of law were "predicated on removing women, and women's speech, from the public sphere" and further legitimized in legal discourse (Landes, 1988, p. 204; Enloe, 2004).

Additionally, Habermas's public is reserved for "legitimate" discourse on political issues impacting *all* people, while the private and familial is perceived as irrelevant and appropriately isolating (Calhoun, 1992; Fraser, 1992; Benhabib,1992). Habermas's limiting characterizations of the public's discourses are: "1) state-related, 2) accessible to everyone, 3) of concern to everyone, 4) and pertaining to common good or shared interest" (Fraser, 1992, p. 128). The problematic definition eliminates issues specifically affecting women, including welfare, child-rearing, domestic violence, reproductive freedoms, and caring of others. "One of the most potent mechanisms for political silencing is dichotomizing 'public' and 'private'" and the idea "that not only women's concerns but women themselves were most 'naturally' kept within the allegedly private sphere" (Enloe, 2004, pp. 73–74). Scholars endorse upending the public's parameters to encourage social advancement, equal representation, and diverse voices and topics otherwise limited or previously excluded from the public sphere (Ryan, 1992).

My purpose for recapping such social theory and the critiques of Habermas's theory is to illustrate how the public and private spheres have become mythical and privileged manifestations in collective imaginations and, accordingly, aligned with traditional gender roles. The literature makes obvious the public sphere's representations throughout the musical and reveals ways that *Hamilton* plays with and inverts public/private as social and theoretical concepts.

READING *HAMILTON* AS A GENDER CRITICISM

Academic literature on *Hamilton* is generally limited but growing. In published analyses, including mainstream media reviews and entertainment blogs, focus is given to racial representation, casting, historical nostalgia, or subversive retelling of American history (Mehltretter Drury, Mehltretter Drury, and Egan, 2021). *Hamilton* is credited as revolutionary in its cultural or political impact, given its unique application of history to address present-day conflicts and controversies (Mehltretter Drury, Mehltretter Drury, and Egan, 2021; Romano and Potter, 2018). The musical is understood for crafting an American story of a founding "father" that unsettles the traditionally whitewashed and privileged assumptions behind the trope of the American Dream. *Hamilton* comments on themes of "public memory, national and cultural identity, and democracy and social change" (Mehltretter Drury, Mehltretter Drury, and Egan, 2021, p. 3). This musical biography brings forth diverse voices and critiques the limited roles of marginalized individuals in America's past. Given this context, some attention has been given to its portrayals of gender and the framing and messages pertaining to gender relations.

In mainstream commentary, reactions are generally mixed, and some critics argue that *Hamilton* is really a show centering on Eliza's agency, legacy, and career in preserving Hamilton's story (El-Mahmoud, 2020; Dray, n.d.). However, despite moments and rhetoric that emphasize the agency of women portrayed in the musical, most feminist critics view the representations of women as traditional and problematic, especially when scenes and lyrics show them stereotypically as sexualized, untrustworthy, or silenced (Wolf, 2018; Harbert, 2019; Harvey, 2019; Berg Paup, 2021). While the historical accuracy and context justify the limited portrayals to a degree, Miranda's strategy of retelling and subverting the historical narrative leaves other viewers longing for developed gender representations and improved presence of women in public and political plotlines (Harvey, 2019; Robbins, 2020; Berg Paup, 2021). Regardless of conflicting interpretations, the show's discourse reiterates and reflects ongoing struggles for women in politics today.

While I see validity in the analyses arguing "the musical is not a feminist work at its core" (Harbert, 2019, p. 261; Wolf, 2018; Berg Paup, 2021), I intend to interrogate the surface reading of representations and context around the women in *Hamilton*. I show how viewing traditional portrayals of the spheres in Act I of *Hamilton* initially reinforces traditional gender roles and limits progressive readings. However, I also diverge from these analyses by arguing that Hamilton's story disrupts normative understandings of the public/private sphere and its gendered elements. Rather than focusing examinations on representations of *Hamilton*'s women, I analyze the story's commentary on masculinity and gender roles of male characters.

Kervin (1990) explains that many gender analyses

> approach the definition of femininity and the representation of women as compared to men, implicitly or explicitly setting up masculinity and the image of the male as the norm, the point from which women's images deviate. This tendency works to naturalize male representations and the definitions of masculinity, shifting attention away from the representations' and definitions' origin within changing belief systems. (pp. 51–52)

Since masculinity is performative, influenced by culture, shifting throughout history, and responsive and reactionary to changes in femininity, "masculinity must be approached not as the normative referent against which standards are assessed but as a problematic gender construct" (Kimmel, 1987, p. 10; see also Kervin, 1990, p. 52). A reading of hegemonic masculinity is necessary for understanding the positioning of men and how "masculinities grapple for cultural power along a continuum," subordinating others to retain power and control (Hatfield, 2010, p. 528). The analysis can then compare how gender roles are positioned against masculine portrayals (Hatfield, 2010).

Following the same method utilized by Hatfield (2010), I examine the spheres and masculine portrayals and constructs in *Hamilton* through a "narrative thematic analysis" to "trace the entire story as it develops and impacts the characters" rather than just limiting analyses to "component themes" (p. 530). *Hamilton* exposes the mythical nature of a participatory public sphere while also critiquing masculine, patriarchal, public conditions. After examining the traditional representations of both spheres, I analyze the attributes and commentary on hegemonic masculinity and its intertwinement with men's roles in the public. I argue that the discourse and performances in *Hamilton* demonize traits of hegemonic masculinity and expose the public's traditional male gender roles as toxic and self-destructive. Although the musical limits explicit, positive representations that advance historical and future roles of women in American politics, *Hamilton*'s narrative operates as a call for audiences to rethink gender tropes and norms in regard to women's agency, influence, and voice in American politics.

TRADITIONAL REPRESENTATIONS OF THE PUBLIC AND PRIVATE SPHERES IN *HAMILTON*

Representations and references to the traditional conception of the public sphere are both explicit and implicit in *Hamilton*'s lyrics, performances, and mise-en-scène, especially in Act I. In "Aaron Burr, Sir," Burr takes an eager and enthusiastic Hamilton to a tavern, or public house. Though the set design remains minimal throughout the musical, the stage changes with the removal of street lampposts and the addition of an A-frame table and makeshift bar. Hamilton and the audience "meet" revolutionary legends John Laurens, Marquis de Lafayette, and Hercules Mulligan, who are congregating, drinking beer from steins, and freestyling. The trio's beatboxing rap introductions symbolize public dialogues or debate, representing the conception of the public. Furthermore, the lighting changes from the initial blue backlights to spotlights as characters enter into this sphere.

The actors perform their arguments through lyrics, enacting public decision-making during the Revolution and crystalizing its powerful idealization and mythical significance in the founding of American democracy. Laurens invites Burr to speak (sing a verse) and "drop some knowledge." Hamilton instigates Burr for his disengagement: "If you stand for nothing, Burr, what'll you fall for?"

The song "My Shot" continues to spur imagination of the public sphere. Although the song also serves as an introduction to Hamilton's ambition, "My Shot" references the social imperative to articulate arguments, in this instance, the claims that supported revolutionary war. In the second verse, Hamilton opines that Britain is "shittin' on us endlessly" and taxing Americans "relentlessly." As he preaches, Laurens, Lafayette, and Mulligan surround him, performing reactionary engagement with his ideas and speech. Throughout the song, verses that characterize and describe Hamilton or operate as internal monologues are performed away from other actors who pose as part of the mise-en-scène, whereas when the various actors engage in arguments about the revolution, they commingle, performing as a participatory public by giving undivided attention around a table or forming and reacting as a crowd. The public is envisioned as Laurens calls to "get this guy [Hamilton] in front of a crowd." Lafayette brings out a platform, a literal soapbox, which Hamilton stands on to pontificate to colonists to "handle our financial situation." The ensemble also serves as members of the "public." Throughout both numbers, the lighting is blue backlights and/or single spotlights on Hamilton when verses are internal monologues, whereas they bump or fade up in white lighting indicating scenes of participatory public deliberation.

Throughout the musical, the public sphere is not just performed in dialogue and song; it is also represented in props, such as pamphlets or newspapers. In "The Schuyler Sisters," Angelica is handed a pamphlet during the sisters' excursion to downtown. Angelica raps, "I've been reading *Common Sense* by Thomas Paine / So men say that I'm intense or I'm insane" making reference to the hysteria associated with women's "extremism," or involvement in politics, given the patriarchal bias of the time. While feminist analyses express disappointment with the performance since any empowerment is mitigated by the women's search for husbands, it is still an example of how Miranda begins to invert the two spheres. Angelica, Eliza, and Peggy are in public, again symbolized by the bright white lighting, the publications as props, and the ensemble's actions around them. During the chorus, a member of the ensemble is featured dancing with a book, signaling the reading and education necessitated by the public.

Another idealistic public deliberation is enacted in "Farmer Refuted," when Hamilton's debate against Reverend Samuel Seabury, a defender of British colonialism, is portrayed. Seabury, standing on a platform, sings portions of "Free Thoughts on the Proceedings of the Continental Congress." Hamilton's lines are inserted through declarative rapping of his opposing arguments, eventually shifting the cadence of Seabury's song. Thus, the debate is opposing in both the content of ideas but also in the way the two singers duel in volume, tone, meter, and key, which is blatantly called out by Hamilton's provocation, "Don't modulate the key then not debate with me" (Harvey, 2019).

These examples in Act I of *Hamilton* portray idealism and virtue of the colonies seeking independence from Britain, which seems unlikely without a vibrant and healthy public sphere. Yet despite the perceived celebration of these ideals, Schudson (1992), in an essay investigating the notion of publics during the Revolutionary era, determines that "the idea that a public sphere of rational-critical discourse flourished in the eighteenth or early nineteenth century, at least in the American instance, is an inadequate, if not incoherent, notion" (p. 146). Schudson's research debunks the belief that eighteenth-century American politics engaged in widespread educated, "rational-critical" deliberation about politics with the population. Based on these facts, the musical film highlights the theatrical and hyped representations of a public sphere and the way the spheres are propagated as imaginary constructions, which leads to troubling implications.

The two spheres are delineated along a public and private binary shortly after the Schuyler sisters are introduced. Besides "The Schuyler Sisters," all other songs featuring women of *Hamilton* are performed in a "private" setting, whereas the men are uninhibited in moving between the "public" and "private" throughout the rest of the musical. Therefore, not only are discussions around politics, war, and the new structuring of the American political system romanticized but the gender roles of men and women are reasserted, especially in Act I, based on implied settings alone.

Further, gender roles performed are grounded in tradition. For Hamilton and masculine-identified characters, identities are constituted by hegemonic masculinity most commonly associated with "'superior' behaviors such as toughness and belonging in the public sphere; heterosexuality, misogyny, and financial power; and business ownership, physical size, and patriarchy" (Abbott and Geraths, 2021, pp. 40–41). Alternatively, the women of *Hamilton* are occupied with courtship, marriage, and child-rearing, all within the realm of domesticity, which certainly minimizes their enfranchisement. This reflects the history of Western women, showing "that traditional modes of drawing this distinction . . . [legitimize] women's oppression and exploitation in the private realm" (Benhabib, 1992, p. 93). As such, the reification of distinctions between the two spheres in *Hamilton* fails to acknowledge the progression and advancement for women today. These initial representations support the critiques that the portrayals of women and their roles are traditional and that the mise-en-scènes confine women to the private sphere (Wolf, 2018; Berg Paup, 2021).

INVERSING AND SUBVERTING REPRESENTATIONS OF THE PUBLIC AND PRIVATE SPHERES IN *HAMILTON*

Before Act I ends, a few performances establish more nuanced relationships that Hamilton and Burr have with the two spheres. Beginning with the song "Dear Theodosia," a lullaby-ballad that serves as love letters to the firstborn children of Burr and Hamilton, the duet symbolically places the men in the private or domestic sphere, symbolized by darker lighting, the single chair as prop, and a softened change in musicality from the loud, fast-paced rapping. Given this is a story of America and one that centers on Founding Fathers, Miranda's retelling tends to privilege the private spheres, which would not likely receive as much attention in history lessons of revolutionary heroes. The private sphere is made equal to, if not more important than, the public sphere; both "settings" are given nearly equivalent attention in the musical based on consideration of the songs' "public" or "private" contexts.

In "Dear Theodosia," tension between the spheres is expressed. Burr sings and admits that "domestic life was never quite my style." The claim establishes the men's insecurities in the sphere that is generally attributed to women, which reasserts the gendered double standard, since *Hamilton* men move between the spheres, but the women of *Hamilton* remain restricted and never revised in a publicly active role. At the same time, Hamilton and Burr expose their weaknesses and *lack* of control in such "private" spaces, since their children's smiles "knock them out" and cause them to admit they "fall apart" even though they thought they were too smart to react that way. "Dear Theodosia" is one of a few songs that garner sympathy for the characters as they admit feelings of naivety and a renewed commitment to their families, resulting from becoming new fathers. Miranda not only elevates the importance of their roles as fathers but as *engaged* fathers. Both Burr and Hamilton explain that their fathers were not around for them and vow to change that trend by promising to be present. Additionally, they sing, "I'll do whatever it takes (I'll make a million mistakes) / I'll make the world safe and sound for you" at the same time. This view of fatherhood is consistent with contemporary or "new age" social expectations of fatherhood, a likely revisionist perspective, given the separate responsibilities of men and women at that time. As the song ends, Burr and Hamilton seem less committed to their roles to intimately and domestically protect their children and, instead, foreshadow their work in public, justifying to "bleed and fight for you," "make it right for you," and "lay a strong enough foundation" to pass on.

If "Dear Theodosia" sets up the choices available to the main characters, "Non-Stop" is the moment that specific paths for their work and attention are declared, which I believe foreshadows their tragic allegories in Act II. Hamilton's ceaseless work ethic is emphasized in "Non-Stop." He agrees to run the treasury before Washington can finish asking for his commitment. As Eliza calls Alexander, asks him to "look around," and croons, "helpless," likely in reference to her perceived state without him, Hamilton's final lines in the song include, "I have to leave" / "They are asking me to lead" and "I am not throwin' away my shot." These lines become part of the medley or mashup of other song motifs as the other leads and the ensemble add, "He never will be satisfied," "Why do you assume you're the smartest in the room?" "History has its eyes on you," and "Just you wait," which positions Hamilton's tragic ending, arrogance, and ignorance.

In Act II, the subtext surrounding the notion of "home" becomes more positive and less demonized. In her essay, Berg Paup (2021) argues that "Miranda emphasizes how important the public sphere is to Alexander when he frames going home as punishment given to him by General George Washington [in Act I's] 'Meet Me Inside'" (p. 112). I contend that the revived value assigned to "going home" in Act II is a direct critique of Hamilton's qualities and his willingness to feed his public ambition. The private sphere is likewise elevated in "The Room Where It Happens," when, telling the story of the Compromise of 1790, Madison and Jefferson compromise District of Columbia as the nation's capital in exchange for Hamilton's debt plan. Madison privately asks Jefferson, "Wouldn't you like to work a little closer to home?" and Jefferson responds, "Actually, I would." Similarly, in "One Last Time," George Washington deciding to go home implies that leaving the public sphere is honorable, imperative, and desirable. In one verse, Washington instructs Hamilton to "take a break," which is significant, since in the performance of "Take A Break," Hamilton chooses work over spending time with his family, another rejection of the private sphere. Washington asks for relaxation, taking a break and offering to share a drink with Hamilton. Washington "teaches" the public how to say "good-bye" to the very sphere he led. Here the private sphere is a reward and privilege. "I wanna sit under my own vine and fig tree . . . At *home* in this nation we've made" [emphasis added]. Washington reminds Hamilton that the goal of independence was to attain comfort in their own private space, thereby privileging it.

HAMILTON: REVEALING THE PUBLIC'S MYTHS

Although *Hamilton* limits women to the private in nearly every scene, the musical's Act II explicitly showcases the influence of women on men. Political affairs are determined in the private sphere in more than one instance. "The Election of 1800" shows Burr campaigning at "homes" and instructing wives, "Tell your husbands to vote for Burr." It is illuminating because it breaks from traditional conceptions of men making decisions, although it also exhibits the critique that *Hamilton* portrays subversive agency and the ideology of Republican Motherhood (Berg Paup, 2021). Still, in this instance, the public is directed by the women, which interrupts the power relations typically imagined in public.

Additionally, the storyline does not explain how ideas manifest independently for Hamilton, instead, it shows Angelica relaying opinions to Hamilton in "Take A Break." As if reading her letter addressed to Alexander, she implores him: "You must get through to Jefferson / Sit down with him and compromise." She encourages him to not give up and that she is cheering for him despite their distance. Thus, Hamilton's eventual willingness to compromise with Jefferson comes from private correspondence with Angelica. Although Angelica and Eliza are inhibited from advancement, the most important and productive endeavors from Hamilton in the second half of the show are credited to their influence.

In "Burn" and "Who Lives, Who Dies, Who Tells Your Story," audiences are shown women's subversive agency at work (although, again, restricted to domesticity). After learning of Hamilton's affair, Eliza engages in erasure to hide her broken heart from the public: "I'm erasing myself from the narrative / Let future historians wonder how Eliza reacted . . . " She also holds the control over Hamilton's private persona, as she literally sets fire to their letters onstage. "I'm burning the memories / Burning the letters that might have redeemed you." Later in "Who Lives, Who Dies, Who Tells Your Story," Eliza asserts control—"I put myself back in the narrative"—securing Hamilton's legacy and Washington's monumentalizing due to her work (and women's work) to tell their story. Women, despite their segregation, controlled the narrative all along. And yet, Eliza asks rhetorical questions: "Will they tell *our* story? Will they tell *my* story?" [emphasis added]. These questions, though unanswered in the musical, are addressed by the production, as critics argue that *Hamilton* really is the tale of Eliza (El-Mahmoud, 2020). As such, "Burn" and "Who Lives, Who Dies, Who Tells Your Story" portray the work of women as the only action that can truly redeem Hamilton's reputation, placing immense value on the women surrounding Hamilton and the domestic sphere. Yet it curbs the progressivism in gender relations. The ending starts to disrupt the traditional gender expectations, but it does not go far inverting it since women's public work is never shown. However, the rhetorical questions are valuable, as they ask who generally controls public narratives and why.

The song that best alters manifestations of an idealized public sphere is "The Room Where It Happens." Although many people today are disillusioned by contemporary politics, *Hamilton* imparts that the "true" principles of democracy and confidence in deliberative ideals faded long before the twenty-first century. In Act II, the Congress is not "working" accordingly ("not every issue can be settled by committee"), and their fighting "isn't pretty." In short, democratic deliberation in representative government is not as imagined, and the public sphere is a guise for political decisions happening in private. It reveals both the exclusionary and secretive nature of deals and compromises on issues that affect the general public. We learn that the success of Hamilton's treasury plan lies in the decisions "that are happening over dinner." In reference to the Compromise of 1790, the song reveals, "No one else was in the room where it happened. . . . No one really knows how the game is played," with lyrics comparing politics to the mystery of dealmaking and secret recipes. Thus, in the spirit of the song, audiences never really learn what was discussed, as Jefferson, Madison, and Hamilton are shown talking and dining onstage but their words are never heard. Democratic principles are referenced only to be minimized: "My God, In God We Trust / But we never really know what got discussed." The performance is furthered by

Burr's exclusion, yet he remains the main narrator/singer. The ensemble sings "Thomas claims" to emphasize that Jefferson's version of events cannot be determined as true. Rather than disclosing what actually happens, Hamilton only sings of his ambition. Miranda keeps the musical number performative of the uncertainty rather than allegorizing details. "We want our leaders to save the day / But we don't get a say in what they trade away." The willingness to keep public interests from the public is exposed, since we do not know what is "sacrificed." Likewise, in "We Know," Hamilton and Madison promise to keep Hamilton's affair secret, assuring him, "The people won't know what we know." Confirming the insidious, private state of politics relayed, Inabinet (2021) describes *Hamilton*'s lasting messages as "the circulation of . . . salacious vice still [governing] American public life" and one that "dramatizes the strength of a system concealing evil underneath layers of virtue display" (p. 136). Thus, the "reality" of the supposed public sphere is that it is a myth in democratic politics and leaders have placed personal ambition over democratic principles. "Public" work is most likely resolved in private spheres of influence.

HAMILTON'S TRAGIC TALE OF HEGEMONIC MASCULINITY

Hamilton communicates warnings about maintaining public/private idealizations most pointedly through character allegories. Hamilton's story reflects prioritizing political ambition and pride over family and his own life, which parallels his relationships with the two perceived spheres. Most importantly, it is his privileging of the public sphere over his private accomplishments that result in his greatest losses and tragedy. As mentioned earlier, in "Take A Break" Hamilton resists the domestic sphere when refusing to vacation up north with his family so he can work. Ultimately, his obsession with work results in his affair. Hamilton, himself, justifies it in "Say No To This," describing himself as sleep-deprived, "weak," "in need of a break," yearning for the companionship of Angelica and his wife, and it was then, at that moment, Maria Reynolds entered his life. Without the support and presence of the other women he desires, Hamilton has an affair with another. As if the affair is not tragic enough, Hamilton confesses to it publicly in "The Reynolds Pamphlet," for, although the confession of the affair is detrimental to his reputation and his family, he will not "sully" his name in accusations of speculation and embezzlement. In this way, making "public" the publication that describes his affair, an event that should stay in the "private," sabotages both any chance of becoming president and hurts his marriage. Hamilton's disregard for the private is emphasized in "The Reynolds Pamphlet," as three lines emphasize that the sexual encounters occurred in his private residence with frequent encounters "at his own house" and followed by the chorus's commentary by a drawn out "damn." The Reynolds Pamphlet's audience is particularly shocked by that violation as shown by the lyrics' repetition.

Likewise, Eliza shames Hamilton for using the public sphere to air publicly their private matters. She lists off the violations, which are publishing the letters written by Reynolds, documenting the affair, and pointing out that to save his reputation, he broke not only their marriage but also their lives. She also asserts that the public is not privy to her heart, their bed, and the knowledge of what happened. Thus, the private sphere is held up as sanctified, a lesson that Hamilton never comes to learn. She also calls out Hamilton's personal insecurity by pointing out his obsession with a legacy and his paranoia and insecurity of how he is perceived by others. It is this claim that further reveals Hamilton's public persona as dangerous and "senseless," one characterized by attributes of hegemonic masculinity, including individualism, breadwinning and ambition, sexual promiscuity, and violence and toughness. Eliza's solo declares the consequences of Hamilton's behavior: tearing her heart and forfeiting their love. In the end, Eliza expresses hope that Hamilton will burn because of his actions.

Eliza's desire manifests as Hamilton succumbs to two other tragedies: the death of his son and his own fatal decision to duel. In "Blow Us All Away" Philip Hamilton, Hamilton's firstborn son, dies in a duel with George Eacker due to Hamilton's own notions of hegemonic masculinity. Hamilton advises his son how to allegedly "end" the matter, "Stand there like a man until Eacker is in front of you / When the time comes, fire your weapon in the air." Although Hamilton discourages the killing of Eacker, Hamilton encourages hegemonic masculinity both by supporting a defense of his honor and advising Philip to duel.

In the duel between Hamilton and Burr, Hamilton again follows "rules" of hegemonic masculinity. In "Your Obedient Servant," Hamilton describes himself as "just a guy in the public eye" trying to do what is best for his country. He claims he has no intention to apologize and also asserts, "I won't apologize for doing what's right." Alluding to his public persona, Hamilton commits to his own "intemperance," as Burr points out, and stubbornly insists on dueling. Burr's ending then becomes equally tragic. The duel that defines Burr's life comes about because he envies and resents Hamilton's power and influence. In "Your Obedient Servant," when Burr references to wanting to "be in the room where it happens," the stage lighting turns a sinister red. Thus, following the public's expectations is not just detrimental for Hamilton, it also secures Burr's infamous legacy as the renowned villain who shot Hamilton and thereby punishes Burr for following in Hamilton's footsteps.

Generally, men and women are disciplined by culture to follow prescriptive gender norms and "not deviate from the script" (Hatfield, 2010, p. 528). However, Miranda's *Hamilton* teaches viewers to tread cautiously around such expectations. I contend the liberal subtext in *Hamilton* criticizes the traditional notions of public life and corresponding gender roles, disparaging such conventions. Miranda's retelling of Hamilton's story teaches viewers that Hamilton's downfall derives from the privileging of his public work and hegemonic masculine persona. Reynolds and Neville-Shepard (2021) identify Hamilton and Burr as "tragic heroes, with their accomplishments and legacies . . . becoming overshadowed by the stubbornness of their competitive spirits" (p. 41). While they argue that *Hamilton* is an allegory of the American Dream and materialistic myth, I conclude that *Hamilton* is also a warning against idealizing the public/private divide and normative gender roles. Feminist theory teaches that "patriarchal gender roles are destructive for men as well as for women" (Tyson, 2015, p. 83). *Hamilton* thus communicates that man's demise comes from a commitment to hegemonic masculine ideals (individualism, extreme ambition, "strength," fear or refusal to fail). Berg Paup (2021) agrees that "Hamilton's masculine honor was at stake," one "that both necessitated a response to a physical challenge and required an avoidance of any discussion of emotion. This ideology of public masculinity is what ultimately led to his demise" (p. 113). Protecting his masculinity resulted in the loss of everything that was once important to Hamilton—his political ambition, the life of his son, and his own life.

CONCLUSION

In the midst of a quarantine, a sizable public was brought together by *Hamilton* on Disney+ (Frankel, 2020; Spangler, 2020; Durkee, 2020). *Hamilton*, the notable text, reminds viewers that screens not only bring forth a public but that "media produce the public sphere and public screen as primal scenes of Being" and "institute the scene or open the spaces from which epistemologies and ontologies emerge" (DeLuca and Peeples, 2002, p. 132). "Publics" are not "real" or inherent, but constructed. It therefore necessitates questioning social constructs because society will often uncritically accept theoretical concepts and media representations without realizing their implications. As such, critics should pay close attention to texts' messages, like those in *Hamilton*, to understand how they invoke social knowledge. After all, since media is among the influences inculcating "gender rules" (Kervin, 1990), it can also change them.

Thus, I conclude that *Hamilton*'s narrative did more than just incite a public when Disney+ brought a Broadway blockbuster into private homes. The story provides a vital subtext, containing richly layered messages and ideologies about the public. It is not sufficient to interpret characters' representations and roles in a vacuum; instead, I endorse using the musical's storyline to understand how the text critiques and constructs history and conditions of future possibility.

Hamilton does invoke familiar and problematic American myths. It glamorizes the Founding Fathers' public and politics and largely places virtuous women and their livelihoods in the domestic/private sphere. However, deeper critical observations illuminate Miranda's metacritiques. His portrayals lead to rethinking public/private spheres and their influence on "gender rules," which, in turn, results in a more progressive understanding of the film's gender representations, challenging initial criticisms that *Hamilton* affirms patriarchal premises.

Despite Act I's familiar representations of the public/private, Act II exposes the public sphere as fictional and troubles the dichotomy to upend conventional assumptions about the public and its value. Furthermore, regardless of conflicting interpretations, contemporary musicals such as *Hamilton* have potential. Though they "draw attention to America's exclusionary history even as they continue to tell stories that centre white male experience," they also "open up the storehouse of cultural memory of the founding era to invite in new interpretations of the past and present" (Harbert, 2019, p. 263). Although *Hamilton* falls short in providing revisionist representations of women in public, Miranda uses a tragic tale of Hamilton, who resists the domestic and clings to his toxic, masculine persona, to show audiences that tropes such as qualities of hegemonic maculinity and portrayals and advancement of women are still limited. Thus, *Hamilton* calls for rewriting scripts of imagined spheres and learning from the problematic, patriarchal narratives; otherwise, society risks continuing to silence the stories of people already marginalized from the public.

REFERENCES

Abbott, J. Y., and C. Geraths. (2021). "Modern Masculinities: Resistance to Hegemonic Masculinity in Modern Family." *Journal of Contemporary Rhetoric* 11, no. 1/2, 36–56.

Arendt, H. (1958). *The Human Condition.* Chicago: University of Chicago Press.

Benhabib, S. (1992). "Models of Public Space: Hannah Arendt, the Liberal Tradition, and Jürgin Habermas." In *Habermas and the Public Sphere*, edited by C. Calhoun, 73–98. Cambridge, MA: MIT Press.

Berg Paup, E. (2021). "Chapter Seven: Patriarchy and Power: A Feminist Critique of *Hamilton*." In *Rhetoric, Politics, and Hamilton: An American Musical*, edited by J. P. Mehltretter Drury and S. A. Mehltretter Drury, 105–23. New York: Peter Lang.

Calhoun, C. (1992). "Introduction: Habermas and the Public Sphere," In *Habermas and The Public Sphere*, edited by C. Calhoun, 1–48. Cambridge, MA: MIT Press.

DeLuca, K. M., and J. Peeples. (2002). "From Public Sphere to Public Screen: Democracy, Activism, and the 'Violence' of Seattle." *Critical Studies in Media Communication* 19, no. 2, 125–51.

Dewey, J. (1927). *The Public and Its Problems*. Athens: Swallow Press/Ohio University Press.

Dray, K. (n.d.). "*Hamilton*: Does the Critically Acclaimed Musical Have a Problem with Its Female Characters?" *Stylist*. https://www.stylist.co.uk/life/hamilton-musical-disney-plus-female-characters-schuyler-sisters-sexism/404847.

Durkee, A. (2020). "'Hamilton' Boosts a Struggling Disney as Broadcast Dominated Streaming Platforms in July." *Forbes*, August 10, 2020. https://www.forbes.com/sites/alisondurkee/2020/08/10/hamilton-boosts-a-struggling-disney-as-broadcast-dominated-streaming-platforms-in-july/?sh=6f6880852500.

Eley, G. (1992). "Nations, Publics, and Political Cultures: Placing Habermas in the Nineteenth Century." In *Habermas and the Public Sphere*, edited by C. Calhoun, 289–339. Cambridge, MA: MIT Press.

El-Mahmoud, S. (2020). "Why I'm Convinced *Hamilton* Is Actually Named after Eliza." Cinema Blend, July 10, 2020. https://www.cinemablend.com/news/2549876/why-im-convinced-hamilton-is-actually-named-after-eliza.

Enloe, C. (2004). *The Curious Feminist*. Berkeley: University of California Press.

Frankel, D. (2020). "Disney Plus 'Hamilton' Viewership Exceeds Those Who've Seen It Live, Research Company Says." NextTV, July 20, 2020. https://www.nexttv.com/news/disney-plus-hamilton-viewership-exceeds-those-whove-seen-it-live-research-company-says.

Fraser, N. (1992). "Rethinking the Public Sphere: A Contribution to the Critique of Actually Existing Democracy." In *Habermas and the Public Sphere*, edited by C. Calhoun, 109–42. Cambridge, MA: MIT Press.

Habermas, J. (1991). *Structural Transformations of the Public Sphere*. Translated by Thomas Berger and Frederick Lawrence. Cambridge, MA: MIT Press.

Harbert, E. (2019). "Embodying History: Casting and Cultural Memory in 1776 and Hamilton." *Studies in Musical Theatre* 13, no. 3, 251–67.

Harvey, T. A. (2019). "Who Tells Your Story? Intersections of Power, Domesticity, and Sexuality Relating to Rap and Song in the Musical, *Hamilton*." Master's thesis, Michigan State University. ProQuest (Publication No. 13879250).

Hatfield, E. F. (2010). "'What It Means to Be a Man': Examining Hegemonic Masculinity in *Two and a Half Men*." *Communication, Culture and Critique* 3, 526–48.

Inabinet, B. (2021). "Chapter Eight: Bondage and Circulation." In *Rhetoric, Politics, and Hamilton: An American Musical*, edited by J. P. Mehltretter Drury and S. A. Mehltretter Drury, 127–44. New York: Peter Lang.

Kervin, D. (1990). "Advertising Masculinity: The Representation of Males in *Esquire* Advertisements." *Journal of Communication Inquiry* 14, no. 1, 51–70.
Kimmel, M., ed. (1987). *Changing Men*. Newbury Park, CA: Sage.
Landes, J. B. (1988). *Women and the Public Sphere in the Age of the French Revolution*. Ithaca, NY: Cornell University Press.
McLaughlin, L. (1998). "Gender, Privacy, and Publicity in 'Media Event Space.'" In *News, Gender, and Power*, edited by C. Carter, G. Branston, and S. Allan, 71–90. New York: Routledge.
Mehltretter Drury, S. A., J. P. Mehltretter Drury, and H. Egan. (2021). "Chapter One: Introduction: *Hamilton* as Cultural and Rhetorical Phenomenon." *Rhetoric, Politics, and Hamilton: An American Musical*, edited by J. P. Mehltretter Drury and S. A. Mehltretter Drury, 31–45. New York: Peter Lang.
Reynolds, M., and R. Neville-Shepard. (2021). "Chapter Three: *Hamilton* and the Entelechy of the American Dream." In *Rhetoric, Politics, and Hamilton: An American Musical*, edited by J. P. Mehltretter Drury and S. A. Mehltretter Drury, 31–45. New York: Peter Lang.
Robbins, H. (2020). "*Hamilton*—The Diverse Musical with Representation Problems." *The Conversation*, June 29, 2020. https://theconversation.com/hamilton-the-diverse-musical-with-representation-problems-141473.
Romano, R. C., and C. Bond Potter. (2018). "Introduction: History Is Happening in Manhattan." In *Historians on Hamilton: How a Blockbuster Musical Is Restaging America's Past*, edited by R. C. Romano and C. Bond Potter, 1–14. New Brunswick, NJ: Rutgers University Press.
Ryan, M. P. (1992). "Gender and Public Access: Women's Politics in Nineteenth-Century America." In *Habermas and the Public Sphere*, edited by C. Calhoun, 259–88. Cambridge, MA: MIT Press.
Schudson, M. (1992). "Was There Ever a Public Sphere? If So, When? Reflections on the American Case." In *Habermas and the Public Sphere*, edited by C. Calhoun, 143–63. Cambridge, MA: MIT Press.
Spangler, T. (2020). "'Hamilton' Drives Up Disney Plus App Downloads 74% over the Weekend in U.S." *Variety*, July 6, 2020. https://variety.com/2020/digital/news/hamilton-disney-plus-premiere-app-downloads-72-percent-1234698795/.
Tyson, L. (2015). *Critical Theory Today: A User Friendly Guide*, 3rd ed. New York: Routledge.
Wahl-Jorgensen, K. (1999). "Ensuring Richness and Diversity of Representation in the Public Sphere: Mass Media as Forums for Democratic Debate." *Journal of the Northwest Communication Association* 27, 24–52.
Wolf, S. (2018). "*Hamilton*'s Women." *Studies in Musical Theatre* 12, no. 2, 167–80.
Wolfson, E. (2020). "The Fourth of July Weekend Threw America's Coronavirus Failures into Stark Relief." *Time*, July 6, 2020. https://time.com/5863324/july-fourth-coronavirus/.

SECTION IV

Revelations about Broadway

Chapter 10

Who Lives, Who Dies, He Tells the Story

Hip-Hop, Antagonist-Narrators, and the Impact of Musical Genre on Storytelling

Max Dosser and Kevin Pabst

How does a bastard, orphan, son of a whore and a Scotsman, dropped in the middle of a forgotten spot in the Caribbean by providence, impoverished, in squalor, grow up to have the story of his life narrated by the man who killed him? While *Hamilton* is deservedly praised for many groundbreaking achievements, it is at the same time indebted to many musical theater traditions and tropes. One such element is the character archetype of Aaron Burr, who serves as both narrator and primary antagonistic force—the person directly responsible for Alexander Hamilton's death. Burr opens the musical with a direct question to the audience, challenging the likelihood of Hamilton's success given his origins. This question immediately sets up the tension that the musical will be focused on a man that Burr believes *should* be his inferior but, in reality, is not. Rather, he exceeds Burr in every capacity that Burr holds dear, intensifying Burr's jealousy and frustration until the rivalry climaxes with their fateful duel. This type of theater production and this antagonist-narrator archetype have their precedents, most notably *Jesus Christ Superstar* with Judas Iscariot—where Judas believes Jesus is out of control and has drifted from the approach that will bring them practical success—and *Amadeus* with Antonio Salieri—where Salieri is tormented by Mozart's genius and seemingly effortless success.

While this antagonist-narrator role has been the subject of much work in literature (including Agatha Christie's *The Murder of Roger Ackroyd* and Vladimir Nabokov's *Lolita*, among many others), less scholarship has centered theater. Despite this, the antagonist-narrator role not only allows for a unique character arc, it also has an undeniable impact on the unfolding of the overall narrative of the work. This type of role is well loved by the theater community, as the actors who originated Burr and Salieri (Leslie Odom Jr. and Ian McKellen, respectively) won Tony Awards for their performances, and Ben Vereen was nominated for originating Judas. The narrator archetypes in musical theater vary, as seen with the Narrator from *Into the Woods*, Emcee in *Cabaret*, and Officer Lockstock in *Urinetown*, as well as Burr, Judas, and many others. Depending on which narrator archetype is deployed, the unfolding of the narrative and the audience's understanding of the production can be impacted, which is one reason why the narrator has been at the center of theatrical innovations throughout the twentieth and twenty-first centuries (Martens and Elshout, 2014).

The narrative of a theatrical production and audiences' understanding of it are also impacted by the music genre of the production. Different genres have distinctive themes, lyrical conventions, and musical aesthetics, influencing not only *what* types of stories are told through song but *how* those stories are told and interpreted. The nature of the rock opera, for example, mandates an abundance of glitz, glamour, and excess, driving the aesthetics of *Jesus Christ Superstar*'s sound, stage, and costume design in very specific directions. Furthermore, rock music mandates specific sounds, lyrical rhyming schemes, and emotional affects. The antagonist-narrator Judas is a sleeveless, diva punk rocker who screams many of his numbers—his vocal performance rife with grit and grain. Conversely, the genre of hip-hop necessitates a much different approach to narrating in *Hamilton*. The dense lyrics and complex rhyming schemes that pack as many words per second into a song as possible enable more to be said, and the emotional vulnerability and authenticity that are key staples of the genre open the way for a deeper dive into the psyche of the antagonist-narrator.

In this chapter, we argue that the possibilities and constraints of the narrator within a theatrical production are dictated not just by narrative archetypes but by musical genres as well. A consistent refrain sung by Burr and other characters throughout *Hamilton* is "who lives, who dies, who tells your story?" The way the stories in musical theater are told—and by extension, the ways audiences understand the narratives and the values implicit within them—are driven by both the narrator archetype and the music genre of the production. We begin by demonstrating how narration and music are intertwined in musical theater and that they shape one another in the production of a narrative. Second, we propose a *genre-dependent narrator model* for interpreting musical narrators that pulls from this unique combination of narrative and genre scholarship. Third, we apply our genre-dependent narrator model to Burr in *Hamilton* as well as to Judas in *Jesus Christ Superstar* and Salieri in *Amadeus*, as the two other most prominent theater antagonist-narrators. Finally, we conclude by looking to the finale of *Hamilton*, in which the narrator shifts. This moment both illustrates Burr's uniqueness among antagonist-narrators and entrenches the importance of considering the performance of authenticity of musical genre in theater narration.

STORYTELLERS AND MUSICAL AUTHORSHIP

There is debate within the field of narratology about who qualifies as the narrator and what exactly makes a narrator a narrator. Thomson-Jones (2007) claims that a narrator is "a fictional agent who tells or shows a story" (p. 79), while Spearing (2015) suggests a narrator has come to mean "a hypothetical but supposedly necessary figure internal to the narrative" (p. 60). These are two drastically different understandings of what a narrator is and how meaning is affected within the story, but both definitions are limited in understanding the complex role of the narrator. Whereas Thomson-Jones's overlooks when the narrator is a real person, such as in documentaries, Spearing's fails to consider that the narrator does not need to be internal to the narrative to be a narrator. Often, the narrator serves as an uninvolved third party—a concept that can be traced back in theater to the narrating function of the Greek Chorus (Margolin, 2014). The various definitions provide the contours of the specific rhetorical dimensions of a narrator, and a point of agreement among many is that "there can be no narrative without a narrator" (Barthes, 1977, p. 109).

A central aspect of the debate centers on the differentiation between the author and the narrator. Currie (2010) argues that "there is no distinction that should or can be made between authors and narrators . . . narratives are communicative artefacts: things made in such a way as to communicate, and not merely to represent, their stories" (p. 65). Hogan (2013), however, posits that "the real author exists as a person in the material world and the narrator does not" (p. 37). The reason that this debate matters for our argument is due to the perceived authenticity of the narrator. Authenticity is a central aspect not only for the believability of the narrator (Doležel, 1980) but also for music genres—particularly that of hip-hop.

While the trickiness and often problematic nature of boxing music within firm genre lines has been written about extensively (Brackett, 2016; Demers, 2010; Drott, 2004; Fellezs, 2011; Holt, 2007), the impact of specific values, traditions, and themes strongly associated with specific genres on the form and function of music is significant. Born (2011) writes that genre operates as "a point of contingent convergence between musical formations and social formations" (p. 385). Building on Holt (2007), who argues that genres are identified with specific cultural values just as much as they are with music, Fellezs (2011) claims that genre can also create and mediate ideas about identities such as race, gender, and social class. Brackett (2016) suggests that genres "may be understood as modes of feeling, and as ways of experiencing embodied emotion" (p. 14), and he provides the most useful conceptualization of genre for our purposes: "The point of articulation between music analysis—the formal or technical description of music—and the social meanings and functions of music" (p. xvi). Additionally, Kelly (2020) maintains that forms such as genre "[impose] order onto content and [dictate] how audiences are invited to understand and relate to particular messages" (p. 22). In these understandings of genre, it is clear that a collection of cultural values that embody unique expressions of identity is just as central to a genre's formation as specific musical techniques, compositionally or performatively.

The coalescence of musical traits and cultural expressions is important for our genre-dependent narrator model, as the distinctions between narrator and author are further nuanced when considering the specific context of music. Negus (2011) maintains that musical authorship is mediated, constructed, and contested and that it exists at many levels, all of which are important to consider when evaluating narrative function in musical productions. While the "real author" is the actual individual who wrote the text, the "implied author" is the constructed and particular sensibility conveyed by the text through the views and values expressed directly or indirectly, which may or may not align with those of the real author. For Negus, the "narrator" is simply the figure that tells the story, or a specific part of it. The narrator and the author, real or implied, are not necessarily the same. This is further nuanced by the function of "persona" within music, the character a performer plays, which similarly may or may not align with the real author, implied author, or narrator of a song. For example, in David Bowie's song "Ziggy Stardust," the real author of the song is David Robert Jones, known professionally as David Bowie; the implied author is the sensibility promoting a rags-to-riches-to-rags-again narrative arc; and the narrator speaks in omniscient third person, singing about the character Ziggy Stardust. Yet the persona in which David Bowie performs while singing this song is Ziggy Stardust himself, even though the narrator of the song is not Ziggy. Thus, authorship, narratorship, and persona are three distinct factors of any given musical text, particularly, as we frame it, within musical theater.

The concept of a narrator in theater studies is similar to that of cinematic and literary narrators. Genette (1993) writes that theater narration comes from the *reading* of the drama and stage directions, and Searle (1975) argues, "The author of the play is not in general pretending to make assertions; he [*sic*] is giving directions as to how to enact a present which the actors then follow" (p. 328). Chatman (1990), however, challenged previous conceptions of the drama narrator by proposing a model where the narrative agency depends on whether the narrative agent is an overt teller figure or an impersonal, covert figure more concerned with showing. Expanding on Chatman's model, Jahn (2001) proposed an alternative model in which the performed text and the scripted text are given separate but related slots in the hierarchy of theatrical narrator performance. Research on theatrical narrators continues to blossom, including Fuchs's (2014) work on omniscient narrators in drama—a title that almost certainly applies to Burr. Burr not only acknowledges his role as narrator but also presents his near-omniscient (as, to be fair, he does not know what occurred in the room where it happened) knowledge through passing his narrating duties to Hamilton for the "Say No To This" number. This moment is important to note, as Burr hands the narration not only to Hamilton but to Lin-Manuel Miranda, who both played Hamilton and wrote the musical. Narratology scholarship seems to indicate that this author-narrator divide is particularly important, and we argue that the musical genre is central to exploring *how* narrators tell their stories.

THE GENRE-DEPENDENT NARRATOR MODEL

With an importance established for the distinction between author and narrator as well as the varying levels of authorship and narratorship in music, we propose a genre-dependent narrator model for interpreting the significance and impact of the narrator on audience perception of musical productions, unfolding over five steps:

1. *Identification of narrator.* Drawing from the works of narratology and musicology cited above, we define the narrator of a theatrical production as the character or figure who conveys the story to the audience. The narrator may be a character in the production who interacts with other characters, an omniscient presence who is not involved in the actual events of the story, or some combination of the two. Furthermore, multiple narrators may exist for a single production. When this is the case, this model can be applied to each individually. Regardless, identifying who the narrator/s is/are and what specific type/s of narrator they are is the first step toward interpreting the impact they have on an understanding of the narrative.

2. *Degree of narrator's authorship.* For the purposes of this step, we refer to Negus's "implied author." The "real author" of a production—the actual individual(s) who wrote the text—rarely, if ever, functions as the narrator in a musical production. While Miranda, the real author of *Hamilton*, does play a narrator in the character of Alexander Hamilton at times throughout the production, it is important to note that in these cases, the narrator is Hamilton, *not* Miranda. For the purposes of this model then, the degree of authorship with which we are concerned is that of implied authorship—the sensibility, perspective, or lens through which the events of the narrative are filtered. In the case of third-person omniscient narrators who are uninvolved in the events of the narrative and who present the story matter-of-factly, supposedly without bias, a degree of authorship may not be readily apparent. In the case of narrators who are also characters involved in the events of the story, however, this level of implied authorship becomes more significant. Identifying the degree to which a narrator's authorship shapes or influences the direct or indirect perspective of the narrative is thus an important step in our model.

3. *Detailing the narrator's persona.* When narrators do possess a level of implied authorship over the telling of the story, analyzing how that particular authorship impacts the narrative can be aided through examining the narrator's persona—the specific character traits and motivations that drive the way the narrator behaves and that shape the ways in which the narrator conveys information to the audience.

4. *Identification of key genre traits.* As music genre influences the tone, aesthetic, and cultural codes of a narrative, parsing out the specific traits, values, and traditions of a musical production's genre is key to determining how the telling of the story is filtered through yet another lens. This step requires additional research, as each production to which this model may be applied could feature multiple musical genres. The key elements of a genre can be identified through a combination of academic scholarship, music criticism, artist testimonials, and fan discourse, so as not to privilege a singular realm of knowledge production. And while problematics with genre still abound, analyzing how popularly understood genre traits help shape the decisions, behaviors, and actions of a narrator is nonetheless a significant step of this model.

5. *Implications.* Using these different lenses through which a musical narrative is filtered—narrator, author, persona, and genre—one then examines how audience understanding of the story being told is affected.

What emotional responses might viewers of a musical have as a direct result of these factors? How do these different filters influence the narration, and to what end? This step is made clearer through comparison to other musical productions with similar stories and/or narrators, and it is for this reason that we offer *Jesus Christ Superstar* and *Amadeus* as points of comparison—to more fully illustrate how audience understandings of musical productions are shaped by the factors we examine in this model.

THE MUSICAL NARRATION OF AARON BURR, SIR

In applying our model to Aaron Burr as well as Salieri and Judas, we must first provide the contours of what the antagonist-narrator is. An antagonistic force in theater, literature, and other media can be many things, but we use the definition provided by Baldick (1996): "The most prominent of the characters who oppose the protagonist or hero(ine) in dramatic or narrative work" (p. 15). The antagonist is often viewed as a villain, but if the protagonist is an antihero or evil, the antagonist can be a sympathetic and virtuous character (think Macduff in *Macbeth*), which many readers may find to be the case with our examples. The way we conceive of the antagonist-narrator archetype, then, is the character or figure who conveys the story to the audience while simultaneously putting up the primary obstacles that interfere with the protagonist's goals. The criteria we use to establish an antagonist-narrator is that the figure must 1) act in opposition to the protagonist, and 2) "tell" the story to the audience (though that telling can take multiple forms).

With our definitions in mind, we now turn to Burr, Salieri, and Judas. While all are antagonist-narrators, their functions in their productions are quite different. Salieri, it could be argued, is the lead character of *Amadeus*, as the narrative is essentially him telling the audience why he plans to kill himself. Judas, on the other hand, is a minimal presence in *Jesus Christ Superstar*, sitting out large portions of the musical. Then there is Burr. Similar to Salieri and Judas, Burr is the first central figure to speak in the production, introducing the audience to the story much in the way we introduced the reader to this chapter. Burr's antagonism is portrayed through his rivalry with Hamilton. While Salieri has a higher position and is able to undermine the genius yet puerile Mozart, Judas is a disillusioned follower of the increasingly self-absorbed Jesus. Burr is neither Hamilton's superior nor his follower. While he prefers to think of them as equals (or even himself slightly above Hamilton), the musical portrays Hamilton in the superior role, with more influence, bravery, and gumption. Just as Salieri undermines Mozart through his influence in the court and Judas pleads with Jesus in an attempt to change his ways, Burr often interferes with Hamilton's goals. But in many ways, Burr does this through *not* taking action. His inaction, his waiting for it, puts him in contrast to Hamilton with his ceaseless, ambitious climbing.

Additionally, while not a required aspect of the antagonist-narrator, Burr, Salieri, and Judas also all directly contribute to the death of the protagonist. Judas provides Jesus's location to Annas and Caiaphas, which leads to Jesus's arrest and death. The fictional Salieri would be pleased he is included in this list, as his goal is to be remembered as Mozart's murderer—a goal that goes unrealized by the end of the play. Even so, there are arguments to be made that through Salieri's undermining of Mozart at court, the sabotage of his rise in the social standing of Vienna, and the pressure he placed on Mozart to compose while he was ill all directly contributed to Mozart's poor health and ultimate death. In contrast to Salieri, there is no doubt that Burr's actions are responsible for Hamilton's death. In one of the few moments where Hamilton does actively undermine Burr—a moment in which the sympathies of the musical seem to shift from the protagonist to the antagonist—Burr challenges Hamilton to a duel after Hamilton refuses to apologize for turning the public against Burr and costing him the presidency. Burr shoots Hamilton, and Hamilton later succumbs to his wounds. While it is clear how Judas, Salieri, and Burr function as antagonists, their narration styles vary greatly and bring into question the level of authorship in each narrative.

This brings us to the second step of the model. In considering the implied authorship of the narrator, it is best to think of it in terms of how the audience relates to the narrator's telling. The implied authorship is high when the narration is such that the audience's assumed understanding of what happens in the narrative is the same as the narrator's, while it is low when the audience may have differing opinions. This is elucidated through the various narration styles of Salieri, Judas, and Burr. Salieri breaks the fourth wall throughout the narrative, even performing an invocation at the start of the show to raise the lights on the audience so he can see as he addresses them. While the audience may not agree with Salieri's actions, the entire narrative is filtered through his memories and his voice. As such, the level of implied authorship in *Amadeus* is extremely high. Judas is on the other end of the spectrum. While Salieri speaks to the audience and even freezes the action in various scenes to offer the audience insight, Judas narrates in the second-person perspective. Rather than speak to the audience, Judas appears to speak his narration to Jesus, even when Jesus is not onstage with him. Judas moves the action along with his songs, and he both sets up the narrative and closes it out, but his role is more rooted in a narrative told by someone else. Some may argue that Judas is not a narrator at all, but that is because the level of implied authorship is quite low. Judas is as much a narrator as Che in *Evita*, El Gallo in *Fantasticks*, and the Narrator in *Into the Woods* (Robinson, 2015).

Burr, however, falls somewhere between Salieri and Judas. Burr does directly address the audience, as evidenced by the very first line of the musical. Burr, however, is also absent for stretches throughout Hamilton, similar to Judas, though not to the same extent. But he certainly is not an ever-present figure in the narrative like Salieri is. Despite his absences, if Burr were the only one to ever address the audience, he would have a very high level of implied authorship, but that is not the case. The first song of the musical, "Alexander Hamilton," ends with all the major characters in the first act telling the audience their relation to Hamilton: "Me, I trusted him," "Me, I loved him," and so on. Throughout that song, different characters take on the role of revealing Hamilton's past, such as George Washington being the one to tell the audience that Hamilton's cousin committed suicide. "Alexander Hamilton" is not the only song where Burr's narrating duties are performed by someone else. As mentioned earlier, in "Say No To This" Burr tells the audience, "Alexander's by himself, I'll let him tell it." Additionally, Angelica and Eliza Schuyler narrate the action in "Satisfied" and "Who Lives, Who Dies, Who Tells Your Story," respectively. As such, while Burr is the antagonist-narrator for the musical, his level of implied authorship falls well below that of Salieri: he has a level of implied authorship over certain parts of the story but not all of it.

How that authorship is perceived by the audience has much to do with Burr's persona, which is the third step of our model. For most of the musical, Burr is a reserved and ambitious politician who seeks to climb the political ladder while stepping on as few toes as possible. His professional philosophy is summed up in his oft-repeated line "talk less, smile more, don't let them know what you're against or what you're for" first sung in the song "Aaron Burr, Sir." Through attempting to build bridges with everyone while alienating no one, Burr does not express support for any particular stance. When Hamilton, conversely, starts achieving far more success through loudly and aggressively expressing his own often divisive views, Burr flares with jealousy, confusion, and frustration.

Yet Burr's apparent opportunism becomes more nuanced as *Hamilton* progresses. Through revelations of complicated relations with his now-deceased parents, the struggle of living up to his familial legacy, and a love affair he must keep quiet, Burr's philosophy of not taking a public stance is recolored from spineless self-ambition to carefully calculated patience, an attempt to assert control over one aspect of his life when he has lost it over so many others. The pains and struggles of Burr's past contextualize his present actions and make him more sympathetic in the eyes of the audience.

That sympathy is aided by the fact that Burr is a likable character played with aplomb by Leslie Odom Jr. Although Burr is reserved, appears outwardly opportunistic, and is the primary antagonist to Hamilton, he is still friendly and even something of a mentor to Hamilton well into the second act of the musical. Indeed, the two consider themselves friends, often joke with each other, and until near the end, seem to share a mutual respect for one another. Despite the demands of his "talk less, smile more" philosophy and its resultant disingenuity in his professional life, the audience is nonetheless incredibly endeared to Burr through his vulnerability and authenticity—two elements that are central to the genre of hip-hop and that also are only expressed by Burr when he directly addresses the audience as narrator, not when he engages with other characters.

Moving to the fourth step of the model, we now identify key traits of hip-hop as a genre. As countless hip-hop artists have revealed across interviews and testimonials, authenticity is a central component to the genres of hip-hop and rap. As Kajikawa (2015) explains, "Rap musicians and fans ascribe great value to authentic expression. . . . Such authenticity . . . is a quality that musicians seek to inhabit but that listeners ultimately ascribe" (p. 6). Authenticity and vulnerability are key to hip-hop's impact on the way that Burr as a narrator functions in *Hamilton*, as evident through three tenets of the genre: the performative codes, musical structure, and cultural values.

As music critic Adam Neely and NYU music technology professor Ethan Hein (2020) discuss in a video essay on the translatability of hip-hop songs to other genres through covers, part of what makes hip-hop feel authentic and genuine is the very staging of vulnerability. Unlike many other genres, most hip-hop artists do not play instruments while they perform. Neely and Hein suggest that instruments like guitars can function as shields, putting a physical barrier between performer and audience and granting singers an additional layer of performance to hide behind. For hip-hop artists, however, there typically is no such shield—nothing between performer and audience. The power and the meaning of the lyrics being sung become more prominent, and the vulnerability of the artist is highlighted.

Authenticity is further facilitated through the lyrical structure of hip-hop. Less beholden to melodic structures, hip-hop music uses rhythm as its primary structural force. This enables a greater range and quantity of potential lyrics. Melodic lines, such as those in pop or rock music, tend to have fewer words per second than rap or hip-hop do, as the vocal performance of melody is more technically difficult to execute at a faster pace than the vocal performance of rhythm. The increase in quantity of lyrics does not necessarily mandate an increase in authenticity and vulnerability, but by virtue of having more lyrics per song to work with, it does enable artists to engage themes in more depth, which can lead to more authentic and vulnerable performances.

Furthermore, authenticity and vulnerability are evident through the unique political commitments of hip-hop. Davis and Gross (1994) describe within hip-hop an "ethos of the subaltern . . . a politically situated sense of cultural ethos . . . [that] challenges dominant cultural and political orders with ideologically subversive schemes" (p. 66). Harrison and Arthur (2019) build upon this by suggesting that one of the primary tenets of hip-hop's very ethos is a committed politics of action and loyalty, manifesting around "generating and promoting counter-knowledge, repurposing property/space as a public good, and maintaining a loyalty to hip-hop and its communities of origin and practice" (p. 15).

Hip-hop-afforded authenticity through performative code, musical structure, and cultural value all influence the narration style of Burr in *Hamilton*. In "Wait For It," Burr's solo number in which he addresses the audience and explains the context driving his own motivations, Burr stands alone center stage, a single spotlight on him. The ensemble is offstage for the first half of the song and remain in the dark when they enter. Burr stands completely still for the first verse and pre-chorus, and afterward only walks a few steps. There is no dancing or intricate choreography, unlike the majority of the songs in *Hamilton*. Burr swings his arms during the final chorus, though the movement is staged more as a gesture than a dance. The very choreography of this number stages an intimate vulnerability: this is just Burr addressing the audience, no frills, no other layers of performance to hide behind, only the words he sings. This staging of vulnerable authenticity is apparent in other numbers, such as "Dear Theodosia" (performed by Burr and Hamilton, both addressing their newly born children) and "Burn" (performed by Eliza, addressing Hamilton), when such intimacy is most effective for the narrative.

The musical structure of *Hamilton*'s hip-hop score facilitates such authenticity. Libresco (2015) found that at 20,520 total words over two hours and twenty-three minutes, *Hamilton* averages 144 words per minute. Such a feat is only possible through the musical genre of hip-hop. The lyrical density enables more nuanced, detailed, and thorough exploration of themes and topics than possible in the slower words-per-minute rates of other genres. And while not the fastest singer in *Hamilton* (that honor belongs to Marquis de Lafayette), Burr would simply be unable to communicate the same depth of emotions and thus the same degree of authenticity in numbers such as "Wait For It," "The Room Where It Happens," "Your Obedient Servant," and "The World Was Wide Enough" in the more limited word count of other genres.

Finally, hip-hop's ethos of committed political action that challenges dominant political and cultural ideologies and promotes counter-knowledge could not be more evident than it is in *Hamilton*. Miranda's initial idea for telling the story of Alexander Hamilton was through a mixtape, so using the genre of hip-hop to tell the story of this immigrant Founding Father was key from the start. In this way, the genre of hip-hop drives the entire narrative. Black, Latinx, and minority individuals are cast as White historical figures. The historical anachronisms and a music genre central to American minority cultures are employed in order to promote a counter-knowledge that challenges dominant hegemonic ideologies about the founding of America. This extends to Burr, as the figure who most directly conveys information to the audience. Burr's narration style is influenced by the hip-hop genre not only through an emphasis on authenticity and vulnerability but also through a committed political action to resist and challenge existing hierarchies of knowledge.

The final step of the model is to look at the implications of the genre on the narrator. As we have explained, Burr's role in the musical is influenced by the tenets of hip-hop, impacting not only how his character is written but how he is received. Through the authenticity and vulnerability displayed through the hip-hop numbers, Burr becomes an incredibly sympathetic figure. *Hamilton* uses hip-hop to shade its characters, preventing them from becoming black and white, good and evil. Rather, the vulnerability reveals the flaws and strengths of all the characters, allowing for greater audience investment. As we discussed the impact of rock music on Judas in our introduction, we now turn to Salieri, who, being steeped in classical music, is both presented and interpreted much differently than Burr and Judas are. Salieri is much more villainous than Burr, and the classical music that infuses the production is not steeped in the same vulnerability and authenticity. Rather, the genre is about precision and perfection—tenets that Salieri aims for in his career. The narration, however, reveals that Mozart, the genius composer, is anything but precise, let alone perfect. The characters hide behind instruments as they perform their beautiful art, and it is only when they are away from the music that their faults are revealed to the audience. In contrast to *Hamilton*, where the music deepens audience sympathy for the characters, the music in *Amadeus* shrouds character flaws. The sympathies for Salieri, Mozart, and others are generated not through how they reflect the tenets of classical music but rather through how their characterizations so clearly conflict with them.

Through the genres of hip-hop, rock, and classical, the narration styles of these productions are vastly altered. Burr and Judas are allowed to expose their flaws, while Salieri must conceal his in an effort to convey refinement. Judas can hide behind a rock persona of glitz, glamour, and heavily melodic lines, while Burr must bear his soul through lyrics that are often more rhythmic in nature. These musical filters influence how audiences react to the narrators and to the narrative overall. Our genre-dependent narrator model does not aim to demonstrate how audience *will* react to a production but rather illustrate how, through the combination of musical tenets and narrator persona, particular themes and narratives can be more readily communicated. The musical genres raise questions about Judas's guilt, Mozart's perfection, and Burr's role in history in ways that would require entirely different methods if the music were inspired by other genres.

CONCLUSION

While Burr is the first character to speak in *Hamilton* and serves as the narrator of the musical, he is absent in the musical's final moments. Instead, Eliza becomes the narrator, taking the viewer far past the time of Hamilton and Burr's rivalry as well as past Hamilton's death. This decision is elucidated by Leslie Odom Jr., who claims that Burr spends the musical in purgatory as his punishment for killing Hamilton. He narrates the events to find out where he went wrong, and only once he relives it all can he find a measure of peace and pass on (Hunt, 2020). This is yet another way that Burr fits with the role of the antagonist-narrator while revolutionizing the archetype. Judas kills himself out of guilt for turning in Jesus, and Salieri spells out his intention to kill himself at the outset of the play. Burr, rather than kill himself, uses his narration to come to terms with his mistakes and pass the torch of telling the story—the story that is no longer about him—to someone else, a move that aligns with the authenticity and vulnerability of hip-hop.

We applied our genre-dependent narrator model to *Hamilton* using *Amadeus* and *Jesus Christ Superstar* as points of comparison in order to illustrate how, while the archetype of the antagonist-narrator is not uncommon in theater, the way Miranda utilized it in writing *Hamilton* revolutionizes the role. Through marrying an antagonist-narrator to hip-hop, Miranda created a character that is able to progress the story while also presenting a nuanced narrative that is never as simple as just his opinion. Our model can be used to analyze various types of narrators and consider not only their role in the narrative but how the genre plays into the potential interpretations. Genre conventions continue to grow and change, within theater and within music. Our hope is that this chapter demonstrates the importance of expanding Aaron Burr's final line of *Hamilton*: let's not only ask not only *who* tells your story but also *how*.

REFERENCES

Baldick, C. (1996). *The Concise Oxford Dictionary of Literary Terms*. Oxford: Oxford University Press.
Barthes, R. (1977). *Image-Music-Text*. Translated by S. Heath. New York: Hill and Wang.
Born, G. (2011). "Music and the Materialization of Identities." *Journal of Material Cultures* 16, no. 4, 376–88. https://doi.org/10.1177/1359183511424196.
Brackett, D. (2016). *Categorizing Sound: Genre and Twentieth-Century Popular Music*. Berkeley: University of California Press.

Chatman, S. (1990). *Coming to Terms: The Rhetoric of Narrative Fiction and Film.* Ithaca, NY: Cornell University Press.

Currie, G. (2010). *Narratives and Narrators: A Philosophy of Stories.* Oxford: Oxford University Press.

Davis, R. C., and D. S. Gross. (1994). "Gayatri Chakravorty Spivak and the Ethos of the Subaltern." In *Ethos: New Essays in Rhetorical and Critical Theory*, edited by J. S. Baumlin and T. F. Baumlin, 65–69. Dallas, TX: Southern Methodist University Press.

Demers, J. (2010). *Listening through the Noise: The Aesthetics of Experimental Electronic Music.* Oxford: Oxford University Press.

Doležel, L. (1980). "Truth and Authenticity in Narrative." *Poetics Today* 1, no. 3, 7–25. doi: 10.2307/1772407.

Drott, E. (2004). "The End(s) of Genre." *Journal of Music Theory* 57, no. 1, 1–46. https://doi.org/10.1215/00222909-2017097.

Fellezs, K. (2011). *Birds of Fire: Jazz, Rock, Funk, and the Creation of Fusion.* Durham, NC: Duke University Press.

Fuchs, B. (2014). "Ventriloquist Theatre and the Omniscient Narrator: *Gatz* and *El pasado es un animal grotesco*." *Modern Drama* 57, no. 2, 165–86. https://muse.jhu.edu/article/547514.

Genette, G. (1993). *Fiction and Diction.* Translated by C. Porter. Ithaca, NY: Cornell University Press.

Harrison, A. K., and C. E. Arthur. (2019). "Hip-Hop Ethos." *Humanities* 8, no. 1, 1–14. https://doi.org/10.3390/h8010039.

Hogan, P. C. (2013). *Narrative Discourse: Authors and Narrators in Literature, Film, and Art.* Columbus: Ohio State University Press.

Holt, F. (2007). *Genre in Popular Music.* Chicago: Chicago University Press.

Hunt, J. (2020). "Hamilton: Why Eliza Replaces Aaron Burr as the Narrator." Screen Rant, August 28, 2020. https://screenrant.com/hamilton-musical-eliza-aaron-burr-narrator-replace-reason/.

Jahn, M. (2001). "Narrative Voice and Agency in Drama: Aspects of a Narratology of Drama." *New Literary History*, 32, no. 3, 659–79. https://doi.org/10.1353/nlh.2001.0037.

Kajikawa, L. (2015). *Sounding Race in Rap Songs.* Oakland: University of California Press.

Kelly, C. R. (2020). *Apocalypse Man: The Death Drive and the Rhetoric of White Masculine Victimhood.* Columbus: Ohio State University Press.

Libresco, L. (2015). "'Hamilton' Would Last 4 to 6 Hours if It Were Sung at the Pace of Other Broadway Shows." FiveThirtyEight, October 5, 2015. https://fivethirtyeight.com/features/hamilton-is-the-very-model-of-a-modern-fast-paced-musical/.

Margolin, U. (2014). "Narrator." In *The Living Handbook of Narratology*, edited by P. Hühn, J. C. Meister, J. Pier, and W. Schmid. Hamburg University. http://www.lhn.uni-hamburg.de/.

Martens, G., and H. Elshout. (2014). "Narratorial Strategies in Drama and Theatre: A Contribution to Transmedial Narratology." In *Beyond Classical Narration*, edited by J. Alber and P. K. Hansen, 81–96. Berlin: Walter de Gruyter.

Neely, Adam. (2020). "Why Are There So Few Rap Cover Songs?" YouTube, September 22, 2020. https://www.youtube.com/watch?v=D_mh1Rq35ZM.

Negus, K. (2011). "Authorship and the Popular Song." *Music and Letters* 92, no. 4, 607–29. https://doi.org/10.1093/ml/gcr117.

Robinson, M. (2015). "Judas, Che and Aaron Burr, Sir! 9 Antiheroes and Narrators of Musical Theatre." *Playbill*, October 19, 2015. https://www.playbill.com/article/judas-che-and-aaron-burr-sir-9-antiheroes-and-narrators-of-musical-theatre-com-367639.

Searle, J. (1975). "The Logical Status of Fictional Discourse." *New Literary History* 6, no. 2, 319–32. https://doi.org/10.2307/468522.

Spearing, A. (2015). "What Is a Narrator?: Narrator Theory and Medieval Narratives." *Digital Philology* 4, no. 1, 59–105. https://doi.org/10.1353/dph.2015.0003.

Thomson-Jones, K. (2007). "The Literary Origins of the Cinematic Narrator." *British Journal of Aesthetics* 47, no. 1, 76–94. https://doi.org/10.1093/aesthj/ayl040.

Chapter 11

Aaron Burr vs. Mike Pence
Curtain Speeches and Controversy

Ryan Louis

My community theater is obsessed with puns. As a season-ticket holder, I experience many grinning-groaning moments of well-crafted wordplay. Before every show, the theater's executive director drums up support for the various cookies, snacks, and alcoholic beverages available (for a nominal price!) at intermission. At the recent musical production of *Matilda*, for example, the bar featured a deliciously spiked Trunchbull Punch. Though I often cringe at the obviousness of this marketing strategy, I understand it. Theaters have to hawk their wares; promote upcoming events; exchange thank-yous. Such efforts are vital to their survival. Broadway is in on the scheme too: voice-overs remind audiences to silence mobile devices, unwrap candy wrappers *now* and, above all, be mindful of important safety protocol. Many use humor; others sound outright threatening. They mean business.

Curtain speeches are ubiquitous in staged theater productions, yet there is no individual study of them and their effects in rhetorical scholarship. This is unfortunate because, as I argue, such examples of public address have important consequences—revealing how rhetors construct an ethics of theatergoing. Though they function practically to convey specific information about refreshments and emergencies, they also act as disciplining tools, highlighting acceptable decorum, and inculcate a theatrical culture vis-à-vis civic society. The genre has discursively influenced contemporary theater by norming and instantiating expectations.

I begin filling in the curtain-sized gap in public address scholarship by detailing the form and function of this understudied rhetorical genre. I do this by discussing three types: pre-curtain, post-curtain, and dramaturgical. I then look to an exemplar from *Hamilton: An American Musical* that, in the aftermath of a volatile election, ignited controversy.

DUELING VICE PRESIDENTS

Directly following *Hamilton*'s curtain call on November 18, 2016, Brandon Victor Dixon (the actor portraying Vice President Aaron Burr) made an appeal from the stage to Vice President–elect Mike Pence—in attendance that night. Pulling out a written statement, Dixon read to the assembled crowd, immediately receiving its whistling praise. He said,

> We are the diverse Americans who are alarmed and anxious that your new administration will not protect us. . . . We truly hope that this show has inspired you to uphold our American values and work on behalf of all of us. All of us. (*Hamilton*, 2016)

The address sparked a public controversy. President-elect Donald J. Trump tweeted the next morning that "our wonderful future V.P. Mike Pence was harassed last night at the theater by the cast of Hamilton, cameras blazing. This should not happen" (Trump, 2016b). Eight minutes later, Trump continued: "The Theater must always be a safe and special place. The cast of Hamilton was very rude last night to a very good man, Mike Pence. Apologize!" (Trump, 2016c).

The reactions to Dixon's address varied based on how individuals interpreted the conventions of the generic form. For Trump, it was a targeted political interruption of theater norms—violating the rules of decorum associated with post-curtain speeches. He intensified the conflict by using the rhetorical strategy of *patriotic correctness*. This contradicted the approach taken by Dixon and Pence. For members of *Hamilton*'s cast and crew, the speech was an obvious extension of the show's dramaturgical themes framing America through imbricating identities. Dixon hybridized the form—combining dramaturgical and post-curtain speaking standards—to encourage a dialogic approach with Pence. Having seen the show that night, Pence likely understood the context of its delivery and, in later communication, supported Dixon's efforts at establishing a courteous mediated dialogue. The initial public address and ensuing controversy, thus, dueled over the form and purpose of curtain speaking. Depending on where you sat that night, only one vice president staged a decorous performance.

In the next section, I theorize the rhetorical genre in which Dixon's address fits. Thereafter, I analyze the *Hamilton* curtain speech and the resulting discourse that played out across a series of tweets and media appearances.

Curtain speeches provide a path to track the controversy and its effects. By exposing the central themes of such rhetoric, I discern two highly polarized readings of the speech.

Though intermission cookies and mixed drinks are important to the well-being of a theater, I contend that a rhetorical understanding of curtain speeches—a generic form much taken for granted—can reveal important consequences about American theatrical traditions.

CURTAIN UP: GENRE AND THE THEATER

Genre has long been studied by rhetorical scholars. With roots in Aristotle's classification of forensic/deliberative/epideictic forms, scholars explore "the stylistic and substantive responses to perceived situational demands . . . to read elements common to many discourses" (Campbell and Jamieson, 1978, 19). Such investigations, Black (1965) says, open opportunities to examine argumentative processes. A rhetorical genre, then, "is a group of acts unified by a constellation of forms that recurs in each of its members" (Campbell and Jamieson, 1978, 20). Because similar rhetoric arises across time and space, the situational constraints of a generic rhetorical action may reliably predict effects.

Engaging genre as a methodology is circumspect, however, when it becomes derivative—that is, when criticism is merely a means to produce a taxonomy. Campbell and Jamieson (1978) argued that "the justification for a generic claim is the understanding it produces rather than the ordered universe it creates" (18). Rowland (1991) has a similar take: criticism of such forms, he said, is useful when "explaining the underlining form of such rhetoric or in evaluating the effectiveness of a given work" (132). To be effective, then, one must consider audience expectations and matters of decorum. And, as when notable rhetors *break the form*, controversy and implications can be far-reaching. Such study "gives the critic an unusual opportunity to penetrate [a genre's] internal workings and to appreciate the interacting forces that create them" (Campbell and Jamieson, 1978, 25).

Though genre analyses can illuminate worlds of implicative rhetoric, rhetorical scholars have yet to focus on the curtain speech. My study of Dixon's address to Vice President–elect Mike Pence requires a brief accounting to establish the form's parameters. As such, I follow Rowland's criteria for classification. I argue curtain speeches are an ontological generic form in which similarities between oratorical examples can be empirically established. Though they are epideictic in manner, they require a specific time and place—encompassing standards that cannot occur anywhere except a place co-constituted as a theater. I agree with Foley (2015), who argues for an expanded understanding of the epideictic. It is "not only to praise the praiseworthy, but also to appraise our ideals of worthiness itself. Epideictic rhetoric evaluates, and that evaluation affirms the values that a community holds, the values that hold a community together" (209).

Curtain speeches extend the form to the stage; curtain speeches help define the responsibilities of a theatrical community and, then, maintain its *decorum*. All public address is rhetorically constrained by institutional and societal customs. Decorum, as Zhang, Z, and Yang (2012) assert, involves the sensibility of a rhetor to accommodate "the economy of a speech (who gets to say what, in what manner, what is better left unsaid, and the like)" (189). Performances of appropriateness, measured by and expressed vis-à-vis rhetorical constraints, are governed by codified rules and cultural norms. Genres are not simply based in occasion "but possess an empirical existence that is held together by the logical force of perceived strategic limitations on effective (or appropriate) discourse" (Rowland, 1991, 135). Like eulogizers, the curtain speaker has some latitude with language, style, and delivery yet remains bound by forces that compel an internally consistent and *decorous* rhetorical form.

Curtain speeches must occur in a place where there is a . . . curtain! Whether literal or metaphorical, theatrical discourse uses the term "curtain" to signify the beginning ("curtain up") and end ("ring the curtain down") of staged performances. Additionally, the genre's form varies based on the *time* in which the rhetor delivers the speech ("pre-" or "post-curtain") and whether it is included as part of a scripted performance (what I call *dramaturgical* curtain speeches).

To determine the components of a curtain speech, the next section briefly analyzes blogs, newspaper articles, and critical responses to past speeches that outline generic limitations. This is not exhaustive; rather, it introduces form and some initial rhetorical implications.

PRE- AND POST-CURTAIN

Like at my local theater, pre-curtain speeches follow familiar patterns. Theater director and critic Joe Patti (2014) calls the curtain speech a "necessary evil," (1) a speech that, delivered before the show, allows latecomers to find their seats without creating disturbances. He suggests that curtain speakers use three to four minutes and ensure that the information does "not negatively impact audience enjoyment . . . [T]he curtain speech is as much a tone setting first impression as the interaction a customer has with your ticket office" (Patti, 2014, 1). Theater consultant SCG Nonprofits (White, 2016) seconds this advice. First, a pre-curtain speech must be an *invitation*:

delivered with directness, brevity, and charm. This may create a positive atmosphere and experience. Second, speakers use the form to introduce themselves and welcome the audience. Third, the speech details events pertinent to the theater's subsistence (e.g., future productions) and offers gratitude to those who may have awarded grants, co-sponsored events, or provided special assistance. Ultimately, the purpose of the speech "is to nurture the ongoing relationship with the audience" and those who contribute to its maintenance (White, 2016).

Many state and federal laws require public facilities (including theaters) to communicate emergency safety information. Therefore, the pre-curtain speech is often a repository for helping audiences locate exits and think through procedures aimed at surviving catastrophe.

Because the curtain speech has the potential to interrupt immersion (pre-curtain) and catharsis (post-curtain), some worry that certain subjects are anathema to its function. Although providing historical and sociopolitical context for a play can be educative, there is a fine line between appropriate monologuing and disruptive politicizing.

Lastly, curtain speeches police decorum by verbalizing a code of ethical theatergoing. Rhetors notably codify the behaviors that produce a "good" theatergoing public. A pre-curtain speech might suggest that it "is totally appropriate to threaten cell-phone scofflaws with some degree of bodily harm" (Rorschach Theatre, 2006). As I explain below, some may also urge civic imperatives—in the dramaturgical or post-curtain versions—that pressure audiences. There is a limit to what speakers can impart, however. A bright-line test exists for when such attempts violate decorum: say what you need to say, but don't *lecture*.

The curtain speech, though necessarily mundane, requires credibility and a fluid delivery style. Board members, theater directors, or cast members conduct it. In person, this means taking center stage to broadcast an individual's community standing. Delivery style is akin to after-dinner speaking: witticisms and humor help establish rapport with the audience. As at *Matilda*'s pre-curtain, my theater's executive director used jovial puns to sell intermission refreshments.

Many critics prefer pre-curtain speeches because performing afterward can interrupt the catharsis or general emotional power of an ending. A speech may be necessary, however, to direct flow of traffic, contextualize an evening's performance within social and political efforts, boost attempts to sell products, and/or notify the audience of after-show events.

Two recent examples of effective curtain speeches include Patti LuPone's pre-curtain address at the July 9, 2015, Lincoln Center production of *Shows for Days* and the post-curtain presentation by *Hamilton* actor Javier Muñoz on November 6, 2016.

On July 8, 2015, near the beginning of Act II, Patti LuPone—a Tony Award–winning actor—disturbed by a patron's flagrant use of her cell phone, walked in character to the offending person's seat and absconded with the phone. Though the theater returned it later, the event created a stir. The next day, LuPone appeared for a pre-curtain speech:

> Basically I'm out here to say 'hi' to you all and dispel any myth that I might do something tonight. [LuPone reenacts the previous evening's event. Audience applauds.] So basically, I'm here to ask all of you to whip out those cell phones, turn them off and come to the theater. [Applause.] I hope you enjoy the show. We love doing it. We love having you as an audience. . . . We do it for you. And, it's always one or two people who ruin it for all of us. So, I'm on your side. I do it for you. Enjoy the show. (Lincoln Center, 2015)

LuPone's standing as a credible actor satisfied the needed ethos. By rhetorically linking cell phone usage during a production to "bad" practice (i.e., one cannot truly "come to the theater" unless the device is turned off), she clarifies a standard of ethical theatrical citizenship. This audience regarded the sentiment as worthy, interrupting the speech multiple times with applause. ABC News (2015) teasingly called her "the cell phone police" and reported that audiences "gave her a standing ovation on Twitter." The speech illustrates two of the many options for meeting generic expectations and conducting an appropriate pre-curtain speech: it welcomes the audience and clearly names behaviors conducive to the theater's decorum.

Javier Muñoz took over the lead role in *Hamilton: An American Musical* from Lin-Manuel Miranda on July 11, 2016. HIV-positive and a cancer survivor, the actor took many medical-related breaks from the show to seek surgery and other treatments. On November 6, 2016, he addressed the audience in a post-curtain speech, offering "a personal testimony of thanks" to that evening's co-sponsor, the Actors Fund of America—a nonprofit organization assisting entertainers with services such as emergency relief:

> In 2002, I was diagnosed—tested positive—with HIV. And I was living in California at the time. I moved back to New York a month later. I didn't know where to go; I had just gotten my green card; I didn't know about the Actors Fund just yet. I went to GMHC [Gay Men's Health Crisis], which was the only place I knew. It was a very tough and hard counselor. Thank God she was. She was intaking me and asked me what did I do for a living. And I said I was an actor. She took off her glasses and said, "What are you doing here? Why aren't you at the Actors Fund?" And it woke me up, and I said, "What's the Actors Fund?" [Applause.] The Actors Fund helped me find my doctor who I still see today; helped me find my insurance coverage; helped me take care of payments for my medications. This is what you gave tonight. I am living proof right

here that what you do makes such a difference. [He cries; applause.] Thank you so much for all you've done; what you will continue to do; and the lives you will help. Thank you so much. [Blows a kiss and steps back.] (The Actors Fund, 2016)

As with LuPone, the actor served as an ethotic force: credible for his standing as the play's lead actor. Further, the testimony is authentic evidence to support his central claim that the Actors Fund is a valuable partner to the theater and community. The applause and positive response by the Actors Fund's (2016) subsequent media release suggests that the speech was effective.

Dramaturgical

Though many curtain speeches are live, playwrights often write one for a show's opening (*prologue*), the end of an act, and/or the final words of the production (*epilogue*). Unlike the extemporaneous versions discussed in the previous section, a dramaturgical curtain speech rarely relies on specific rules of decorum. It may act as a polemic or compel the audience to reflexively engage with the play's themes. Often, it is an overtly persuasive communiqué. Despite its exemption from some rules of decorum, it remains attached to the form and function of the genre.

Perhaps most famous for employing this device was Shakespeare. His prologues (*Romeo and Juliet*: "Two households, both alike in dignity, in fair Verona, where we lay our scene") and epilogues (*A Midsummer Night's Dream*: "And, as I am an honest Puck") serve to provide important contextual information for the audience—nixing the need for board members to stand up and say anything—or to act as a charge for the audience to go in peace and return another time. Two examples illustrate the rhetorical effects of dramaturgical curtain speeches: the final monologue of *Angels in America: Perestroika* and the musical toast concluding *Hadestown*.

Commonly referred to as the "We Will Be Citizens" speech, playwright Tony Kushner's appeal for equal rights—delivered by the play's protagonist, Prior Walters, at its conclusion—has the actor directly address the audience in front of Central Park's Bethesda Fountain:

> The fountain's not flowing now, they turn it off in the winter, ice in the pipes. But in the summer, it's a sight to see. I want to be around to see it. I plan to be. I hope to be. This disease [AIDS] will be the end of many of us, but not nearly all, and the dead will be commemorated and will struggle on with the living, and we are not going away. We won't die secret deaths any more. The world only spins forward. We will be citizens. The time has come. Bye now. You are fabulous creatures, each and every one. And I bless you: More Life. The Great Work Begins.

Though overtly political, the speech is germane to the play's diegetic elements—elegiac and a little magical. It is, like the curtain speeches examined above, redolent of epideictic traditions. This strengthens its power. Theater critic Jean Howard (2013) argues that, through this speech, "Kushner challenges his audience to renewed and refashioned political engagement. . . . Partly this meant a serious engagement with history as a way of disrupting a sense of historical inevitability and opening audiences to the possibility of change." It is, like Shakespeare, an invitation and a charge made by the central (and therefore ethotic) character about important events to come.

A second example is from the day after *Hadestown* won Best Musical at the 2019 Tony Awards. The cast and crew cleverly combined dramaturgical and post-curtain speaking. *Hadestown* fits into a new tradition of productions employing post–curtain call numbers not to advance plot but to tell "the audience how to feel about the story they have just seen and what they should tell their friends" (Soloski, 2019). These post-show "numbers serve three distinct purposes—to brighten the mood, to offer intimacy, to send the audience into the night with a parting gift" (Soloski, 2019). The curtain "falls" on *Hadestown* after the song "Return to Hell II." Not exactly an uplifting send-off, director Rachel Chavkin designed an additional number, "We Raise Our Cups," to honor the (failed) efforts of its protagonist. The song is a literal toast asking the cast and audience to "drink up. . . . And spill a drop for Orpheus." As the song progresses, the instructions continue. It ends: "To Orpheus and all of us / Goodnight, brothers, goodnight." (Andres M, 2019)

This curtain speech—like Muñoz's—offered community gratitude and influenced the audience's post-show emotional and physical well-being. After winning the 73rd Tony Award for Best Musical, Chavkin and several members of the production walked onstage. She spoke:

> Some of you maybe know this, but usually we end the show with a toast. And we'll allow [actor] Amber Gray and our beautiful company to do that properly in a moment. But we just wanted to thank you all for being here tonight because it's a very special night. [Applause.] The nominations, the awards: it's a culmination of an over 12-year journey for this show that began in Vermont. It means the world to be celebrating it here with you and for us to be here at the [Walter] Kerr [Theatre] and with this extraordinary company—both those you see and those you do not see, below. [Applause.] So raise a sippy-cup if you have one, or a hand if you don't; but cheers to our beautiful company, onstage and off. To all of you . . . thank you. (Andres M, 2019)

They pour and raise cups of champagne as the cast sings its final dirge. In this way, the director hybridizes the generic form. The speech reflected the success of the play's hero and the heroics of the musical's cast and crew. Both purposes advanced the established generic form.

In the next section, I consider the structure and purpose of curtain speeches—emphasizing how they satisfy multiple exigencies from theatrical and community partners. By recognizing VIPs, establishing sociohistorical contexts, policing behaviors, providing information about safety protocol and, finally, marketing products, they rely on epideictic modes in a specialized range of time and space. My examples illustrate how generic constraints may overlap, become salient, and lead to audience compliance with normative standards of decorum. More specifically, I take up the controversy of Brandon Victor Dixon's post-curtain speech. As *Hamilton*'s antagonist, Vice President Aaron Burr, he hybridized generic elements and created a polarized understanding of appropriate theater decorum.

CONSTRUCTING A CURTAIN CONTROVERSY

When Vice President–elect Pence arrived at the Richard Rodgers Theatre on November 18, 2016, the crowd met him with both a chorus of jeers and some light applause. He would later label this greeting as "what freedom sounds like" (Bradner, 2016). After the curtain call, he again heard crowd disapproval as Dixon stepped up to address him in his post-curtain speech:

> You know, we had a guest in the audience this evening. [Laughter.] Vice President–elect Mike Pence: I see you're walking out, but I hope you will hear [audience booing] just a few more moments. There's nothing to boo here, ladies and gentlemen, nothing to boo. We're all here sharing historic love. We have a message for you, sir; and we hope that you will hear us out. [Dixon pulls out paper from his back pocket.] And I encourage everybody to pull out your phones and tweet and post because this message needs to be spread far and wide, okay? [Reading from script:] Vice President–elect Pence we welcome you and we truly thank you for joining us here at *Hamilton: An American Musical*, we really do. We, sir, we are the diverse America who are alarmed and anxious that your new administration will not protect us, [applause] our planet, our children, our parents or defend us and uphold our inalienable rights, sir. But we truly hope that this show has inspired you to uphold our American values and to work on behalf of all of us. All of us. [Massive applause.] Again, we truly thank you for sharing this show, this wonderful American story told by a diverse group of men and women of different colors, creeds, and orientations. [Applause] (*Hamilton*, 2016)

For the most part, the speech followed the traditional form and function of a curtain speech. It contained a decorous sentiment similar to those discussed in the previous section. It utilized polite address ("ladies and gentlemen"; three uses of the word "sir"), welcoming acknowledgment ("we truly thank you for sharing this show"), and it made efforts to police audience behavior ("There's nothing to boo here"). Pence, ushered from the theater by security personnel during the curtain call, stopped to hear Dixon's speech. Afterward, with Pence out the door, Dixon turned to the audience and asked for their donations to Broadway Cares/Equity Fights AIDS, a nonprofit supported by many Broadway productions. This turn "made it clear that the purpose of the speech wasn't just to shame Pence but to remind the audience that the diverse America *Hamilton* celebrates is something worth defending" (Lind, 2016). Yet the overt political message did breach genre and Broadway norms. For New York theater, it "was a deeply felt and altogether rare appeal from the stage" (Mele and Healy, 2016).

The following Monday, November 21, Dixon appeared on the ABC talk show *The View*. He described the speech as a collaborative process:

> As a group, the producers and the creators came up with what we thought the message we wanted to deliver from the show and the cast would be and we shared it with everybody and then everybody kind of made their comments and contributions and then we decided that it was important for us to take the stage and let our message be heard. (ABC News, 2016)

The *New York Times* reported that the chief architects of the address were three men: the show's creator, Lin-Manuel Miranda; director Thomas Kail; and lead producer Jeffrey Seller. Seller acknowledged his role and the constraints of the implicit rhetorical boundaries of curtain speeches. A pre-show appeal, he argued, would have made the message less prevailing. The group debated "whether it was appropriate to inject a political statement into the night, and that those involved decided to wait until the end of the performance" (Mele and Healy, 2016).

Though there was no direct dialogue between "vice presidents" (one acting a part, one yet to take office), a mediated conversation played out over the next several days in the press. On Sunday, November 20, Pence appeared on the CBS news show *Face the Nation*. Host John Dickerson referenced Dixon's curtain speech directly—pointedly asking the vice president–elect, "Why do you think they're alarmed and anxious?" Pence responded,

> First off, we took my daughter and her cousins to the show Friday night. And, John, if you haven't seen it yet, it's a great show. I'm a history buff and my hat's off to the cast and to the extraordinary team that brought *Hamilton* to the public. We really enjoyed being there. I heard the remarks that were made at the end. What I can tell you: I wasn't offended by what was said. I'll leave to others whether that was the appropriate venue to say it. But I want to assure people

who were disappointed by the election results—people are feeling anxious about this time in the life of our nation—that President-elect Donald Trump meant exactly what he said on election night: that he is going to be the president of all the people of the United States of America. . . . I just want to reassure anyone, including the actor who spoke that night, that President-elect Donald Trump is going to be president of all the people. And I couldn't be more honored to stand with him. (Schultheis, 2016)

Pence's assurance of unity, though platitudinous in its evasion of how the administration might achieve it, was clearly conversant with Dixon's argument. He advanced a courteous and dialogic tone, making plain his intention to reassure "the actor who spoke that night."

In his appearance on *The View* the next day, Dixon thanked Pence for "hearing" his message: "I'm very grateful for Vice-President-elect Mike Pence for staying there and listening to what we had to say. . . . I'm also grateful for his words yesterday, his response to it. It's encouraging" (ABC News, 2016). In an interview with CBS *This Morning*, the actor offered appreciation for Pence's response and continued to use dialogic metaphors to characterize their interaction: "I know some people have said that a one-sided conversation, or a lecture, is not a conversation, but it was the beginnings of a conversation, I hope, that we can continue to have" (Morgan, 2016).

For the most part, then, the curtain speech—despite its unorthodoxy—seemed to achieve its objective: to create an opportunity for redress. That is, of course, until the intensifying rhetoric of President-elect Trump. In addition to the two tweets referenced at this chapter's outset, Trump posted a third on Saturday, November 19, codifying his position on the matter: "Very rude and insulting of Hamilton cast member to treat our great future V.P. Mike Pence to a theater lecture. Couldn't even memorize his lines!" (Trump, 2016d). By labeling the speech "a theater lecture" and adding a personal insult, the President-elect undermined the rhetoric of Pence and Dixon. It effectively displaced attempts to frame successive communication as dialogic.

Sunday morning, before Pence's appearance on *Face the Nation*, Trump again tweeted about the incident, concretizing what would become the dominant media message—a powerful sentiment of aggrievement: "The cast and producers of Hamilton, which I hear is highly overrated, should immediately apologize to Mike Pence for their terrible behavior" (Trump 2016a). These invectives subverted the cordiality promoted by both Dixon and Pence. By employing a metonymic framework, he mostly eschewed any critique against Dixon—the exception being his attack about unmemorized lines—or the specific people who crafted the speech. Trump chunked the characters, play, and theater into a single object (e.g., *Hamilton*) and accused it of being indecorous. In a measured response to Trump, Dixon attempted to reestablish dialogue by using the same indicators of politeness as during his exchanges with Pence: "@realDonaldTrump conversation is not harassment, sir. And I appreciate @mike_pence for stopping to listen" (Dixon, 2016). In the end, the curtain speech created two oppositional forms of communication: one dialogic, the other a stonewalling censure.

At the heart of Trump's argument—echoed by many supporters in the days following the event via the hashtag "#BoycottHamilton"—was his characterization of theater as a "special and safe space" that had been besmirched by the political targeting of Mike Pence. Responding to this, Lin-Manuel Miranda tweeted: "Proud of @HamiltonMusical. Proud of @BrandonVDixon, for leading with love. And proud to remind you that ALL are welcome at the theater" (Miranda, 2016). This exchange traded on whether targeted political rhetoric was *appropriate* for a post-curtain speech. Pence refused to take a side. Recall that during his interview with Dickerson, he responded, "I'll leave to others whether that was the appropriate venue to say it" (Schultheis, 2016). Dixon, speaking to CBS News on November 21, 2016, offered a defense:

> Our show is a very political show. I mean, we tell an American story with a diverse group of Americans and they said, you know, this is an important moment and we want to seize it. . . . Is it appropriate or the right venue? . . . When you have an opportunity to speak with your elected representative, you take it. You do it as respectfully as possible, but you take it. That is their job. (Morgan, 2016)

Dixon was arguing that the musical's content justified a political interjection. Put another way, because it was *Hamilton* and not, say, *Oklahoma!*, the cast and crew had a civic obligation to upend the generic conventions of curtain speeches to advance a position.

To many, *Hamilton* is a mythopoetic phenomenon that fuses dramaturgy and a desired civic reality. The cast, crew, and many of its fans celebrate this, engaging in their own acts of self-mythologization to construct the play as politics par excellence. In the introduction to his book of *Hamilton* cast portraiture, photographer Josh Lehrer proselytizes that the musical "*forces* audiences to see the nation's development and the world from an unexpected, even subversive perspective" (Lehrer, 2019; emphasis mine). The official chronicle of *Hamilton*'s rise to fame further exhorted, "The widely acclaimed musical that draws from the breadth of America's culture and shows its audience what we share doesn't just dramatize Hamilton's [1776] revolution: It continues it" (McCarter, 2016). These suggestions that the show simultaneously exhibits and transforms the ideas and identities of America's founding generation are, in themselves, wildly dramatic. And though less lyrical, Dixon's statement to CBS News (quoted above) drew the same conclusion.

In other media promoting the musical, interviews confirmed an ideology underpinning *Hamilton*'s on- and offstage presence. PBS aired "Hamilton's America" in 2016. In it, the musical's director, Thomas Kail, admitted that "what we're trying to do with this cast and the larger gesture of this show is say: 'Here's a group of people [the founders] you think you can't relate to, maybe we can take down some of those barriers that allows reflection to be truer'" (Horwitz, 2016). In the same episode, Leslie Odom Jr. (the actor who originated the role of Burr) added,

> There's something incredibly pure and fun about the casting that our imaginations really will let us take these leaps and that we don't have to be so closeminded, especially in the theater. That it can be about—be whatever we want it to be. (Horwitz, 2016)

By framing casting choices as a political act, Dixon, Kail, and Odom Jr. elevate *Hamilton* beyond a revolutionary theatrical experience to a revolution of day-to-day rhetorical practice.

With regard to curtain speaking, such viewpoints expand perceived generic norms. Because dramaturgical curtain speeches are less bound by specific rules of decorum—operating within the diegetic constraints of the play's narrative and not necessarily the immediate political norms of the bioenergetic—direct political appeals are more legible and appropriate. This was the framework Dixon used for the speech after the curtain call. Though cheered by many, it assumed that audiences were familiar with *Hamilton*'s cultural-political repute.

With the rising power of a newly elected Trump, however—who was quick to consider the musical "overrated"—a political curtain speech seemingly unrelated to the dramaturgy, was ripe for his ire. The musical is inarguably:

> A cultural phenomenon; [but] for a certain subset of fans, it's a beacon for a progressive America.... The clash between the cast (and audience) of *Hamilton* and the incoming Republican administration [was] about demographics and values—but it's also about who really gets to speak for America. (Lind, 2016)

Dixon's curtain speech, in its plea for the administration to work with "all Americans," including those of "different colors, creeds and orientations," presupposed that the show's ideological centering of multiculturalism was universal.

But President-elect Trump had not seen the show that night. He had not experienced the diegetic potential for heightening revolutionary values through a transformed historical rendering. He only saw a post-curtain speech calling out a duly elected member of his administration. As such, Trump eschewed the substance of the address and framed it as a breach of civic virtue. Despite Miranda's insistence that the speech was an example of "leading with love," conservative allies of the president-elect enacted what political analyst Alex Nowrasteh (2016) calls *patriotic correctness*: a strategic response to rhetoric judged insufficiently nationalistic. Patriotic correctness, like its close cousin political correctness, enables ideologues to police speech and behaviors. *Patriotic* correctness attempts to curtail rhetoric that fails to be "a full-throated, un-nuanced, uncompromising defense of American nationalism, history and cherry-picked ideals" (Nowrasteh, 2016). Lacking deference to supposed national iconicity will, thus, lead practitioners to insult, ostracize, or suppress violators with policy initiatives or tweets.

Vice President–elect Pence, however—in addition to the cast and crew of *Hamilton*—comprehended a hybridized curtain speech that utilized dramaturgical traditions in a post-curtain format. Within this logic, the entreaty functioned like the scripted speeches at the end of *Angels in America* and *Hadestown*. Miranda, Kail, and Seller, the masterminds of the speech, *cast* Dixon. In character as Vice President Burr, he could more appropriately address Pence; Burr/Dixon represented Pence's diplomatic counterpart. The speech, therefore, acted as an extension of ideas presented by the play, synthesized into a distinct and formidable monologue, performed by a relevant and important character at the show's close. The worlds of rhetoric and drama—a separation already marginal—merged. *Hamilton*, like all historical dramas,

> rhetoricizes history and helps invent a usable tradition, in the same way epideictic rhetoric does. Each performance is always an occasion that brings history into dialogue with the present. . . . As such, theater intervenes in the present moment in an interested, addressed, or simply rhetorical way. (Zhang, Z, and Yang, 2012, 190)

Dixon's curtain speech rhetoricized the drama because it was an extension of it.

The central clash that sparked the controversy was less a political disagreement and more the by-product of collapsing the generic forms. By composing the address through a lens of dramaturgical curtain speaking—a natural ending to a political show necessarily punctuated by a call to arms—Dixon became susceptible to complaints of violating rules of decorum. Trump and his supporters did not share the generic frame and were, therefore, able to sidestep the speech's substantive concerns. By assessing the address as a post-curtain speech, they had a clearer case for accusing Dixon of interrupting the sanctity of the theater, creating unnecessary anti-cathartic effects, and perpetuating a direct attack against acceptable and patriotic decorum. At a press event, a reporter asked Trump about the situation. He said simply, "They were very inappropriate" (Associated Press, 2016).

Despite this, Dixon and Pence engaged in a series of profitable mediated exchanges—focusing on the importance of dialogue as a democratic necessity. Trump's response, fueled by a perceived breach of decorum, augured tweets that demanded apologies, castigated alleged rudeness, and utilized insinuations of anti-American harassment.

Had the speechwriters more thoroughly considered the generic constraints of curtain speeches, it is not difficult to imagine the emergence of a richer dialogue. Though it may have been regarded as especially unorthodox, a speech made before the curtain call, during the musical's finale, or couched as an epilogue may have been more effective. Despite satisfying many generic expectations (e.g., politeness, welcomed acknowledgment, speaker's ethos, policed decorum), hybridizing a post-curtain speech with assumptive dramaturgical elements failed to effectively shape a dialogue that assuaged the fears of *Hamilton*'s diverse cast (and, by extension, its core fan base) to a new conservative administration. Though it reaffirmed *Hamilton*'s ostensible values to many audience members that night, it also gave Trump an opportunity to ignore the speech's concerns and construct a political adversary through patriotic correctness.

CURTAIN DOWN: EPILOGUE

The sketch comedy series *Saturday Night Live* parodied the incident. On November 19, 2016—the day after Dixon's curtain speech—Alec Baldwin and Beck Bennett played their recurring roles as Trump and Pence, respectively, offering the following exchange:

Trump: I heard you went to see *Hamilton*, how was that?

Pence: It was good, I got a free lecture.

Trump: I heard they booed you.

Pence: Absolutely.

Trump: I love you, Mike. You're the reason I'm never going to get impeached. (King, 2016)

Baldwin portrayed his character as a foil to Pence's straight man—reasoning that Trump's impulsive behavior could be effectively mitigated by the stoically composed Pence. In one sentence, Bennett encapsulated Pence's response to the controversy: the show was good, it violated an implied standard of decorum, but there was a free gift, so it wasn't *that bad*. Baldwin's response, though predictive, was poignant: Pence, given the opportunity, would hold the administration together because he would take a dialogic path.

What would have happened if Trump had been the person representing the administration that night at the Richard Rodgers Theatre? Only four nights before, the actor who originated the role of George Washington, Christopher Jackson, had left the show. His replacement, Nicholas Christopher—himself a newly minted president—may have been the one to step forward and ask for redress: "I wanna give you a word of warning. . . . I want to warn against partisan fighting. . . . And if we get this right / We're gonna teach 'em how to say good-bye."

REFERENCES

ABC News. (2015). "Patti LuPone snatches phone away from audience member." [Video]. YouTube, July 10, 2015. http://www.youtube.com/watch?v=43mB4QuXGTEandfeature=emb_logo.

———. (2016). "*Hamilton* Star Calls Pence's Response 'Encouraging.'" [Video.] YouTube, November 21, 2016. http://www.youtube.com/watch?v=LCL4CuRy8c8andfeature=emb_logo.

ABC Players. (2011). "Creativity at the Curtain: Texts of Milford [NH] Area Curtain Speeches." September 10, 2011. http://www.abcplayers.org/history/spotlight/2011_09-10-extra.pdf

The Actors Fund. (2016). "*Hamilton* Special Performance—Curtain Speech by Javier Muñoz." [Video.] YouTube, November 7, 2016. https://www.youtube.com/watch?v=RGzpDOm113Qandfeature=emb_logo.

Andres M. (2019). "*Hadestown* First Curtain Call and Speech after Tonys 2019." [Video]. YouTube, June 11, 2019. https://www.youtube.com/watch?v=M5ST6UAyr1o.

Associated Press. (2016). "Trump: 'Hamilton' Cast Was 'Very Inappropriate.'" [Video]. *USA Today*, November 20, 2016. https://www.usatoday.com/videos/news/nation/2016/11/21/trump:-'Hamilton'-cast-'very-inappropriate'/94187678/.

Black, E. (1965). *Rhetorical Criticism: A Study in Method*. Madison: University of Wisconsin Press.

Bradner, E. (2016). "Pence: 'I Wasn't Offended' by Message from 'Hamilton' Cast." [Video]. CNN, November 20, 2016. http://.cnn.com/2016/11/20/politics/mike-pence-hamilton-message-trump/index.html.

Campbell, K. K., and K. H. Jamieson. (1978). "Form and Genre in Rhetorical Criticism: An Introduction." In *Form and Genre: Shaping Rhetorical Action*, edited by K. K. Campbell and K. H. Jamieson, 9–32. Speech Communication Association.

Dixon, B. [@BrandonVDixon]. (2016). "@RealDonaldTrump conversation is not harassment sir. And I appreciate @mike_pence for stopping to listen." [Tweet].

Twitter, November 19, 2016, 8:07 a.m. https://twitter.com/brandonvdixon/status/799977281875755008?lang=en.
EBZB Productions. (n.d.) "Suggested Curtain Speech: General Audiences." http://www.ebzb.org/ curtainspeeches/ebzbcurtainspeech.pdf.
Foley, M. (2015). "Time for Epideictic." *Quarterly Journal of Speech* 101, no. 1, 209–12.
Hamilton. [@HamiltonMusical]. (2016). "Tonight, VP-Elect Mike Pence attended #HamiltonBway. After the show, @BrandonVDixon delivered the following statement on behalf of the show." [Tweet]. Twitter, November 18, 2016. https://twitter.com/hamiltonmusical/ status/799828567941120000?lang=en.
Horwitz, A., dir. (2016). *Great Performances*, season 44, episode 4, "Hamilton's America." Executive producers D. Horn, J. Kamen, L. Miranda, J. Seller, D. Sirulnick, J. Wilkes. RadicalMedia; The John D. and Catherine MacArthur Foundation; PBS.
Howard, J. E. (2013). "Tony Kushner's Angel Archive and the Re-Visioning of American History." *Emisférica* 9, no. 1. https://hemisphericinstitute.org/en/emisferica-91/e91-essay-tony-kushners-angel-archive-and-the-re-visioning-of-american-history.html.
King, D. R., dir. (2016). *Saturday Night Live,* season 42, episode 7. Donald Trump Prepares, cold open. Aired November 19, 2016. Executive producer L. Michaels. Broadway Video; SNL Studios; NBC. [Video]. http://www.nbc.com/saturday-night-live/video/donald-trump-prepares-cold-open/3428575.
Lehrer, J. (2019). *Hamilton: Portraits of the Revolution.* New York: Rizzoli International Publications.
Lincoln Center. (2015). "Patti LuPone's Curtain Speech." [Video]. YouTube, July 10, 2015. https://www.youtube.com/watch?v=nleN2q7fIIQandfeature=emb_logo.
Lind, D. (2016). "Donald Trump's Feud with the Cast of *Hamilton*, Explained." Vox, November 21, 2016. https://www.vox.com/policy-and-politics/2016/11/21/13699046/trump-hamilton-pence-apologize.
Lipari, L. (2007). "The Rhetoric of Intersectionality: Lorraine Hansberry's 1957 Letters to the *Ladder.*" In *Queering Public Address: Sexualities in American Historical Discourse*, edited by C. E. Morris III, 220–48. Columbia: University of South Carolina Press.
McCarter, J. (2016). "Introduction." In *Hamilton: The Revolution*, by L. Miranda and J McCarter, 11. New York: Grand Central Publishing.
Mele, C., and Healy, P. (2016). "Pence Draws a Reaction at 'Hamilton.'" *New York Times*, November 19, 2016. http://www.nytimes.com/2016/11/19/us/mike-pence-hamilton.html.
Miranda, L. [@Lin-Manuel]. (2016). "Proud of @HamiltonMusical. Proud of @BrandonVDixon, for leading with love. And proud to remind you that ALL are welcome at the theater." [Tweet]. Twitter, November 19, 2016, 2:29 a.m. https://twitter.com/Lin_Manuel/status/799892301187338241.
Morgan, D. (2016). "'Hamilton' Star Responds to Trump: 'There's Nothing to Apologize For.'" [Video.] CBS News, November 21, 2016. https://www.cbsnews

.com/news/hamilton-brandon-victor-dixon-mike-pence-donald-trump-theres-nothing-to-apologize-for.

Nowrasteh, A. (2016). "The Right Has Its Own Version of Political Correctness. It's Just as Stifling." *Washington Post*, December 7, 2016. https://www.washingtonpost.com/posteverything/wp/2016/12/07/the-right-has-its-own-version-of-political-correctness-its-just-as-stifling.

Patti, J. (2014). "What to Do about Curtain Speeches?" *Butts In Seats: Musings on Practical Solutions for Arts Management* (blog), May 20, 2014. https://insidethearts.com/buttsintheseats/ 2014/05/20/what-to-do-about-curtain-speeches/.

Rohrschach Theatre. (2006). "The Art of the Curtain Speech." *Rorschach Theatre Blog*, July 6, 2006. https://rorschachtheatre.blogspot.com/2006/07/art-of-curtain-speech.html.

Rowland, R. (1991). "On Generic Categorization." *Communication Theory* 1 (May), 128–44.

Schultheis, E. (2016). "Mike Pence: 'I Wasn't Offended' by 'Hamilton' Cast Member's Comments." [Video]. CBS News, November 20, 2016. https://www.cbsnews.com/news/mike-pence-i-wasnt-offended-by-hamilton-cast-members-comments/.

Soloski, A. (2019). "But Wait, There's More!" *New York Times*, December 22, 2019. https://www.nytimes.com/2019/12/18/theater/musical-finales-curtain-calls.html.

Trotter, M. (2006). "Gregory, Yeats and Ireland's National Theatre." In *A Companion to Modern British and Irish drama 1880–2005*, edited by M. Luckhurst, chapter 7. Hoboken, NJ: Blackwell Publishing Ltd.

Trump, D. [@RealDonaldTrump]. (2016a). "The cast and producers of Hamilton, which I hear is highly overrated, should immediately apologize to Mike Pence for their terrible behavior." [Tweet]. Twitter, November 20, 2016, 6:22 a.m. Twitter has since suspended the account of @RealDonaldTrump.

———. (2016b). "Our wonderful future V.P. Mike Pence was harassed last night at the theater by the cast of Hamilton, cameras blazing. This should not happen." [Tweet]. Twitter, November 19, 2016, 8:48 a.m. Twitter has since suspended the account of @RealDonaldTrump.

———. (2016c). "The Theater must always be a safe and special place. The cast of Hamilton was very rude last night to a very good man, Mike Pence. Apologize!" [Tweet]. Twitter, November 19, 2016, 8:56 a.m. Twitter has since suspended the account of @RealDonaldTrump.

———. (2016d). "Very rude and insulting of Hamilton cast member to treat our great future V.P. Mike Pence to a theater lecture. Couldn't even memorize his lines!" [Tweet]. Twitter, November 19, 2016, 6:32 p.m. Twitter has since suspended the account of @RealDonaldTrump.

White, C. (2016). "How To Give a Great Curtain Speech." SCG Nonprofits. https://scgnonprofits. com/how-to-give-a-great-curtain-speech/.

Zhang, P., Y. Z, and X. Yang. (2012). "The Rhetorical-Theatrical Sensibility as Equipment for Living." *ETC: A Review of General Semantics* 49, no. 2, 186–96.

Chapter 12

Hamilton and the Genre of the Politicized Broadway Musical

Following the Rhetorical Tradition, Twisting the Rhetorical Tradition

Theodore F. Sheckels

The Broadway musical has a ragged history. Several have attempted to tell it, but its lineage is difficult to pin down. There were, back through the centuries, forms of musical theater one might point to as precedents, but what emerged in the theaters of New York City sprung more from the desire to provide entertainment—and make money—than from the desire to imitate European forms such as the French or Viennese operetta or the London works of Gilbert and Sullivan or even American ones such as the minstrel or vaudeville variety shows (Patinkin, 2005; Kenrick, 2017). Most certainly, some of the Broadway theatrical entrepreneurs were aware of what, in a lighter vein, had been staged elsewhere; and they borrowed ideas. However, any precise lineage is very difficult to establish.

Clearer than the lineage is that there were in the twentieth century two categories of shows that emerged: the revue, which featured a loose collection of acts; and one telling a story, usually simple and romantic, embellished with singing and, eventually, some dancing. Slowly, the revue faded, and the one offering a story, in the hands of artists who took the Broadway musical seriously, became more sophisticated. Thus, we have had throughout the past several decades shows that one might dismiss as "fluff" along with shows that attempt to do more than just entertain (and make money). To this day, there are those on Broadway trying simply to entertain the masses and those on Broadway trying to do more.

The creative artists behind a Broadway musical are many: the book writer, the composer, the lyricist, the choreographer, the set designer. Many of these have taken their particular art seriously; some have taken the show as a whole seriously, collaborating with others involved and striving to work the pieces together. These creative artists wanted to "say something," using the resources of the musical genre to do so. Thus, quite a few Broadway musicals attempt to make a social or political statement, more often than not a left-leaning one that reflects the politics of both the New York audience and the artists. This grouping of shows is loosely defined, but the boundaries are sharp enough and the examples numerous enough to suggest that such politically attuned musicals constitute a genre.

In this chapter, I will explore that genre, arguing that six rhetorical techniques are commonly used by these shows that attempt to offer commentary. Then I will consider the Broadway musical *Hamilton*, largely the work of Lin-Manuel Miranda, in this generic context. *Hamilton*, I will argue, relies on these rhetorical techniques and gives them a unique twist. John Schilb (2007) in *Rhetorical Refusals* outlines how writers often take what is expected and, to various degrees, play with these expectations. Miranda's work fits this description: aware of what was common in the genre, Miranda follows suit but with a rhetorical legerdemain that marks *Hamilton*, on the whole, as strikingly different.

THE POLITICIZED BROADWAY MUSICAL

Show Boat (1927) and *Oklahoma!* (1943) are often pointed to as Broadway landmarks. The first marks the point at which the genre should have matured into something serious; the second marks the point at which the genre does finally mature. Given this trajectory, it is not surprising that, in between, there were musicals that took both artistry and political commentary seriously, including *Strike Up the Band* (1930), *Of Thee I Sing* (1931), *Face the Music* (1932), *Flying Colors* (1932), *Life Begins at 8:40* (1934), *Red, Hot, and Blue* (1936), *I'd Rather Be Right* (1937), *Pins and Needles* (1937), *The Cradle Will Rock* (1938), and *Knickerbocker Holiday* (1938). And yet, in almost all of these cases, the political commentary was both awkwardly added and strikingly weak, usually because the political commentary was incidental and watered down to avoid offending the sympathetic but nonpartisan paying customers. These musicals echoed the people's (well, the New York City people's) support of FDR and the American effort in World War II. *Show Boat*, in raising the matter of racial discrimination, took a risk. *Oklahoma!*'s risks were artistic, not political; but in succeeding, *Oklahoma!* gave the genre a seriousness that opened the door for more artistic and political risk-taking.

After *Oklahoma!*'s success, the political commentary in many Broadway musicals was both more integral to the show and more strongly stated, including *South Pacific* (1949), *The Pajama Game* (1954), *West Side Story* (1957), *How to Succeed in Business Without Really Trying* (1961), *Stop the World—I Want to Get Off* (1962), *Oliver!* (1963), *Fiddler on the Roof* (1964), *Cabaret* (1966), *Hair* (1968), *A Chorus Line* (1975), *Evita* (1979), *Les Misérables* (1987), *Miss Saigon* (1991), *Rent* (1996), *Urinetown* (2001), *Hairspray* (2002), *Avenue Q* (2003), and *In the Heights* (2008). The political focus might be race or sexual orientation or poverty or US foreign policy. The topics vary, but, treated as a genre, one can discern six rhetorical strategies being used to make a statement.

Slipping In the Telling Statement

Audiences expected the story to be "lite" and probably romantic. *South Pacific*, for example, is a World War II story, but it is more about the antics of sailors and nurses on a Pacific island than war, and it features not one but two romances. The romances cross social lines—a sailor from prim-and-proper Philadelphia with a Polynesian girl, and a nurse from Little Rock, Arkansas, with an older French man who, she and the audience find out later in the show, had a relationship with a Polynesian girl that produced two children. Polynesian is "of color" but probably not processed that way by the audience, who see the South Pacific natives as "colorful" but not "of color." But as the sailor Joe and the nurse Nellie back away from these relationships, the audience sees racial prejudice surface. For example, the song "You've Got to Be Carefully Taught" turns what is emerging in the musical into its devastating theme. The song shocks. It is not that no one saw the theme emerging, but what seemed to be marginal was suddenly central—and could not be ignored.

Racial tension was, of course, more noticeable in *West Side Story*. But it was not White versus Black, and it could be easily overlooked as gang versus gang or Jets versus Sharks (even though the latter gang was cast with several African Americans based on dancing ability). But then, the sometimes funny, always energetic song "America" comes along. Just like "You've Got to be Carefully Taught," "America" puts racial discrimination center stage. There is much artistry to be admired in *West Side Story*: Leonard Bernstein's score, Stephen Sondheim's lyrics, Jerome Robbins's choreography—and it was easy to become lost in "the show," but then "America" is sung and danced onstage and we hear what it is like to be "not White" in America. Ultimately, each show could make its political message blatant. What these two classic musicals reveal, however, is the rhetorical power of suddenly confronting the audience with a message that was present but somewhat latent.

Humanizing Victims

The political statements Broadway artists were making almost always focused on victims of oppression. In making such statements, artists needed to be careful not to essentialize the victims as just victims. Instead, they needed to be humanized so the privileged audience would see them as people. For example, with Joe in *Show Boat*, its creators come very close to creating a stereotype, albeit one with a magnificent voice. But Joe (and other "slaving" African Americans we see in some renditions of the musical) is not the only victim: there is also Julie LaVerne, dismissed from the performing company on board the *Cotton Blossom* because she has Black African blood. The extent of her role varies from version to version, but in all, she is humanized not only as a victim of southern law but as the main character Magnolia's noble friend. *Show Boat* is set after the Civil War; thus, there is no slavery per se, but some renditions visually remind viewers of the South's slavery past as well as its racist, late nineteenth-century present.

A more striking example of humanization comes many years later with *Rent*. It deals not with victims of racial prejudice but with victims of prejudice tied to sexual orientation and HIV/AIDS, which in the 1980s was ravaging the gay community. Public attitudes toward those suffering wavered between sympathy and antagonism in this historical moment. *Rent* played a major role in making the former the dominant reaction by portraying those suffering from HIV/AIDS as likable young men and women with complex life stories. Drawn together in New York City by their aspirations, they were individuals first and combatants against the epidemic second.

Endowing Victims with Carnivalesque Energy

Theorist Mikhail Bakhtin (1984) explores the "carnivalesque" in his study of French satirist Rabelais. Bakhtin sees in the medieval carnival, which featured the grotesque mockery of authority, the satirical energy evident in Rabelais. Others have found this same energy in the satirizing and protesting of any number of power-down groups. For example, the women's marches in many cities on January 21, 2017, exhibited grotesque mockery and satirical energy. The "carnivalesque," then, is a tool used in ideological battle: it is at the core of social protests, highlighting the protester's enthusiasm and underscoring their grievances.

As a lighter form of popular entertainment, the Broadway musical tilts in the former direction. We see it among the power-down Puerto Ricans in *West Side Story* in the dance at the gym scene and on a tenement roof singing and dancing to "America." We see it in *Rent* during the "La Vie Boheme" scene at the show's midpoint. We see it in *Hairspray* at the show's "Can't Stop the

Beat" conclusion, previewed by the dance scene in Motormouth Maybelle's record shop. There, the power-down groups are illustrated by both race and weight. And we see it Lin-Manuel Miranda's *In the Heights*, where oppression is in the background of several stories focused on ways of integrating into "mainstream" society, including Cuban immigrant Abuela Claudia's story, with its emphasis on the poor-paying jobs she had to endure in Mayor LaGuardia's NYC. Some accept the need to fit in, some reject the idea, and many waver, but all exhibit the energy that commands attention.

Creating Parallels

In *Show Boat*, parallels are struck between Julie's and Magnolia's stories. The structure is a typical subplot/plot one, with points where the two converge. Similar is the structure of the much later *Hairspray*, but here the subplot (racial discrimination) becomes so dominant that it overwhelms the ostensible plot (discrimination against the overweight). But there is yet another parallel functioning in *Hairspray*, between what is occurring on the Baltimore teen dance show and what is occurring in society at large. After all, the Civil Rights Movement was not about the *Buddy Deane Show* (the real dance program thinly disguised by the *Corny Collins Show*) but about more profound instances of discrimination.

Broadway shows can strike parallels between diagetical elements or between something onstage and something off. *Hairspray* does both, for instance. Other illustrative examples of creating a parallel with something in society are *A Chorus Line* and *Cabaret*. The first is ostensibly about a group of young women and men who pine for a role in an upcoming Broadway show. Ironically, should they succeed, they acquire the total anonymity exhibited so well in the closing number "One." But the absorption of their personal stories into chorus line oblivion is only part of the show's message, for they represent workers more broadly, who at work become part of whatever the capitalist "machine" has graced them with as employment. A Marxist-tinged parallel lurks beneath the show's surface with its choreographed dancing and its poignant songs.

The second, *Cabaret*, strikes a parallel between the emerging evils of Nazi Germany and the present evils of 1960s America. The Kit Kat Klub's initials being KKK offered a clue. For those who missed the parallel, performances through the years have featured, before and/or after performances, montages of Civil Rights images, emphasizing the show's point that it is easy to become self-absorbed and miss the evil. *Cabaret*, it might also be noted, used the telling song, as did *South Pacific* and *West Side Story*. The decadent host sings a comic love song to his gorilla lover, only to end it by noting that what others saw in her—that he overlooked—was not that she was a gorilla but that she was Jewish. Comedy yields to a powerful indictment of growing Nazi prejudice—and parallel prejudice in the United States.

Foregrounding the Stories of Victims

Broadway creators tended to put onstage people who either looked like those in the audience or were comic exaggerations. There was an assumption that people would not come to a show that depicted "the other." There was undoubtedly prejudice on the presumed audience's part but also the matter of identification. The predominantly White, predominantly upper- and upper-middle-class audience could not connect with the stories of African Americans or Hispanic Americans. There were shows that tried to offer these stories, but they did only moderately well at the box office. Even shows with magnificent scores, such as *Porgy and Bess* (1935), did not change that fact.

Broadway creators could, however, show nonethnic victims. Although *Gypsy* (1959) focused more on Mama Rose's attempts to live vicariously through her daughters' stage careers, the show did bluntly depict the plight of vaudeville-type performers as the American stage turned away from variety shows and toward the risqué. Daughter Louise's plight—starve or strip—was not only an analogy for the situation of others in show business but also depicted all those caught in a changing economy. With *West Side Story*, victims acquire color; and with *Rent*, they acquire nonheterosexual orientations. The portrayal of victims does broaden, but, as Miranda brings *In the Heights* and *Hamilton* to the stage, there are few portrayals of African Americans or Hispanic Americans and, thus, few opportunities for performers from these groups. In histories of Broadway, several shows are pointed to as the first "Black" musical or the first Latinx-Hispanic musical. The very fact that historians seem to be in a continual search for "the first" suggests that racial or ethnic "others" have not been *fully* embraced by Broadway (Green, 2014). *In the Heights*, for instance, is noteworthy because it provided major Broadway roles for these actors, singers, and dancers. The show also foregrounds their stories, most of which feature characters who are torn between their ethnic heritage and their desire to succeed in the largely White-defined American context.

Playing with the Music

Just about everyone knows what proverbial "show tunes" sound like. A few pioneers have attempted to change the music, such as Gershwin with *Porgy and Bess* and Bernstein with *West Side Story*. They created masterpieces but inspired few others. The major break with "show tunes" was the infusion of rock music, with *Hair* and *Jesus Christ Superstar* (1971) initiating the departure, which then degenerated into "jukebox" musicals, some of which, including *Jersey Boys* (2005) and *Beautiful* (2014), were well-designed and entertaining. Critics would note, throughout recent decades, the departures. However, except for forays into jazz (offered with its African American roots often obscured), these departures were from one White-defined form to another White-defined form. The Four Seasons' music was not ethnic, and the Carole King-Gerry Goffin songs (or the Barry Mann-Cynthia Weil songs) sung by African American performers were not strikingly African American.

In the Heights struck critics as different because it made use of both Latin music and rap or hip-hop. Miranda offered a mix of musical types in the show, but what struck people were his strongly ethnic departures from either "show tunes" or the increasingly popular rock scores. Stressed in these comments was the assumption that Miranda was as intentional in his use of the musical styles of "others" as he was in offering starring roles for "others." Although the cases are quite different, what Miranda was trying to do in *In the Heights* was legitimize such music just as Galt MacDermot, Gerome Ragni, and James Rado tried to do in *Hair*. Rock was now acceptable on Broadway—as were Miranda's styles. One might say that *Hair* brought the counterculture of the 1960s to Broadway. More profound, however, was the cultural "work" Miranda was attempting.

HAMILTON

Before considering *Hamilton*'s use of the Broadway musical genre, consider how Lin-Manuel Miranda's adaption of Ron Chernow's biography gave Miranda both a challenge and an opportunity. *In the Heights*, *West Side Story*, and *Rent* dealt with present-day New York City. Other shows took audiences back in time: *Hairspray* to the 1960s, *South Pacific* to the 1940s, *Cabaret* to the 1930s. But no one had chosen to deal with contemporary issues by focusing on a subject as far back in time as Miranda did. The challenge was generating interest in such an old, historical subject. The opportunity was provided by facts that Chernow's biography of Hamilton introduced but did not stress: that Hamilton was ethnically "other"; he was mistreated by his supposed "betters"; and his story (not to mention wife Eliza's) was largely ignored by those who had documented American history.

Miranda's character Usnavi in *In the Heights* sings of his arrival, as an infant, from the Dominican Republic. Likewise, the *Hamilton* cast sings of Alexander Hamilton's arrival from Jamaica in the show's opening number. Miranda arguably saw another Usnavi, but this one would not be running a bodega in Washington Heights; this one would have a much "larger" story. Miranda would choose to enact both roles on the Broadway stage, signaling that his rhetorical goals were quite similar even though the two alter egos were quite different. Usnavi's story would invite the audience to consider the plight of a marginalized population, living day-to-day, wondering whether they fit better here or back "where they came" from because the "American Dream" seemed only a distant possibility. Hamilton's story would invite the audience to consider the plight of not just the denizens of Washington Heights but a huge group of people denied the "American Dream" from the nation's beginning to the present day.

It is easy to portray Miranda as new to Broadway, and therefore, naïve about its traditions when *In the Heights* debuted. To the contrary, Miranda, though still a university student when the seeds of the show were planted, was well aware of what was typical. In fact, in both *In the Heights* and *Hamilton*, he follows—but departs from—tradition, with the departures not as radical as some suggest. This chapter has thus far charted six techniques the genre uses to insinuate a political message. *Hamilton* uses the six, with a twist sometimes aptly termed "revolutionary."

Slipping In the Telling Statement

What does he *not* do? He does not insert a song such as *South Pacific*'s "You've Got To Be Carefully Taught" to hit the half-aware audience with the political message. Given the different way in which Miranda creates a parallel, such a blunt dose of messaging was not necessary: the message was before the audience's eyes throughout the show. The closest Miranda comes to inserting a "telling" song is including three pieces sung by King George III. They are comic, but they are also musically quite different from most of the show's fare. Their style—perhaps best described as 1950s rock, by being so strikingly different and therefore discordant, calls attention to how the bulk of the musical is not in the pop or rock style stereotypical in the genre. Rather than insert a song that is in itself telling, Miranda inserts three pieces that, because they are so very "White" and sung by a character depicted as so very "White," draw our attention to the message the show as a whole, as staged, delivers by simply being. The telling statement, then, does not deliver the message; rather, it draws attention to the message by being discordant in sound and in appearance. Put another way, Miranda flips the traditional strategy.

Humanizing the Victims

In most of the shows discussed in this chapter, the audience sees the victims directly, including the Puerto Ricans in *West Side Story*, the HIV/AIDS sufferers in *Rent*, and the Caribbean immigrants in *In the Heights*. *Hamilton* works differently. The audience sees Hamilton directly, but he is only the metonymic representative of the many victims whose stories have not been told and, worse, who have not been embraced by a nation committed to liberty and equality. Those others are glanced at—in comments about slaves, in comments about immigrants, and in Angelica Schuyler's pledge to tell Jefferson to "include women in the sequel." More so than these glances is the staged reality of people of color playing the very White revolutionary roles. We see who has not been included when we look at an African American George Washington or Thomas Jefferson, an Asian American Eliza Schuyler Hamilton, and a Latinx American Alexander Hamilton. This view, of course, is based on the initial casting, but, even as casts changed, the roles were still enacted by performers of color.

Humanizing victims usually entails offering their full stories and thereby removing them from the stereotype of "victim." Miranda's rhetoric works differently. He humanizes them by giving them the very human stories of the men and women the actors of color are portraying: Christopher Jackson, an African American, becomes a very human George Washington who confesses weaknesses and fear and acts nobly as general and president, and Miranda becomes a principled but flawed Alexander Hamilton.

Endowing with Carnivalesque Energy

While in development, *Hamilton* critics wondered how a presumably boring story about an early American known mainly for being on the ten-dollar note could become an entertaining Broadway show. Quickly, skeptics discovered the energy Miranda and colleagues gave the show by a combination of its ensemble numbers and how the show was choreographed and staged. Just like its hero, the show is "non-stop." Contrast it to *1776* (1969), which won fans because it was witty even though it lacked dynamism. *Hamilton* offers considerable wit in its fast-paced lyrics, but it also offers the energy of "My Shot" and the Yorktown battle sequence. Again, this energy is, on one level, associated with our forebearers but, on another, with those long-"othered" in the nation who are enacting the roles of those forebearers in the show.

Constructing Parallels

Most shows of this type require the audience to recall *a* while watching *b*. Sometimes, it is easy, such as watching Tracy Turnblad in *Hairspray* suffer discrimination because of her heft while recalling the discrimination suffered by African Americans on the *Corny Collins Show*. But sometimes the rhetoric is more difficult: moving from the growing Nazi oppression of Jews in *Cabaret* to the oppression of African Americans in the audience's present requires more conscious effort. Miranda eliminates the distance between *a* and *b* by presenting both within the characters onstage. The audience sees Washington or Jefferson, the *a*, but also sees the actor of color portraying the Founding Father while also representing those not embraced by the message of liberty and equality being offered in his day, the *b* in the parallel. Miranda is innovative in constructing a parallel like this. His desire to do so also explains, rhetorically, his insistence on casting performers of color. He was not just trying to offer Broadway roles to those normally excluded. He had a rhetorical and political intention.

Foregrounding the Victims' Story

Miranda's show is about those Alexander Hamilton interacted with professionally, such as his fellow patriots and fellow politicians. The show is also about Hamilton's interactions with his wife, her sister, his son, and his short-term lover Maria Reynolds. To the extent that this particular story from the nation's early history had not been fully told and to the extent that Hamilton, because of his background, was a victim, Miranda puts a victim's story very much center stage. However, Miranda suggests that there are many, many other victims whose stories have been neglected. Some were victimized by being marginalized, such as Eliza Hamilton. Others were oppressed or enslaved. Their stories percolate throughout the musical, including the characters of Angelica, who speaks of oppressed women; John Laurens, who speaks of his dream of forming a regiment of freed slaves; and Lafayette and Hamilton, who speak of their immigrant status. The show also foregrounds the narratological issues of both what gets told and who does the telling.

Along with Chernow, Miranda centers Hamilton's story. He is no longer the forgotten Founding Father. Late in the show, Eliza's story, which extends for decades beyond her husband's death, is centered. *Hamilton* then addresses what gets told, but, beginning with Washington's advice to Hamilton in Act I, the show also stresses who offers the narrative. Washington suggests that his own story might be told in any number of ways. The same with Hamilton and that of any other historical figure. What can one do? One can try to gain control of one's narrative. In the show, Hamilton does so in ways that backfire—trying to free himself from charges of corruption by confessing his illicit liaison. More in control—and saluted for it—is Eliza. She takes herself out of the narrative after her husband's confession. Then, after her son Philip's death, she puts herself back in and, after Alexander's death, she commits herself to not only saluting his legacy but extending the narrative through her actions. *Hamilton* then addresses the question of who does the telling.

Perspective is a common concern among those who study narratology. In Wayne C. Booth's *The Rhetoric of Fiction* (1961), he suggests that expanding the study of perspective beyond the simplistic division into three paths (first person, third-person limited, third-person omniscient) of the "New Critics" is the key to understanding how narratives work. Broadway musicals tend to have an invisible third-person omniscient feel, but many have tried to insert instances of first-person perspective, such as *A Chorus Line*. Miranda goes farther insofar as he becomes meta-critical, inviting the audience to reflect on the perspectives *not* chosen. Silencing them, Miranda suggests, silences the marginalized. Miranda, I would argue, is under no illusion that Eliza will become *the* storyteller after the curtain closes; however, he has both pushed her forward and suggested strongly that any "accepted" rendition of history ought to be interrogated to discover what has not been said. What has often "not been said" are, of course, the victims' stories. In a meta-critical manner, Miranda has indeed foregrounded their narratives—less by presenting them full onstage and more by suggesting their existence if only one were to have the "right" storyteller.

Playing with the Music

Hamilton is often described as a "hip-hop" musical, but that description is misleading. There are many different types of music in the show. Consider how "My Shot," "Wait For It," "What'd I Miss," and "Hurricane" align side by side. They are as different from each other as they are all different from the ditties George III sings. Similarly, Miranda's *In the Heights* is not entirely "hip-hop" and Latinx. As a Broadway artist, Miranda knew how to mix styles *and* that doing so was required to sustain audience interest.

With this preface in mind, one must note that Miranda does indeed bring to the fore musical types not usually dominant on the Broadway stage. Furthermore, he brings to the fore musical types associated with those who are power-down in society. If "show tunes" are thought to be the music of a privileged theatergoing class, and if rock is thought to be the music of a newer generation of Broadway fans, then Miranda is putting side by side with these musical options another style: a style associated with an even newer generation, as well as groups not typically embraced by Broadway—as performers, as characters, as audience members.

The target audience for a Broadway show must be considered. Historically, it was a New York City audience. Then tourists became the target audience. The former delighted in lighter fare and "show tunes"; the latter was far from monolithic. Some hunted for nostalgia; some hunted for spectacle; some hunted for the delight that Disney shows provided. But there was also an audience seeking innovative production techniques and challenging ideas.

This might be a younger, well-educated, and left-leaning audience. A survey of recent Broadway musical fare reveals shows primarily pitched at these different audiences. *Hamilton* was not *Hello Dolly!* (in revival) or *Spiderman* or *Frozen*. Those were pitched at other audiences. From the beginning, reports on *Hamilton*'s creation made clear that Miranda was assuming he would have this last group with him in the Richard Rodgers Theatre. Perhaps he was surprised at the number, but their dominance was such that a negative reaction to attendance by Vice President–elect Pence was likely—and occurred. There was communitatis (as the term is used by performance studies scholars) present, and, in large measure, it was created through the music. Ignoring its variety, the audience valorized the music as different and as representing those who did not usually "speak" through Broadway and were now being allowed to. Thus, *Hamilton* became a "hip-hop musical" when it really was far more than that.

Undoubtedly, more than just the music drew this particular audience to the show. The other twists on the genre played a role, but it was the music that propelled *Hamilton* to its box office success. This rhetorical dynamic would not be unusual: after all, the shows are musicals, and audiences old and new left the theater humming songs not thinking about messages. It is worth recalling the same essential audience that propelled *West Side Story* to success in 1957 also propelled *The Music Man* that same year, with Meredith Willson's creation, not the Bernstein/Sondheim one, winning the Tony. Audiences departed theaters humming "Tonight" or "Seventy-Six Trombones," not focusing that moment on the serious message in the Bernstein-Sondheim show as opposed to the rather silly one in Meredith Willson's. Miranda's choice of music was a strategic way of bringing those stories into focus as both the initial audiences reflected and as the show built its predominant audience.

CONCLUSION

The publication of the musical's story in *Hamilton: The Revolution* (Miranda and McCarter, 2016) fueled the view that *Hamilton* was revolutionary. The rhetorical reading offered in this chapter suggests that that assessment is both untrue and true. It is untrue insofar as *Hamilton* was not the first politically tinged Broadway musical. There was a wave, with questionable sophistication, between the Broadway landmarks *Show Boat* and *Oklahoma!* And there was another wave, with much greater sophistication, soon after. From these musicals there has emerged a genre with distinct rhetorical traits, such as recurring ways in which the creative teams delivered the show's political message. Miranda did have a generic tradition to place *Hamilton* in. Miranda had common techniques to use, and he used them. There is little that is revolutionary in proceeding in this manner.

However, *Hamilton*'s creative team gave the inherited rhetorical traits twists, some slight and some sharp. Very much in line with what Schilb outlines in *Rhetorical Refusals*, *Hamilton* followed generic expectations only to a point and then deviated so that the show could either make or reinforce the political point. I will let others judge whether this was "revolutionary" or not, but it was clearly rhetorically astute and rhetorically effective. Miranda and his team saw ways to work with—but also depart from—the genre, and they delivered a message that resonated with the audience in multiple ways. A Broadway audience is accustomed to receiving a musical in a predictable manner, with variations from genre to genre. *Hamilton*, by adhering to the genre of a politicized musical, allows the audience to behave in its accustomed manner. But by twisting the expectations, *Hamilton* adds extra nuances to the audience's repertoire. The audience, for example, must pay attention to who is performing the show's roles and to meta-critical, narratological matters. *Hamilton* brings such into the show, and, by doing so, *Hamilton* plays with the politicized musical genre and delivers a message that, in its emphasis on diversity, exceeds what one typically finds in that Broadway form.

REFERENCES

Bakhtin, M. (1984). *Rabelais and His World.* Translated by H. Iswolsky. Bloomington: Indiana University Press.

Booth, W. C. (1961). *The Rhetoric of Fiction.* Chicago: University of Chicago Press.

Green, S. (2014). *Broadway Musicals: Show by Show*, 8th ed. Milwaukee, WI: Applause Theatre and Cinema Books.

Kenrick, J. (2017). *Musical Theatre: A History*, 2nd ed. London: Bloomsbury.

Miranda, L-M., and J. McCarter. (2016). *Hamilton: The Revolution.* New York: Little, Brown.

Patinkin, S. (2005). *"No Legs, No Jokes, No Chance": A History of the American Musical Theatre.* Evanston, IL: Northwestern University Press.

Schilb, J. (2007). *Rhetorical Refusals: Defying Audiences' Expectations.* Carbondale: Southern Illinois University Press.

Index

abolition, 50, 57–60, 62
    abolitionist, 24–25, 35, 50
Adams, John, 73
    "The Adams Administration" (song), 73, 76
aesthetic(s), 6, 8–10, 101–15, 170, 174
"Alexander Hamilton" (song), 55, 62, 71, 96, 139, 177
Amadeus (the musical), 169, 171, 175, 180–81
American Dream, 16–22, 24–27, 152, 162, 210
Aristotle, 53, 187
authenticity, 79, 103, 170–71, 178–81
authorship, 171–74, 176–77

Bakhtin, Mikhail, 206
Baldwin, Alec, 199–200
Bernstein, Leonard, 205, 208, 214
Biden, Joe, 2, 26, 39, 127, 141, 145
Biggie Smalls, 110–11
Black American rhetorical style, 106
Black, Edwin, 187
Black Lives Matter (BLM), 7–9, 117–34
Blackness, 102
"Blow Us All Away" (song), 161
Booth, Wayne C., 213

Broadway, 1–2, 6, 35, 67, 87–89, 91, 93, 101, 109–12, 117, 123–24, 131, 139, 149, 162, 185, 194, 203–15
    See also theater
Brown, Michael, 102
"Burn" (song), 159, 179
Burr, Aaron, 1, 23, 35, 48–51, 56–57, 96, 101, 121, 126–28, 143, 154, 156–57, 158, 160, 161–62, 169
    "Aaron Burr, Sir" (song), 48, 154, 177
    as antagonist narrator, 169–71, 175–81
    duel with Hamilton, 1, 55, 60, 96, 127, 161
    as narrator, 26, 73, 173

Cabinet Battle(s), 21–22, 24–25, 111, 140–41
#CancelHamilton, 47–48, 62–63, 124–25
Chernow, Ron, 32–33, 91, 140, 209, 212
choreography, 1, 16, 103, 105, 110, 204, 207, 211
    Burr's choreography, 179
    Hamilton and Jefferson's dance choreography, 23–24
    King George's dance choreography, 73, 76

West Side Story's dance
    choreography, 205
Civil Rights Movement, 93, 207
Clinton, Hillary, 16, 39
cognitive behavioral theory,
    138, 142, 145
costume(s), 24–25, 75, 105, 110, 170
COVID-19, 118, 120, 149
    coronavirus, 2, 141
curtain speeches, 185–202
    decorum and, 189, 193–94
    dramaturgical curtain speeches,
        188–89, 191, 196, 199
    form and, 189

"Dear Theodosia" (song), 48, 51, 56–57,
    156–57, 179
Declaration of Independence, 21
democracy, 2, 21, 23, 27, 38
    Jeffersonian democracy, 16
Democratic Party, 16, 18–19, 26–27
    Democrats, 16, 18, 26–27
Dickerson, John, 194
Diggs, Daveed, 123, 127, 140
disability, 68–70, 74–75, 77–80
    disability studies, 68–69, 80
    disability drag, 79
Disney+, 2, 7, 47–48, 62, 70, 121–24,
    139, 145, 149, 162
Dixon, Brandon Victor, 186, 193–99
duel(s), 55, 110–11, 155, 161, 186
    Burr vs. Hamilton duel, 1, 55, 60,
        96, 101, 127, 161, 169, 176
    Laurens vs. Lee duel, 49
    Philip Hamilton vs. George
        Eacker duel, 161

"The Election of 1800" (song), 158
emancipation, 59–63

"Farmer Refuted" (song), 155
federalism, 101
femininity, 153
Ferguson, Missouri, 102
Floyd, George, 2–3, 118, 120, 124, 126

Founding Father(s), 2, 9, 24, 57, 61–63,
    92, 95, 121, 124, 139–40, 144, 156,
    163, 179, 212
frame analysis, 102, 106–8, 112
Frankfurt School, 5–6
Franklin, Benjamin, 36, 140

gender, 5, 8–9, 69, 89, 103, 120, 124,
    149–65, 172
    gender norms, 154, 162
    gender roles, 152–53, 156, 162
genre, 91, 101, 103, 144, 170–74,
    178–81, 185–88, 191, 194, 204–5,
    209–10, 214–15
    generic form, 186–87
Goldsberry, Renée Elise, 120–22
Groff, Jonathon, 67, 69–73, 75–76, 80

Hadestown (the musical), 90, 97,
    191–92, 198
Hair (the musical), 208–9
Hairspray (the musical), 207, 209, 211
Hamilton, Eliza/Elizabeth, 17, 47–48,
    51–52, 55–58, 96–97, 122, 125, 130,
    141, 152, 155, 157–59, 161, 177,
    179, 181, 209, 211–13
Hamilton, Philip, 47, 161, 212
Harris, Kamala, 16
"Helpless" (song), 141
Hemings, Sally, 25
hip-hop music, 1, 5, 15, 71, 91, 101–
    103, 108–12, 122, 144, 169–71,
    178–81, 209, 213–14
"Hurricane" (song) 21, 213

"I Know Him" (song), 73–74, 76, 78
immigrant(s), 5, 8–9, 16, 19–20, 23,
    25–27, 40–42, 94–97, 125, 137–47,
    179, 207, 211–12
    immigration, 9, 36–37, 40–43,
        55, 137–47
individualism, 19, 21, 161–62
intersectionality, 106
In the Heights (the musical), 139, 205,
    207–10, 213

Jackson, Christopher, 31, 39, 41, 121, 200, 211
Jay-Z, 108–9
Jefferson, Thomas, 9, 15–30, 33, 62, 96, 111, 123, 140–41, 158–60, 211–12
Jesus Christ Superstar (the musical), 169–70, 175–76, 180–81, 208

Kaepernick, Colin, 126
King George III, 9, 50, 67–82, 87–88, 90–91, 210, 213

de Lafayette, Marquis, 25, 48, 50, 52–53, 58, 62, 123, 125–26, 137–38, 140, 145, 154, 179, 212
Laurens, John, 9, 47–65, 125, 129, 137, 154, 212
    Laurens Interlude, 9, 48, 51, 53–55, 57–63
Lee, General Charles, 49
LuPone, Patti, 189–91

Madison, James, 22–23, 26, 33, 123, 158–60
Manhattan, New York, 109
Martin, Trayvon, 118–19
masculinity, 111, 162
    Hamilton's toxic, masculine persona, 163
    hegemonic masculinity, 153, 156, 160–61
    hypermasculine, violent hip-hop discourse, 110
    masculinist biases, 151
McConnell, Mitch, 22, 141
"Meet Me Inside" (song), 157
Miranda, Lin-Manuel, 1–3, 31–32, 87–88, 90–92, 95–96, 101, 108–9, 117–18, 121–22, 123, 124, 125–26, 129, 138–40, 144, 149, 152, 155–57, 160, 162–63, 173–74, 179, 181, 190, 194, 204, 207–15
    Miranda's interpretation of Hamilton and Thomas Jefferson, 22–27
    Miranda's interpretation of Washington's Farewell Address, 34–43
    Miranda on Black Lives Matter, 121
    Miranda on *Hamilton*'s diverse cast, 95, 144
    Miranda on King George III, 67–68, 77–78
    Miranda on Laurens's death, 60
    Miranda on "the scream," 47
    Miranda's performances at the White House, 15, 139
    Miranda's relationship with fans, 131
    Miranda responds to #CancelHamilton, 63
    Miranda responds to Mike Pence controversy, 196, 198
Mulligan, Hercules, 48, 50, 52–53, 58, 123, 129, 154
Muñoz, Javier, 189, 192
The Music Man (the musical), 214
musicology, 173
"My Shot" (song), 49–50, 96, 110, 124, 154, 211, 213
    remix of, 16

narrative, 17, 18
    genre-dependent narrator, 173
    narrative agency, 173
    narrative analysis, 60, 63
    narrative coherence, 58–60
    narrative fidelity, 58–60
    narrative method, 53–54
    narratology, 171–73, 213
    rhetorical dimensions of, 171
Nas, 109
neoliberalism, 89, 94
New York City, 1, 21, 25–26, 55, 97, 101, 103, 109, 138–39, 141, 190, 194, 203–4, 206, 209, 213
    See also Manhattan, New York
"Non-Stop" (song), 20–21, 48, 55, 58–59, 157

Notorious B.I.G. *See* Biggie Smalls

Obama, Barack, 2, 15, 18, 20, 22–24, 32, 36, 39–40, 102, 121, 139
Odom Jr., Leslie, 121, 127, 170, 177, 181, 197
Oklahoma! (the musical), 196, 204, 214
Onaodowan, Okieriete, 123
"One Last Time" (song), 31–32, 36–43, 158

Pence, Mike, 10, 88–89, 92, 140, 185–87, 193–96, 198–200, 214
performance [theory], 91–93, 97, 214
popular culture, 3–8, 16, 77
    and hegemony, 5–6, 180
    vs. high culture, 4–5
public memory, 16–18, 20, 27, 34–35, 42–43
public and private spheres, 123, 149–65
privilege, 4, 77, 91, 117, 119–20, 123, 127–29, 152, 156, 158
    Broadway audiences as privileged, 206, 213
    Hamilton as underprivileged, 109
    Thomas Jefferson as privileged, 20
public address, 32, 185–86, 188

rap music, 1, 6, 71, 91, 96, 109–11, 124, 144, 154–56, 178, 209
R&B music, 101, 144
Rent (the musical), 131, 205–6, 208–9, 210
Republican Motherhood, 151, 158
Republican Party, 22
    Democratic Republicans, 26
    Republicans, 18, 20, 22–23, 27
revolution, 50, 56
    American, 16, 71
    Revolutionary War, 1, 24, 26, 54, 60, 72
Reynolds, Maria, 160–61, 212
Reynolds Pamphlet, 21, 55, 160–61

"The Reynolds Pamphlet" (song), 73, 76, 160
rhetoric, 32–35, 48, 53–54, 63, 69–70, 79–80, 91, 93–94, 102–6, 109, 145, 185–88, 190–91, 197–98, 204, 212–15
    invitational rhetoric, 97
    See also public address; popular culture
"The Room Where It Happens" (song), 23, 158–59, 161, 179
Roosevelt, Franklin Delano, 204

"Satisfied" (song), 177
Saturday Night Live, 199
"Say No To This" (song), 160, 173, 177
Schumer, Chuck, 141
Schuyler, Angelica, 130, 155, 158, 160, 177, 211–12
Schuyler, Eliza, 177, 211
    See also Hamilton, Eliza/Elizabeth
Schuyler sisters (characters), 126, 156
"The Schuyler Sisters" (song), 155–56
Seabury, Samuel, 128–29, 155
1776 (the musical), 90, 211
Shakespeare, 191–92
Show Boat (the musical), 206–7, 214
slavery, 2, 9, 17, 25, 27, 47–51, 57–63, 92, 97, 102, 111, 119, 124–26, 130, 137, 139–40, 145, 206
    slaves, 18, 35, 50, 62–63
    slaveholder, 20, 24
    slave owner, 25
social media, 62, 108, 117–18, 130–31
Sondheim, Stephen, 205, 214
Soo, Phillipa, 122
the South, 25–26, 111, 206
South Pacific (the musical), 205, 207
"Stay Alive" (song), 49
"The Story of Tonight" (song), 50, 52, 56, 96

"Take A Break" (song), 158, 160
Taylor, Breonna, 118, 120, 124, 126

"Ten Duel Commandments"
  (song), 110–11
"That Would Be Enough" (song), 96
theater, 3, 5–6, 89, 169–72, 175,
  181, 203, 213
  See also Broadway
"Tomorrow There'll Be More of Us"
  (song), 47–48, 52, 56, 61
Tony Award, 1, 31, 90, 97, 101, 121,
  139, 170, 190, 192, 214
Trump, Donald, 2, 19–20, 26, 36,
  40, 43, 89, 92, 118, 124, 137–45,
  186, 195–200
Twitter, 47, 62, 121, 124, 190

Virginia, 23, 26, 111

"Wait For It" (song), 179, 213
Wallace, Christopher. *See*
  Biggie Smalls.
Washington, George, 9, 17, 23, 25,
  31–33, 36–43, 49, 55, 60, 87, 102,
  111, 121, 126, 129, 140, 157–59,
  177, 200, 211–12
  Farewell Address, 9, 31–46

"Washington On Your Side"
  (song), 23
"We Know" (song), 139, 160
West Side Story (the musical),
  205, 210, 214
"What Comes Next?" (song),
  72–74, 76, 78
"What'd I Miss" (song), 23, 26, 213
Whiteness, 9, 79, 87, 89–90, 94–95, 119
White rhetorical style, 106
White supremacy, 102, 119
"Who Lives, Who Dies, Who Tells
  Your Story" (song), 97–98, 159,
  169–70, 177
work ethic, 21, 24
"The World Was Wide Enough" (song),
  55, 96, 179

"Yorktown (The World Turned Upside
  Down)" (song), 3, 25, 41, 50, 72, 95,
  137–40, 211
"You'll Be Back" (song),
  71–72, 74, 76–78
"Your Obedient Servant"
  (song), 161, 179

About the Authors

Max Dosser (MA, Wake Forest University) is a PhD candidate in the communication department at the University of Pittsburgh. His research interests largely fall within the fields of media studies and cultural studies, with particular focus on genre (speculative fiction in particular), fandoms, and music communication. He is the co-founder and editor of the speculative fiction literary magazine *Flash Point SF*.

Jessica L. Gehrke (MA, Washington State University) is completing her PhD in communication with a concentration in rhetorical leadership at the University of Wisconsin–Milwaukee. She is an assistant professor in the Department of Professional Communication at Wisconsin Lutheran College. She teaches courses in public address, intercultural communication, professional communication, and public relations. Her research interests include how public memory is shaped through popular culture.

Caleb George Hubbard (MA, communication, West Texas A&M University) is a currently a PhD candidate in the Department of Communication at the University of Oklahoma. His research interests are in analysis of popular culture and political communication. A large amount of his research interest centers around fandom and celebrity studies, specifically how these topics have an influence/impact within civic life. In spring 2021, Hubbard received the Outstanding Graduate Student award at the University of Oklahoma for his research, service, and teaching. He has published in the *Atlantic Journal of Communication*.

Jacob Justice (PhD, University of Kansas) is an assistant professor of speech communication and the director of forensics in the Department of Writing and Rhetoric at the University of Mississippi. Jacob completed his MA in communication studies at the University of Kansas and his BA in political science and communication at Wayne State University in Detroit, Michigan. His research has been published in *Rhetoric & Public Affairs* and *Argumentation & Advocacy*.

Nancy J. Legge (PhD, Penn State University) is a professor of rhetoric in the Department of Communication, Media, and Persuasion at Idaho State University, where she also serves as the basic course director. She teaches rhetorical theory, rhetorical criticism, popular culture, persuasion, and image repair. Her research interests emphasize rhetorical analysis of popular culture, crisis and image repair theory, and the rhetoric of persuasive attack. Her research is published in *Rhetoric, Politics, and Hamilton: An American Musical, Communication Reports, Journal of International Crisis and Risk Communication Research*, and other journals and book chapters. She is the coauthor of *Business and Professional Communication: Plans, Process, and Performance*.

Ryan Louis (PhD, University of Kansas) is associate professor of communication studies at Ottawa University in Ottawa, Kansas (not to be confused with our consonant friends in Canada). He received his master's in performance studies and rhetoric from Hofstra University in New York and completed his PhD in rhetoric. His research celebrates the intersections of performance and rhetorical theories—centering civic engagement within pedagogy, theater, and forensics. He manages the Pi Kappa Delta National Archives, a resource for the study of historical oratory and performance.

Ailea G. Merriam-Pigg (MA, applied anthropology, San Jose State University; MA communication arts, University of Wisconsin–Madison) is a PhD candidate in the communication arts department at the University of Wisconsin–Madison. She is a researcher and teacher of digital communication and performance. Her research has a particular emphasis on marginalized populations and portrayals. It explores how power is centralized and disrupted, and her interest in performance is bolstered by over twenty-five years as a performer herself.

Kevin Pabst is a communication PhD student at the University of North Carolina at Chapel Hill focusing in media studies. He holds an MA in communication from Wake Forest University and a BA in communication studies from the University of Alabama. His research interests include music formats, sound studies, genre, and forms of power within music industries and cultures.

Judith P. Roberts (PhD, University of Southern Mississippi) is program coordinator and associate professor of communication and media studies at

Louisiana Tech University and co-publisher of the *Lincoln Parish Journal*. She teaches a variety of undergraduate courses, including media law, social media, copy editing, and practical reporting. Her current research focuses on the intersection of politics and religion.

Sarah Mayberry Scott (PhD, University of Memphis) is an assistant professor at Arkansas State University. She teaches communication courses in theory, argumentation, and gender. Her research focuses on rhetorics of disability and ableism. Her recent publications include "Sonic Lessons of the Covid-19 Soundscape," for *Sounding Out!*, "Situated Listening: Toward a More Just Rhetorical Criticism," in *Rhetoric and Public Affairs*, and "Sound and Silence in *A Quiet Place*" in the anthology *Representations of Disability in Film, TV and Print Media*.

Theodore F. Sheckels (PhD, Penn State University) is Charles J. Potts Professor of Social Science and professor of English and communication studies at Randolph-Macon College. He teaches a variety of political communication, rhetoric, and public address classes. His research focuses on the presidency, state politics, and contemporary Canadian, Australian, and African literature. He has authored, coauthored, edited, or coedited over fifteen books including *Celluloid Heroes Down Under: Australian Film, 1970–2000* (2002); *The Political in Margaret Atwood's Fiction* (2012), and *The Rhetoric of the American Political Party Conventions, 1948–2016* (2020).

Talya Peri Slaw is an instructor of speech in the Department of Writing and Rhetoric at the University of Mississippi. She completed an MA in communication studies at the University of Kansas and BAs in political science and communication at Wayne State University in Detroit, Michigan. Her research includes a publication in an edited volume based on the proceedings of the twenty-first annual NCA/AFA Alta Summer Conference on Argumentation.

Erika M. Thomas (PhD, Wayne State University) is an associate professor and the co-director of forensics in the Department of Human Communication Studies at California State University, Fullerton. Her areas of study include rhetorical criticism and theory, critical/cultural theory, and argumentation. Her work has most recently been included in *Transmedia and Public Representation: Transgender People in Film and Television* (Peter Lang), and in the journals *Women & Language* and *Relevant Rhetoric*.

Jonathan Veal studied rhetoric in the communication studies master's program at San Diego State University. He has presented papers at both the Western States Communication Association and the National Communication

Association. He has taught courses in public speaking, persuasion, and gender studies. His research interests center on aesthetics, particularly in relation to music. He currently lives in Tustin, California, where he works in the private sector in media and music.

Luke Winslow (PhD, University of Texas at Austin) is an assistant professor of rhetorical studies in the Department of Communication at Baylor University. He joined the faculty at Baylor in 2020 after teaching for six years in the School of Communication at San Diego State University. His teaching and research interests include contemporary rhetorical criticism, political communication, and rhetoric and religion. His first book, *Economic Injustice and the Rhetoric of the American Dream*, was published by Lexington Books in 2017. His second book, *American Catastrophe: Fundamentalism, Climate Change, Gun Rights, and the Rhetoric of Donald J. Trump*, was published by Ohio State University Press in 2020. He lives in Waco, Texas, with his wife and three children.

www.ingramcontent.com/pod-product-compliance
Lightning Source LLC
Chambersburg PA
CBHW020117010526
44115CB00008B/865